EDUCATION IN FIFTEENTH-CENTURY ENGLAND

THE JOHNS HOPKINS UNIVERSITY STUDIES IN EDUCATION

No. 35

EDITED BY

FLORENCE E. BAMBERGER

EDUCATION IN FIFTEENTH-CENTURY ENGLAND

BY

CLARA P. McMAHON

GREENWOOD PRESS, PUBLISHERS
NEW YORK   1968

To My Mother

Acknowledgment

The author expresses sincere appreciation to Dr. Florence
E. Bamberger, Dr. Sidney Painter, and Dr. Richard E.
Thursfield of the Johns Hopkins University for their valu-
able contributions in the preparation of this dissertation.

TABLE OF CONTENTS

CHAPTER I

INTRODUCTION

Just as intermittent streaks of lightning flash across the midnight sky and suddenly illuminate the shadows of darkness, revealing for a split second the salient features of the land beneath it, so glimpses into the all-too-rare documents of fifteenth-century England permit us to obtain a brief but clear-cut picture of the educational scene of that century. The fifteenth century was a period of crystallization, a period in which the educational ingredients of the early middle ages were slowly being filtered out and the remaining ones were crystallizing into the modern design for education. University, secondary, elementary, and vocational education were all part of this crystalline formation, and were all present to aid in the later symmetrical design.

Cause cannot be separated from result, and in like manner educational history cannot be divorced from the cultural and intellectual trends of the time. The philosophy that permeated these educational efforts of the fifteenth century was Scholasticism,[1] decadent though it was becoming, and it is impossible even to mention education without taking into account this philosophical background, built up by the accumulation over a number of years of the thoughts, beliefs, reasonings, and writings of such outstanding philosophers and intellectual figures as Abelard, Aquinas, Roger Bacon, and Duns Scotus, to mention but a few.

To some people, Scholasticism means the Middle Ages; to others, it is equivalent to triviality; to still others, it is synonymous with " whited sepulchre," a dazzling, brilliant

---

[1] Scholasticism as herein used refers to the various schools of philosophy embraced by the great Schoolmen, who engaged in controversies over purely philosophical matters, but who accepted the authority of the Church in defining dogma. For an excellent discussion of the varying meanings of Scholasticism, see Maurice de Wulf, *History of Medieval Philosophy* (third edition, translated by P. Coffey; London: Longmans, Green & Co., 1909), pp. 101-116.

front of imposing philosophical thought that unexpectedly crumbles to dust when the slightest pressure of intelligent reasoning is applied to it. For centuries Scholasticism has been accused of being little more than a working-over of Aristotelian dogmas; of being barren and sterile of any degree of originality. Francis Bacon was one of the first of a long line of such accusers:

> This kind of degenerate learning did chiefly reign amongst the schoolmen; who, having strong and sharp wits, and abundance of leisure, and small variety of reading, but their wits being shut up in the cells of a few authors (chiefly Aristotle their dictator) as their persons were shut up in the cells of monasteries and colleges, and knowing little history, either of nature or time, did out of no great quantity of matter and infinite agitation of wit spin out unto those laborious webs of learning which are extant in their books.[2]

But it was the latter period of Scholasticism that gave rise to the criticism of Erasmus, Francis Bacon, John Locke, *et al.*, and unfortunately, for many centuries, it was this period rather than the great period of its culmination that was regarded as typical Scholasticism. It can readily be seen how easily the absurd dialectical disputes and impassioned quarrels which engaged certain so-called philosophers of the fifteenth century have left a stigma that has blotted out, to a great extent, the contributions the great Scholastics have made in the field of culture and learning.

Modern research has revealed many hitherto unknown facts about the Scholastics. Far from being narrow-minded, uncritical pedants who marked time for three centuries, they were men of great learning and profound discrimination, men who were masters of the Scriptures and of the writings of the patristic fathers, men who possessed great acumen. Predestination, freedom of will, the nature of God, election, and reprobation were only a few of the questions endlessly discussed by the Scholastics. The purpose of Scholasticism was to find proof for the doctrines which the Church had already formulated, and for the statements in the Bible which they accepted

---

[2] Francis Bacon, *Advancement of Learning*, p. 25, cited by Ernest A. Moody, *The Logic of William Ockham* (N. Y.: Sheed and Ward, Inc., 1935), p. 12, n. 1.

on faith because they believed it was inspired.[3] Bound as they were by their deference to authority, nevertheless they must be considered as pioneers in opening up new fields of thought.

Porphyry, the Neo-Platonist of the ninth century, was the first to set off the spark in the philosophic controversy between Realism and Nominalism, the controversy which was to permeate Scholasticism. He stated it thus in his Introduction to *Isagoge*:

With regard to genera and species, whether they have actual subsistence, or consist merely in pure thoughts, and whether, if they do subsist, they are corporeal or incorporeal; transcendent, or immanent in, and related to, sensible things, I shall not endeavor to decide, and this for the reason that the question is an extremely profound one, requiring another and deeper investigation.[4]

This problem, of the nature of knowledge, then, or the question of universals, was the problem that all the Scholastics attacked, and which produced a spirit of inquiry that refused to be downed. The philosophy which maintained that universals possessed reality in the highest degree was called Realism. There were two kinds of Realism—the first held that universals had an independent existence apart from individual objects, and that they existed *before* the individual objects, and was known as Platonic Realism, Ultra-Realism, or Extreme Realism; the second said that such universals, possessing a real existence, existed only *in* the individual objects, and was called Moderate Realism, or Aristotelian Realism. The former, in other words, held the object of a universal idea to be universal and one, while the latter held it to be particular and multiplied with the multiplication of individuals.[5] Nominalism, on the other hand, denied the existence of objective universal conceptions, and maintained that they were merely

[3] J. Franklin Messenger, *An Interpretative History of Education* (N. Y.: Thomas Y. Crowell Co., 1931). p. 85.
[4] Cited in Thomas Davidson, *A History of Education* (N. Y.: Charles Scribner's Sons, 1900), p. 163; cf. John Edwin Sandys, *A History of Classical Scholarship* (Cambridge: University Press, 1903), I, 239 and 506; and Joseph Rickaby, *Scholasticism* (London: Constable and Co., 1911), pp. 2-3.
[5] Rickaby, *op. cit.*, p. 4.

names, representations without content and reality, a " mere concept of the mind." Genera and species have no real existence; only individuals really exist, and generic and specific terms are due merely to the more or less arbitrary necessities of thought and the convenience of speech.[6]

Nominalism came into great disrepute in the eleventh century through the teachings of Roscellinus, who, applying the doctrine to the dogma of the Trinity, caused great offense and was required to recant by the Ecclesiastical Council of Soissons in 1092.[7] For many years afterwards Nominalism remained quiescent; it was not until Ockham in the fourteenth century that it became active once more. Abelard, Roscellinus' great pupil, and later one of his greatest critics, because of his brilliance in debate and because of his magnetic personality, dominated the educational world in the early twelfth century. His theories tended toward Moderate Realism, and his career is of special interest to the student of the history of education because of his very large contribution to the popularity of dialectical scholarship.[8] Abelard waged a relentless war on behalf of the supremacy of human understanding, and on freedom of religious thought apart from ecclesiastical authority. It is to him, also, that we are indebted for the " scholastic method," [9] as demonstrated in his

---

[6] Cf. also Friedrich Ueberweg, *History of Philosophy* (translated from the fourth German edition by George S. Morris; N. Y.: Scribner, Armstrong, and Co., 1876), I, 366: " Nominalism is the doctrine that only individuals have real existence, and that genera and species are merely subjective combinations of similar elements, united by the aid of one and the same concept (*conceptus*), through which concept we think the manifold homogeneous objects which it includes, and under one and the same word (*nomen vox*), which word, for want of a sufficient number of simple proper names, we employ to express at once the totality of homogeneous objects included under the concept. Of Nominalism there are two varieties, according as stress is laid on the subjective nature of the concept (conceptualism), or on the identity of the word employed to denote the objects comprehended under the concept (Extreme Nominalism, or Nominalism in the narrower sense of the term). The formula of Nominalism is: *universalia post rem.*"
[7] *Ibid.*, p. 372.
[8] Frederick Eby and Charles F. Arrowood, *The History and Philosophy of Education Ancient and Medieval* (N. Y.: Prentice-Hall, Inc., 1940), p. 745.
[9] While this method had been used earlier, it received a great impetus in the hands of Abelard. The author is assuming the reader's famili-

book *Sic et Non*, in which he raised a series of questions on Church teachings, and gave evidence for both sides, without rendering a decision. This type of reasoning did much to stimulate free inquiry, which was exactly what Abelard wanted.[10]

The passion the Scholastics possessed for compiling, organizing, and classifying human knowledge is shown in the eagerness with which they seized on the work of Peter the Lombard, somewhat the junior of Abelard. Despite the fact that his work could claim no particular originality or literary inventiveness, it became the chief textbook in the universities for centuries to come. His compendium was known as the *Quatuor libri sententiarum*, commonly called the *Book of Sentences*, and included the statements of recognized authorities of the Church on particular questions. The book was divided into topics, and proofs were brought forward for the solution of each question without summarizing the best answer. Peter's method differed slightly from Abelard's since a decision was reached, a decision both " positive and orthodox."

Twelfth-century England was illuminated by the¹ clear, steady glow of light that emanated from John of Salisbury. Born in England and educated in France under such eminent instructors as Abelard, William of Conches, Alberich, Gilbert, Robert Melun, and a host of others, he received a thorough training in theology and philosophy, and soon became known as the most learned man of his time. Our knowledge of him and his time has been gleaned from his two most important works, the *Metalogicus*, which concerns the study of logic, and the *Polycraticus*, which Reginald Poole calls " an encyclopedia of the cultivated thought of the twelfth century," [11] and

---

arity with the method of syllogism: statement of major premise, minor premise, with arguments for and against, and the conclusion.

[10] " Therefore this present collection is made, as a basis for discussion in the schools, after the fashion recommended by Aristotle to all serious students. For by doubting we come to enquiry, and through enquiry we grasp the truth, as the Truth Himself hath said: ' Seek and you shall find, knock and it shall be opened unto you.' " Preface to Abelard's work, as quoted on p. 120 in George G. Coulton, *Studies in Medieval Thought* (London: Thomas Nelson and Sons, Ltd., 1940).

[11] Reginald Lane Poole, *Illustrations of the History of Medieval*

which is the framework for an ideal government. Combined with his study of theology and philosophy were his humanistic tendencies, rather unusual for his age. Terence, Vergil, Horace, Ovid, Lucan, Statius, Persius, Martial, Juvenal, Sallust, and Seneca are but a few of the Latin authors whom he had read and quoted. He railed against the many petty quibbles which the theologians engaged in, and against their methods of teaching logic and dialectics. He held it to be unfitting to spend too much time on problems of this kind, or to devote all one's life to them alone, and charged even Aristotle with subtilizing.[12]

Up until the beginning of the thirteenth century, the scholars of the Middle Ages had access to very few of Aristotle's works. Since his theories were known only through garbled and inaccurate translations of other writers, the Church had recoiled in alarm from Aristotle. With the thirteenth century renaissance and the subsequent introduction of better Greek-Latin and Arabic-Latin translations of Greek, and the translations of Jewish and Arabian works, Aristotle's theories were seen to be more and more compatible with ecclesiastical dogmas, and the Church's vigilance was relaxed. Examination of his *Metaphysics, Physics, Psychology*, and *Ethics* led to his becoming the bulwark of scholastic philosophy, and throughout the thirteenth century his supremacy was unchallenged. With the rise of the universities in this era and the inclusion of the *Metaphysics* and *Physics* of Aristotle in the arts curriculum, it may be inferred that the genuine Aristotle was being distinguished from the Platonic conception of him. Better and purer translations were sought for; John of Salisbury had led the way, with Robert Grosseteste, following in his footsteps as a translator, but it was two Dominican friars, Henry of Brabant and William of Moerbeke, who were responsible for the translation of nearly the whole of Aristotle's works from the Greek.

Robert Grosseteste may rightly be remembered as one of

Thought and Learning (second edition, revised; N. Y.: The Macmillan Co., 1920) p. 190.
    [12] Ueberweg, *op. cit.*, I, 401.

the "earliest leaders of thought at Oxford, as a promoter of Greek learning, and as an interpreter of Aristotle." [13] Born about 1175, in suffolk, he was educated not only at Oxford, but also at Paris, and returned to Oxford to become its Chancellor. He was elected Bishop of Lincoln in 1235, and thus began a rather stormy career of quarrels and antagonisms between himself and the chapter which had elected him. The deans and canons of the chapter felt that he had no right to visit them; he should concentrate on the diocese. After a number of years, the issue was settled at Lyons by a papal bull of 1295, which acknowledged Grosseteste's claims. Hated by some, loved and admired by many, recognized by all as an indefatigable worker with a burning zeal for setting aright many of the abuses of the Church, he was a man who, at the time of his death in 1253, had made an unusual impression on his age. Matthew Paris, his contemporary, and one who did not consider himself his friend, because Grosseteste (in Paris' opinion) was a persecutor of the monks, says of him:

> He was a manifest refuter of the pope and the king, the blamer of prelates, the corrector of monks, the director of priests, the instructor of clerks, the support of scholars, the preacher to the people, the persecutor of the incontinent, the sedulous student of all scripture, the hammer and the despiser of the Romans. At the table of bodily refreshment he was hospitable, eloquent, courteous, pleasant, and affable. At the spiritual table, devout, tearful, and contrite. In his episcopal office he was sedulous, venerable, and indefatigable. [14]

An eager student of the classics, Grosseteste was instrumental in giving new life to them, especially with regard to Aristotle. He translated, or caused to be translated, many works from the Greek, and was the force behind better translations of Aristotle. Together with Adam de Marisco and Roger Bacon, he urged the study of the physical sciences and theology. His versatility in writing was great; he has been called a French poet, an agriculturist, a lawyer, a physician, and a preacher. [15] His voluminous works (letters, sermons,

[13] Sandys, *op. cit.*, I, 556.
[14] Quoted in Henry Richards Louard's "Robert Grosseteste," *Dictionary of National Biography*, VIII, 721.
[15] Hastings Rashdall, *Universities of Europe in the Middle Ages* (new edition in three volumes, edited by F. M. Powicke and A. B. Emden; Oxford: Clarendon Press, 1936), III, 241.

2

works on theology, commentaries on Aristotle and Boethius, poems, treatises on husbandry, and innumerable translations of both Latin and Greek), his boundless energy, his humanistic tendencies, and his vigorous personality all contributed toward making him a powerful influence on English scholars. Professor Louard says:

> Probably no one had a greater influence upon English thought and English literature for the two centuries following his time than Bishop Grosseteste; few books written then will be found that do not contain quotations from ' Lincolniensis.' [16]

Roger Bacon was a meteor-like splash of light against the pedantic darkness of Scholasticism. He was inextricably bound with the Scholastics, yet he struggled unceasingly to free himself of their metaphysical entanglements. He was, perhaps, born too soon to be fully appreciated; not until the eighteenth century did it become known that he " was more than an ingenious alchemist, a skilled mechanician, and perhaps a dabbler in the black arts." [17]

Few facts are available about him; not even is the date of his birth or death certain. He was born about 1214, in or near Ilchester, Somersetshire, and began his studies at Oxford, where he came under the influence of such renowned men as Robert Grosseteste and Adam de Marisco, both of whom he admired greatly. From Oxford he went to the University of Paris, where he was made a doctor, and where he joined the Franciscan Order. He returned to England *circa* 1250, and some seven years later fell under the suspicions of his Order.[18] He was kept in close confinement for the next ten years, until the fortunate rise of his friend Guy de Foulques to the Papacy as Clement IV gained him release. It was because of Clement's request that Bacon wrote his main works, the *Opus Majus*, the *Opus Minus* (*Secundum*), and the *Opus Tertium*. After the death of his friend he was obliged to atone for his opposition to the spirit of his time by

---

[16] *Op. cit.*, p. 720.
[17] Robert Adamson, " Roger Bacon," *Dictionary of National Biography*, I, 848.
[18] Sandys, *op. cit.*, I, 567.

another imprisonment, which may have ended in 1292.[19] His death occurred in England some two years later.

Bacon was primarily interested in the study of languages and sciences, and he urged with great vehemence their further study. He fully appreciated the value of the writings of the ancients, but at the same time condemned the excessive authority attributed to the *ipse dixit* of Aristotle.[20] Even though Bacon protested vigorously against the Scholastics' philosophic way of thinking, he accepted in his own fashion many of the tenets they held. He upheld these dominant medieval convictions: the entire truth of the Scripture; the absolute validity of the revealed religion, with its dogmatic formulation; also the universally prevailing view that the end of all the sciences is to serve their queen, theology.[21]

The things he hammered against in his relentless attack upon the clergy and the education of his own times were the constant neglect of observation and experiment, and the utter and absolute dependence on and deference to authority. But, as Rashdall points out, unlike other medieval thinkers, orthodox or unorthodox, Bacon saw that the study of Greek was the true key to the meaning of Aristotle, and a knowledge of the Bible in the original the true foundation for a fruitful study of theology.[22] The study of languages and mathematics were closely interwoven. Bacon says:

Next to languages . . . I hold mathematics necessary in the second place, to the end that we may know what may be known. It is not planted in us by nature, yet is closest to inborn knowledge, of all the sciences which we know through discovery and learning. For its study is easier than all sciences, and boys learn its branches readily. Besides, the laity can make diagrams, and calculate, and sing, and use musical instruments. All these are the *opera* of mathematics.[23]

Perhaps because he was so entirely free from the enveloping restraints of scholastic speculation, perhaps because of his too-abusive criticisms of his contemporaries, or perhaps be-

[19] Ueberweg, *op. cit.*, I, 459.
[20] Rashdall, *op. cit.*, III, 245.
[21] Henry Osborn Taylor, *The Medieval Mind* (second edition; London: Macmillan and Co., Ltd., 1914), II, 515.
[22] Rashdall, *op. cit.*, III, 245.
[23] Chap. XXIX, *Opus tertium*, quoted by Taylor, *op. cit.*, II, 528.

cause his attack on scholastic methods was too premature, the fact remains that Roger Bacon made but a slight impression on his contemporaries. It remained for a later generation of Ockhams and Duns Scotus' to create the fatal breach.

But it was Thomas Aquinas, the Italian Dominican, who

> . . . brought the Scholastic philosophy to its highest stage of development, by effecting the most perfect accommodation that was possible of the Aristotelian philosophy to ecclesiastical orthodoxy.[24]

His work, the *Summa Theologica*, was a harmonious whole, an edifice of " human learning, ingenuity, industry, and piety " which has never been equalled, and his system of theology is still the bulwark of the Roman Catholic Church. Aquinas was a Moderate Realist, and he was convinced of the primacy of the true over the good, of knowledge over will. He denied that there was an irreconcilable difference between faith and reason, and declared that faith was the complement of reason. Aquinas is important in the progress of education not only because of the great body of scholarship he produced but because of the pattern he set in philosophical studies.[25]

The beginning of the fourteenth century was simultaneous with the advent of a new school, as opposed to the Thomistic one. The Scotist school was founded by Joannes Duns Scotus, about whose head centuries later controversies were still raging. Scotus was the beginning of the end of Scholasticism, the rupture that was to mean the final break-up of the system. Scotland, England, and Ireland, all three have been claimed, at one time or another, as his birthplace, and the year 1264 or 1275 as his birthdate. If his death occurred, as is commonly supposed, in 1308, at Cologne, then in a short span of time Duns Scotus crammed in a lifetime of learning.

> If indeed he was so young when death came to him, he presents the most remarkable instance of intellectual productiveness and industry in the history of the race.[26]

---

[24] Ueberweg, *op. cit.*, I, 440.

[25] Eby and Arrowood, *op. cit.*, p. 750: " The minute division of problems and examination of every aspect of them is the very essence of the Scholastic method."

[26] William J. Townsend, *The Great Schoolmen of the Middle Ages* (N. Y.: G. E. Stechert and Co., 1920), p. 248.

Among medieval thinkers Duns Scotus was distinguished not
only by breadth and depth of learning—he was familiar with
the logical treatises of Porphyry and Boethius, and the works
of the great Arabian and Jewish schoolmen, such as Averroes
and Avicebron, not to speak of Christian writers—but by
originality and acuteness of intellect.[27] Some of his works
included *Commentaries on Aristotle, Commentary on the
Book of the Sentences*, known as the *Opus Oxiense*, and
treatises on grammar, logic, theology, and metaphysics. It is
in these writings that one becomes aware of the reason for
the title " Doctor Subtilis " that was bestowed on him. His
mind possessed the power of " exquisite discrimination "; he
was one of Thomism's most penetrating critics. His strength
lay rather in acute, negative criticism of the teachings of others
than in the positive elaboration of his own.[28] His power for
drawing subtle distinctions and differences was overwhelming
in its logical consequences; he carried his endless discrimina-
tions to such extremes that reaction set in against him. Hence
the term " Dunce " was derisively applied to whoever cared
for such a line of reasoning, and it has since degenerated, in
modern parlance, to the meaning of stupidity. Scotus' position
as a Realist and his desire for such scientific exactness may
perhaps be traced to Robert Grosseteste and Roger Bacon,
both of whom, it will be remembered, taught at Oxford, where
Scotus was located, and where he may have felt an anti-
Thomistic spirit.

Strict adherence with regard to the theological dogmas of
the Church and the philosophical doctrines corresponding with
their spirit, and skepticism with regard to the arguments by
which they were supported were characteristic of Duns
Scotus.[29] His growing distrust of reason as a basis for faith
was typical of the Scotist followers. Scotus may be summed
up as follows: He was a destroyer of systems (St. Thomas,

[27] J. M. Riggs, " Duns Scotus," *Dictionary of National Biography*,
VI, 217. Cf. also Taylor, *op. cit.*, II, 543: " His learning was complete: he knew the Bible and the Fathers; he was a master of theology,
philosophy, astronomy, and mathematics."
[28] Ueberweg, *op. cit.*, I, 452.
[29] *Ibid.*

St. Bonaventura, Giles of Rome, Robert of Middleton, God frey of Fontaine, Henry of Ghent were attacked) ; all his writings suffer from an excessive use of distinctions and fre quent ambiguity of thought; his system was only a statement, colored by personal variations, of the great, general scholastic synthesis; he laid extreme emphasis on the distinction between philosophy and theology; he proclaimed the subordination of philosophy to theology; he was a voluntarist (the will is superior to the intellect) ; and the characteristic and original element in him was his formalism.[30]

With William of Ockham came in that trend of Scholasticism of dabbling in national, political, and ecclesiastical questions of the time. Flourishing about the first half of the fourteenth century (he died in 1347), William of Ockham became famous for his quarrel with the popes concerning imperial and papal authority on temporal matters, and for his view on evangelical poverty. In 1327, Pope John XXII issued a bull against him, charging him with having uttered "many erroneous and heretical opinions," and excommunicated him.[31] In 1339 the students were warned against his writings, and the following year the University of Paris prohibited his teachings.[32] In spite of all this, the Ockhamist (or Terminist, as it was sometimes called) School continued to flourish.

Ockham followed Duns Scotus not only temporally, but also in some respects philosophically; both admitted the practicality of theology with its separation from philosophy. They differed, however, on several points. Scotus conceived the function of logic to deal with thoughts, while Ockham proceeded on the supposition that logic was concerned not with thoughts or things, but with terms arbitrarily imposed by ourselves.[33] Ockham shows the influence of Scotus in his critical methods and his negations; but he " denied the

[30] Based on a discussion in De Wulf, *op. cit.*, pp. 368-360.

[31] T. Bruce Birch, editor, *De Sacramento Altaris of William of Ockham* (Burlington, Iowa: Lutheran Literary Board, 1930), p. xiii.

[32] *Ibid.*, p. xv.

[33] Reginald Lane Poole, "William of Ockham," *Dictionary of National Biography*, XIV, 802-807.

validity of the metaphysical constructions whereby Duns Scotus sought to rebuild what his criticisms had cast down or shaken." [34]

Some important authorities, such as Gilson, Ueberweg, and Poole, class Ockham as a Nominalist, and agree that the title " Venerabilis Inceptor " was given to him because he re-established Nominalism. He recognized the particular alone as being real; the universal was a mere conception of the thinking mind. He divided the cognitions of the mind into two kinds: intuitive (the knowledge by which we know what a thing is or is not), and abstractive (knowledge which arises from the discrimination and comparison of objects presented through the senses).[35]

Others, including Rickaby, Taylor, and De Wulf say that it is wrong to call Ockham a Nominalist; [36] that is, he by no means denied the existence of Universalist Ideas in the mind. What he did deny was that they stood for anything specifically common to a multitude of individuals; he argued that they stood for all the individuals to whom they were applicable. The saying ascribed to him, " Entities are not to be multi-plied beyond necessity," is indicative of his stand against the multiplication of distinctions.

Some of the terms and distinctions used by Ockham in his logical works have been called innovations, but Ernest A. Moody [37] points out that they have been found in the works of other Scholastics and in some of the treatises ascribed to Duns Scotus.

Moody writes somewhat later:

The novelty of Ockham's position was its full separation of the sphere of natural knowledge from that of faith, and from the meta-physics that took God as its starting point, and the relation of the finite to the infinite as its problem. Ockham was a man of science,

---

[34] Taylor, *op. cit.*, p. 548.
[35] Townsend, *op. cit.*, p. 276-277.
[36] Rickaby, *op. cit.*, pp. 51-63; cf. also Taylor, *op. cit.*, II, 551: " It was not so very great a leap from the realism of Duns, which ascribed a certain objective existence to general ideas, to the nominalism, or rather conceptualism of Occam, which denied it, yet recognized the real existence and necessary functions of universals, in the mind.";
and De Wulf, *op. cit.*, p. 423.
[37] *Op. cit.*, p. 25.

whose theology was neither incompatible with his philosophy and meta-physics, nor confused with it. His method was analytic, and his principles those yielded by analysis of determinate subjects of investigation—each problem being distinguished and stated through reference to the *kinds of things* involved in that single problem, and its solution sought in its own terms, or by its ' proximate middle.' [38]

Ockham had many followers, good and bad, and his influence was felt until the end of the fifteenth century. The " preposterous use of logic " was due in the main to men who mistook the shell for the kernel.

The struggle between Realism and Nominalism did not close with Scotus and Ockham ; a reaction against the Realism of Scotus took place in the ranks of other Realists, and John Wycliffe must be acknowledged as one of the leaders in this revolt. Scholasticism was in its death throes ; the spirit of energy injected by him did not prolong its life. Wycliffe is much more famous as a reformer than as a Scholastic, yet it was Wycliffe's prestige as a Schoolman that gave so much weight to the reform movement which he inaugurated ; this was the first time the established Church principles were assailed, not by some obscure fanatic, not by some mere Revivalist, but by a Doctor in " the second school of the Church." [39]

Wycliffe was educated at Oxford, probably at Balliol, and remained there to become the most important teacher of his time. Because he helped to mold so many student minds, because he was the teacher *par excellence* at Oxford, which had been the intellectual centre of Scholasticism throughout the fourteenth century, because his views had been so thoroughly disseminated throughout Oxford, and consequently throughout the country, Oxford suffered from the anathema that was levelled against Wycliffe and his followers. Lollardy was quick to attract the resentment of the Church because of its attack on the temporal and political power of the clergy (with

---

[38] *Ibid.*, p. 307.

[39] Rashdall, *op. cit.*, III, 266. Cf. also George Macaulay Trevelyan, *England in the Age of Wycliffe* (N. Y.: Longmans, Green and Co., 1935), p. 170: " The method by which he arrived at his conclusions was in appearance the scholastic method then recognized. Without such a basis his theories would have been treated with ridicule by all theologians. . . ."

the resultant lack of moral discipline) and the later attack against the intellectual beliefs taught by the Church. The ecclesiastical repression which followed the collapse of the Wycliffite heresy meant the extinction of a vigorous and earnest scholastic thought.[40] Oxford received a blow that sounded the death-knell of Scholasticism in 1411 when its franchises were taken from it. Even though Scholasticism lingered on through the fifteenth century, it no longer throbbed with the pulse of life; a new spirit was stirring. The decline is characterized by De Wulf:

> The decay of scholasticism followed closely on its period of maturity. The causes that undermined its influence on the history of subsequent philosophical thought, corroded the great monument by a slow but steady and persistent process of disintegration. The succeeding generations were unequal to the task of preserving the work achieved by the master minds of the thirteenth century. Broadly speaking, we may attribute the decay of scholastic philosophy to three main groups of hostile influences: dearth of philosophers, the relaxation of studies, and the steady inroads of antischolastic systems.[41]

Hampered by the narrow confines of the scholastic method, the authority of the Church, and the slight scope of its interests, nevertheless Scholasticism had succeeded in awakening a spirit of inquiry that would not be downed, in opening up new fields of intellectual thought, and in presenting to generations to come an analytical and logical method of thinking that did much for progress. As measured by present-day standards, it fell short of meeting requirements, but considered as a step in the advance of the thought life of the immediately preceding centuries, it was remarkable.[42]

[40] Rashdall, *op. cit.*, III, 270.
[41] De Wulf, *op. cit.*, p. 413.
[42] Messenger, *op. cit.*, p. 98.

CHAPTER II

THE UNIVERSITIES

Early History of Oxford and Cambridge

An historian of the fifteenth century, writing of the early beginnings of Oxford University, would have had no hesitancy whatsoever in setting forth a most elaborate explanation of its foundation, tracing its origin at least to King Alfred, if not earlier. In fact, there appears in the Chancellors' and Proctors' Book, a register kept by these officials of the university from about 1425 on, this readily-believed account of the founding of Oxford:

In the testimony of the majority of chronicles, many places throughout the world at various times are said to have promoted the growth of schools; of all the schools still existing amoung the Latins, it has been discovered that the University of Oxford is first in foundation, more general in the universality of studies, firmer in its profession of Catholic faith, and more outstanding in its multiplicity of privileges. Ancient histories of Britain hint at the priority of its foundation: for it is said that, when long ago, the warlike Trojans, under the leadership of Brutus, triumphantly seized this island, then called Albion, later Britain, and finally England, certain philosophers accompanying them unanimously agreed on the selection of a place on this island for habitation, and named it Grekelade (Cricklade). These Greek philosophers have to this day left traces of their schools. Not far from this place Oxford is known to be situated, which, because of the charm of neighbouring streams, meadows, and woods, antiquity once called Bellesitum; later the Saxons named it Oxford (because of a nearby ford), and chose it as the location for their schools. The more abundant universality of studies in this place is more clearly observed, because in other schools there is so much emphasis on one or more studies that many, or at least some, of them appear to be excluded. At Oxford, however, each study is so taught that one which is rejected may be considered unworthy of the name. Indeed the purity of the Catholic faith in the doctrines has been so safe-guarded, thanks to divine favor, that even the memory of a heresy that sprouted there several times does not exist, which the skill of Catholic doctors and the watchful care of those in charge have not crushed out at its birth. In addition, royal power has so exalted this University, adorned by the many privileges conferred on it by Roman Pontiffs and Bishops, that even the citizens of the place seem to be under the sway of scholastic authority. It is possible, however, that because of the difficult

16

passage across the sea, and the location of the island, that its renown and fame are less well-known to certain far regions, yet it is known to enjoy prerogatives to no small degree. . . .[1]

This treatise, commonly called the Oxford *Historiola*, was incorporated in the records of the university with the evident intention of impressing other schools and universities with the antiquity of Oxford's existence, a device that was common to all kinds of institutions, and one which, as will be seen a little later, was also used by Cambridge University. This *Historiola* was drawn upon time and time again by historians wishing to write a glorious account of the origin of Oxford.

It was this account on which John Rous, fifteenth-century author of *Historia Regum Angliae*, based his theories of Oxford's foundation.[2] In the sixteenth century, during Queen Elizabeth's reign, a controversy arose between John Gaius and Thomas Gaius, representing respectively Cambridge and Oxford, regarding the rival claims of both universities to be the more ancient. It was during this controversy that the Alfred myth of Oxford's origin came to be firmly fixed, a story which such historians as Bryan Twyne and Anthony Wood seized on in their histories of Oxford, and which has dominated other histories until the end of the nineteenth century. The earliest instance of King Alfred's founding Oxford occurs in a passage in Ralph Higden's *Polychronicon*, a chronicle beginning at the creation of the world and continuing until 1357 A. D. Two other chroniclers, Brompton and Hyde, both of Edward III's reign, repeat the myth with some additions, as does Thomas Rudborn, writing his *Historia Major* about the year 1440. Credence and momentum were given to the story by a passage falsely inserted in Asser's *Life of Alfred* (the so-called Camden passage). This Camden passage was not the only imposture connected with the Alfred

---

[1] *Munimenta Academica, Libri Cancellarii et Procuratorum* (edited by Henry Anstey; London: Longmans, Green, Reader, and Dyer, 1868), II, 367-368. Writer's translation. Hereafter referred to as *Mun. Acad.*

[2] This paragraph is based in general on Chapter II, " The Mythical Origin of Oxford," pp. 5-62, of James Parker's *The Early History of Oxford* (Oxford: Clarendon Press, for the Oxford Historical Society, 1885).

myth. University College, Oxford, faced with a lawsuit that could be dismissed if the king's patronage were secured, deliberately seized on this story of Alfred's foundation in order to make it appear that it had always been a royal foundation, even though up until then the college had made no claim that anyone other than William of Durham (its true founder) had been its originator.

Cambridge, too, had its wonderful tales of mythical founders, and vied with the claims of Oxford as to the priority of its ancient and royal foundation. Such illustrious personages as the Spanish prince Cantaber, King Arthur, and the Saxon King Sigebert of the seventh century were hailed as founders by one or another enthusiastic followers of Cambridge, and even supported by royal charters and papal bulls later proved to be fictitious.[3] Such eminent philosophers as Anaximander and Anaxagoras were said to have been brought to Cambridge as tutors,[4] and Alcuin and Bede to have been among its first teachers.[5] Dyer[6] has collected these ancient charters and bulls and printed them in his collection: the charter of King Arthur (531 A. D.) ; a bull of Pope Honorius I (624) ; the charger of King Cadwalder (681) ; and the bull of Pope Sergius I (699) being among the more outstanding of the false ones. In 1430 the originals of these pretended bulls were stated to have been lost or destroyed for at least seventy years, but copies of them were received in evidence on a judicial investigation that took place relative to the ecclesiastical jurisdiction of the university. Their validity was recognized by the Pope's Delegate, whose sentence was duly confirmed at Rome.[7]

The repetition of these myths by historian after historian

---

[3] Charles Henry Cooper, *Annals of Cambridge* (London: Warwick and Co., 1842), I, 1-3.

[4] *Ibid.*, I, 2.

[5] James Bass Mullinger, *The University of Cambridge* (Cambridge: University Press, 1873). p. 66; Hastings Rashdall, *The Universities of Europe in the Middle Ages* (edited by F. M. Powicke and A. B. Emden; Oxford: Clarendon Press, 1936), III, 276.

[6] *The Privileges of the University of Cambridge* (edited by George Dyer; London: Longman and Co., 1824), I, 55-56. Hereafter referred to as *Privileges*.

[7] Cooper, *op. cit.*, I, 182-183.

has done much to cloud over the true origins of the universities, but at long last the veil of mist which has covered them for so many centuries has been pierced, and we are now able to trace out the beginnings, even though they are still vague and somewhat hazy.

There is evidence that there were schools of Oxford before the middle of the twelfth century.[8] These schools at first probably owed their academic importance to the commercial prominence of Oxford. The growth of such religious houses as the Convent of Godestow, the Abbey of Oseney, Abingdon, Saint Frideswyde, etc., increased the company of clerks in Oxford, and can hardly have failed to stimulate schools and teaching.[9]

One recent explanation for Oxford's early importance as a study centre is this:

It is hard to say just why Oxford, rather than the capital or some great cathedral city, should have become the site of the earliest university in England, but its location in the heart of rural England is highly significant. For England was, until very recently, rural: the county and parish furnished the bases of its social and economic life. Oxford was easy of access from all parts of England, but few cities of the country could have been further removed from the foreign influences which were drawn to the courts of the King and of the great princes of the Church. Medieval Oxford was enfolded and nourished by England. No medieval university aligned itself more closely with the aspirations of the nation in the midst of which it was located than did the oldest university of the English-speaking world.[10]

There is, however, no indication of Oxford as a *studium generale*.[11] Dean Rashdall [12] has put forth an interesting hy-

[8] In collecting evidence to show the existence of schools at Oxford before the year 1167, Rashdall, *op. cit.*, III, 16-21, has submitted two letters from a certain Theobaldus Stampensis, written before 1117, in which he is described as "Master at Oxford" or "Doctor at Caen"; a passage in the Oseney Chronicle which mentions the presence of Robert Pullen, theologian, at Oxford, in 1133; and the somewhat doubtful evidence that the Lombard Jurist Vacarius taught at Oxford in the year 1149.

[9] Charles Edward Mallet, *A History of the University of Oxford* (New York: Longmans, Green, and Co., 1924), I, 17.

[10] Frederick Eby and Charles Flinn Arrowood, *The History and Philosophy of Education Ancient and Medieval* (N. Y.: Prentice-Hall, Inc., 1940), p. 781. Cf. also Herbert E. Salter, *Medieval Oxford* (Oxford: Clarendon Press, 1936), p. 90.

[11] By the term *studium generale* is meant the resorting of students to one particular place from all parts. The term "University," as used then, meant merely the corporate body of masters and scholars.

[12] Rashdall, *op. cit.*, III, 9-16.

pothesis about the growth of such a *studium generale* there between the years 1167 and 1190, one which has been generally accepted as the most plausible. He attributes the sudden rise of the *studium generale* to a migration of students (such as gave rise to other universities), presumably from Paris. This would account for Oxford's unusual freedom from ecclesiastical authority, even at its very beginning. Henry II had bitterly quarreled with Thomas Becket, with whom the French king had sympathized, and about the year 1167 had issued ordinances requiring the return of all English scholars studying at Paris under pain of losing their benefices. According to Rashdall, these recalled students settled at Oxford, the spot most likely to attract them, and even then beginning to come into its future fame as a home of learning.[13] However humble its beginning may have been, Oxford's medieval splendor, its brilliant and famous professors, its political and ecclesiastical entanglements, its pulsing, throbbing life, and turbulent and riotous throngs soon made Oxford a force to be reckoned with, and an intellectual centre second to none.

The first half of the thirteenth century saw at least three important occurrences: (1) the beginning of Oxford's ascendancy over the town, coincidental with the founding of Cambridge University, (2) the installation of endowments in the form of " chests " for poor scholars, and (3) the introduction of the collegiate system.

[13] Arthur F. Leach assails Dean Rashdall's theory. In his *Educational Charters and Documents* (Cambridge: University Press, 1911), p. xxiv, he says: " As these documents [the ordinances] contain no mention of Paris, Oxford, or students, they have no real claim to inclusion. Both were proclamations of Henry II, one forbidding any ecclesiastic, regular or secular, from going between England and France without a passport, another ordering all clerks who held English benefices to return to them without delay on pain of deprivation. Both were aimed at Becket, the first to prevent adherents joining him in his exile to France, the second to deprive him of the assistance of the Italian and French clerks beneficed in England. University students were not as a rule beneficed. As Dr. Rashdall himself in a note does ' not assert that the connexion of the migration,' which itself is not even shown to have existed, ' with Oxford is direct or immediate,' *cadit quaestio*. It is more historical to seek the origin of Oxford in a proved congregation of masters and scholars in 1130-1149 than in a hypothetical migration of 1167." However, since it is after this " hypothetical migration " that references to Oxford become numerous, in all probability Rashdall is correct in his theory.

The chartered history of Oxford, and the beginning of its ascendancy over the town, began with a rather violent incident in the winter of 1208-09.[14] A clerk killed a townsman, and the citizens, unable to apprehend the real culprit, hanged several innocent clerks in his stead. When King John, embroiled with the Pope, refused to interfere, the university body (with the exception of a few) protested by abandoning their schools and migrating to Cambridge, Reading, Paris, etc. The Pope triumphed over John, however, which meant that the townsmen were obliged consequently to capitulate to the Legate and acknowledge the rights of the university. The terms imposed on them were as follows: [15] the townsmen were to excuse the scholars of one-half the rent of all halls let to them in the town for a period of ten years; to pay yearly fifty-two shillings for the use of poor scholars and to feast one hundred of them every year on Saint Nicholas' day; to sell to the scholars all provisions at a just and reasonable rate; if they arrested a clerk, to deliver him to the Bishop of Lincoln or other proper authority, on being required to do so; all townsmen convicted of the above offense, to come without shoes, hats, or cloaks to the graves of the clerks who had been hanged, and, followed by the other townsmen, to give them proper burial. Thus was the way paved for the accruing of other privileges to the University of Oxford.

This exodus of masters and scholars from Oxford to Cambridge marked the beginning of Cambridge as a *studium generale*.[16] As in the case of Oxford, Cambridge, too, had been the centre for a school in connection with the conventual church at Ely, the Augustinian Priory of Barnwell. The earliest legal recognition of Cambridge as a university seems to be disputed. Mullinger,[17] following Cooper,[18] contends that the first evidence of such recognition was a writ of Henry III (1217) commanding all clerks who had been excommunicated for their adhesion to Louis, son of the king of France, and who had not been absolved, to depart the realm before the

---

[14] Mallet, *op. cit.*, I, 31.
[15] *Mun. Acad.*, I, 1-3.
[16] Rashdall, *op. cit.*, III, 276-278.
[17] *Op. cit.*, p. 84.
[18] *Op. cit.*, I, 37.

middle of Lent. "If (as it seems very probable)," says Cooper, " the word *clerk* is used in this writ as denoting a scholar, this appears to be the earliest authentic legal instrument referring to the existence of a University at this place." [19] More than likely Rashdall is correct in assuming that nothing definite concerning the *studium generale* of Cambridge can be claimed for that university until the year 1229, when Henry III offered an asylum to the dispersed scholars of Paris. Fuller [20] says, " We easily believe the greatest part of the strangers repaired to Oxford; though Cambridge no doubt did share in them her considerable portion." Still a third view is offered: Leach [21] thinks that a royal writ commanding the sheriff of the county to repress the disorders of the clerks and scholars should be considered the first mention of Cambridge as a university. If the actual naming of Cambridge should be the criterion then Leach is correct in his assumption; but the inference in *Literas Patentes ad Universitatem Parisiensum transmissas pro Scholaribus invitandis, ut se studii causa in Angliam transferant*, on which Rashdall bases his belief that Cambridge is included, is strong enough for contending that here can be found Cambridge's first legal recognition.

The maintenance of poor scholars, the second characteristic feature that had its origin in the thirteenth century, began in 1219, when the Abbot and Convent of Eynsham undertook to pay, on behalf of the townsmen of Oxford, the yearly pension which they were obliged to pay to the university for the maintenance of poor scholars, and also promised " to feed once a year one hundred poor Scholars, to each of whom they give two pence, to be paid annually on the same day." [22] Twenty-one years later Robert Grosseteste, Bishop of Lincoln, having decided that this money was not being allocated to its

---

[19] Dr. Sidney Painter of the Johns Hopkins University has found that Cooper mistook the name Kent for the abbreviation of Cantebrigge, and that consequently the writ in question does not refer to Cambridge at all.
[20] Thomas Fuller, *The History of the University of Cambridge* (London: Thomas Tegg, 1840), p. 18.
[21] *Educational Charters*, p. 148.
[22] *Mun. Acad.*, I, 4. Marginal note.

proper use, issued an ordinance regulating the same.[23] The money, with any additional bequests, was deposited in Saint Frideswyde's Priory, and

> . . . one of the brethren of that Priory, appointed by the Prior and approved by the Chancellor, along with two discreet persons to be elected by the University, shall have the custody thereof. It shall be lent to poor Scholars upon proper pledges being given for the same; such Scholars must not hold a benefice of the value to ten marks. If the pledge be not redeemed within a year, it may be sold. . . . The aforesaid guardians of this money shall annually render an account before auditors appointed by the University for this purpose. . . .[24]

This system of regulating endowments, the " chest " system, with a few minor changes and additions, remained in existence for several hundred years.

The third great event that occurred in the thirteenth century was the introduction of the collegiate system. Students were accustomed to boarding together in certain inns or halls in order to cut down their expenses, and, although these halls were gradually brought under the control of the universities, the students were to a great extent without any restrictions, and consequently lived riotously. However, in 1249, William of Durham died, and left a sum of two hundred and ten marks to be invested in rents for the support of ten or more masters of arts studying theology; [25] and in 1280 a hall was purchased for their residence, later called Great University Hall, where they were gathered under a single roof for the advancement of their learning and improvement of their discipline.[26] Soon after this a second Oxford College was founded, Balliol. John de Balliol, a wealthy baron, persuaded to do penance for his sins, established a society of scholars which must have been in existence before June, 1266, because a King's Writ at that time mentioned such a group.[27] This piece of evidence makes Balliol College actually the first college in Oxford, although

[23] *Ibid.*, I, 8-10.
[24] *Ibid.*, I, 9-10.
[25] Rashdall, *op. cit.*, III, 170.
[26] F. C. Conybeare, " University College," *The Colleges of Oxford, Their History and Traditions* (edited by Andrew Clark; London: Methuen and Co., 1891), p. 5. Hereafter referred to as *Colleges of Oxford*.
[27] *Calendar of Scotch Documents*, edited by Bain, p. 478, quoted by Mallet, *op. cit.*, I, 98, and Rashdall, *op. cit.*, III, 180, n.

3

its formal charter was not given until 1282. But it was Walter de Merton who inaugurated a series of changes which gradually and fundamentally altered conditions of life for Oxford students and masters alike,[28] when in 1263 he made over his Manor House and estate to a group of scholars. The statutes, issued in 1274, " are justly regarded as the archetype of the College system, not only in the University of Oxford, but in that of Cambridge, where they were adopted as a model by the founder of Peterhouse, the oldest of Cambridge Colleges." [29] Merton's idea took root and bore fruit because it was inspired by a true sympathy with the needs of the university, where the subjects of study were then as " frivolous as it was the policy of Rome to make them," where religious houses with the Mendicant Friars almost monopolized learning, and where the streets were the scenes of outrageous violence and outbreaks. The aim of Walter Merton was this: to combine monastic discipline with secular learning, and so to create a great seminary for the secular clergy.[30] The scholars, preferably members of Walter de Merton's family, were to study in some university,[31] where they were to hire a hall and live together. After completing a year's probation in the arts school, they were to proceed to theology; however, some few were allowed to study canon and civil law. In addition to all this, provision was made for twelve young boys, too poor to further their education, to live near the college and to study under their own grammar master. In general, the scholar was to be " chaste, peaceable, humble, poor, of good conduct and capacity for study . . .He must talk Latin in chambers, and abstain from noise, and be subject to expulsion if guilty of serious misdeeds." [32] By 1274 Merton College was permanently established at Oxford, and was well

[28] Lowell Joseph Ragatz, *Glimpses of Oxford during the Thirteenth, Fourteenth, and Fifteenth Centuries* (Washington: Paul Pearlman, n. d.), p. 10.

[29] George C. Broderick, " Merton College," *The Colleges of Oxford*, p. 59.

[30] *Ibid.*, p. 60.

[31] This was at the time of the Oxford migration to Cambridge, Northampton, and Paris.

[32] Mallet, *op. cit.*, I, 116.

on its way toward becoming the home of famous men of the future.

Only one college was founded at Cambridge in the thirteenth century, and that one was Peterhouse. In 1280, Hugh Balsham, Bishop of Ely, conceived the idea of introducing a body of secular scholars into the ancient Hospital of St. John,[33] but such dissension and strife arose among the brethren and scholars that the experiment was unsuccessful. Several years later the bishop decided, for the sake of peace, to separate them and to found a separate college for the scholars.[34] In such fashion did Peterhouse come into existence.

With the dawn of the fourteenth century the two universities had entered into a turbulent and violent life. For almost a hundred years their existence had been one marked by altercations and battles between townsmen and clerks,[35] by jealousies between the Northerners and Southerners,[36] and by the violent and dissipated actions of the clerks themselves.[37] They were able to assume privilege after privilege because of their effective threats of ceasing their lectures and withdrawing from the towns unless their demands were granted.[38] But it was Oxford which took the lead in the fourteenth century, rapidly becoming more powerful and domineering than Cambridge, whose " academic prerogatives and liberties were considerably slower in their growth and somewhat less magnificent in their final development . . ." [39] One contributing factor to this superior renown of Oxford was the presence there of such renowned Scholastics as Duns Scotus, William of Ockham, and John Wycliffe. The fame of a university depended for the greater part on the popularity and influence of its teachers—the more popular a lecturer was, the greater the crowds that were attracted to his side to listen to his teach-

---

[33] *Educational Charters*, pp. 222-224.
[34] *Ibid.*, pp. 224-231.
[35] *Mun. Acad.*, I, 36-37, 46-55, 67-69; *Documents relating to the University and Colleges of Cambridge* (London: Longmans, Brown, Green and Longman, 1852). Hereafter referred to as *Documents*.
[36] *Mun. Acad.*, I, 20.
[37] *Ibid.*, 16-18, 24; *Documents*, I, 2, 3.
[38] *Mun. Acad.*, I, 43-45.
[39] Rashdall, *op. cit.*, III, 279-280.

ings—and Oxford consequently became the intellectual centre of the fourteenth century, not only for England but for France, since Ockham and Duns Scotus, the outstanding scholastic philosophers of the time, were associated with Oxford. This state of affairs was not true for Cambridge. Even that very loyal historian, Thomas Fuller, ardent advocate of Cambridge as he was, had to admit:

> Note by the way, that Oxford was most fruitful of defenders and sufferers for the truth, from the coming of Wickliff till the rising of Luther; during which time Cambridge was but barren of famous confessors. But Cambridge, in the reign of king Henry VIII. afforded more martyrs and witnesses of the truth, whilst Oxford was more generally guilty of superstition. . . . And thus the God of truth was alternately furnished with champions, first of the one then the other University; till both at last (after the perfect Reformation) became the fruitful nurseries of Protestant worthies, to the envy and admiration of all Christendom.[40]

Rashdall, too, emphasizes the sterility of Cambridge at this time:

> Up to the end of the fourteenth century . . . Cambridge was a third rate University; . . . Not a single [great] Schoolman can be shown to have taught at Cambridge: it is hard to produce the name, I will not say of a great man but of a prominent ecclesiastic, who studied at Cambridge before the middle of the fourteenth century. . . . It was not till Oxford had become impregnated with the Wycliffite heresy that Cambridge came into fashion . . .[41]

The founding of colleges went on in measured tread, not only in Oxford, but also in Cambridge, during the fourteenth century: five at Oxford,—Exeter, Queen's, Canterbury, Oriel, and New College; and six at Cambridge,—Michaelhouse, University Hall, later called Clare Hall, Pembroke, Gonville, Trinity, and Corpus Christi. One innovation of this century that received royal imitation and support in the fifteenth and later centuries was the founding of a college with an attendant school to prepare the younger students for college entrance. This was the origin of the English Public Schools.

In 1314, Walter de Stapeldon, Bishop of Exeter, founded Stapeldon Hall, soon better known as Exeter College, for

[40] Fuller, *op. cit.*, pp. 88-89.
[41] Rashdall, *op. cit.*, III, 284. The word " great " has been omitted in the Powicke and Emden edition, but is in the original version, II, ii, 552.

fellows born or resident in Devon and Cornwall, eight from the former and four from the latter county; he also founded a grammar school at Exeter, to prepare boys for Oxford.[42] By a charter dated 6 December 1324, and confirmed by Edward II 20 December, at Nottingham, Adam de Brome founded Oriel College in *sacra theologia et arte dialectica studentium*.[43] Just one year later the college was taken over by the king, who then became its nominal founder. Legally, the name of the college was St. Mary's College; actually, it was known by the name of the house in which the students resided: Oriel. The year 1341 saw the start of the college which was to be the first to have a queen as patroness and foundress. "The Hall of the Scholars of the Queen" was established by Robert of Eglesfield, confessor and chaplain to Queen Phillipa, and its aim, as set forth in the statutes, was "the cultivation of Theology to the glory of God, the advance of the Church, and the salvation of souls." [44] Canterbury College, which did not survive the Dissolution, was founded in 1362 by Simon Islip, Archbishop of Canterbury, who attempted to unite Regulars and Seculars on the same foundation.[45] But it was New College, founded in 1379, that stood out as the most significant endowment of the fourteenth century, just as Merton dominated the thirteenth century colleges. For the first time in the history of Oxford a college became not merely an eleemosynary institution, but a great ecclesiastical corporation which vied both in the splendor of its architecture and the dignity of its corporate life with the Cathedral chapters and the monastic houses.[46] William of Wykeham, Bishop of Winchester, was granted a charter for New College in 1379, although it had already been in existence as early as 1375.[47] The purpose for which New College

---

[42] Charles W. Boase, "Exeter College," *The Colleges of Oxford*, p. 76.
[43] C. L. Shadwell, "Oriel College," *The Colleges of Oxford*, p. 88.
[44] J. R. Magrath, "Queen's College," *The Colleges of Oxford*, p. 125.
[45] Rashdall, *op. cit.*, III, 211.
[46] Hastings Rashdall, "New College," *The Colleges of Oxford*, p. 155.
[47] Mallet, *op. cit.*, I, 288; Rashdall, *Universities of Europe in the Middle Ages*, III, 214.

was founded was to increase the supply of clergy, the lack of which the statutes declared was caused " *ex pestilentiis, guerris et aliis mundi miseriis.*" [48] The distinctive feature of Wykeham's foundation was, in addition to New College with its seventy fellows, the provision for another college, Winchester, to prepare younger students for entrance into Oxford University. Heretofore such provision had been limited to the presence of a grammar master teaching the younger students, as at Merton's and Queen's. But now the first English Public School was born, the prototype of which was to become famous the world over. From the scholars at Winchester were to be selected the seventy scholars of New College. These younger scholars were to be taught by the older fellows who were to be paid by the college and who were consequently the fore-runners of the tutorial system. Of the seventy fellows, at least twenty had to proceed to law, ten for civil, ten for canon. This shows an interesting tendency of the latter part of the fourteenth century to swing away from the study of scholastic philosophy to ecclesiastical and civil law, a tendency that by the end of the fifteenth century was to have reached its peak and to have begun its downward journey as a result of the attendant evils that followed upon a too-zealous attention paid by ecclesiastics to mundane affairs.

The University of Cambridge, too, was not lacking in its share of college foundations in the fourteenth century. The first of these was Michaelhouse, founded in 1324 by Hervey de Stanton, Chancellor of the Exchequer, and Canon of Bath and Wells. All students were to be priests or at least in holy orders when admitted, and all were to study theology.[49] Just two years later, Richard de Badew,[50] Chancellor of Cambridge, founded University Hall. Elizabeth de Burgh, Countess of Clare, augmented the foundation by bestowing advowsons on it, and in return for her generosity she received all the founder's rights.[51] Having bestowed the name of Clare

---

[48] *Educational Charters,* p. 352.
[49] Rashdall, *Universities of Europe in the Middle Ages,* III, 301.
[50] So Cooper and Fuller spell it. Rashdall gives the name as Baden.
[51] Mullinger, *op. cit.,* p. 251; Rashdall, *Universities of Europe in the Middle Ages,* III, 303.

Hall on it, Lady de Burgh issued statutes for it in 1359. The fellows were to be twenty in number, of whom six were required to be in priests' orders at the time of their admission. Two might study civil law, one canon law, and one medicine: the rest were to be artists or theologians.[52] In the short space of five years four other colleges sprang up. Pembroke (1347), whose foundress was Marie de St. Paul, was the only college in an English university where preference was given to natives of France already studying at either university.[53] The reason for this preference is plain to see: Marie de St. Paul was a Frenchwoman. Gonville (1348), named for its founder, Edmund Gonville, had as its main object the promotion of the study of theology: the study of canon law for two years was permitted, but not obligatory.[54] The founder, at his death, left a sum of money to William Bateman, Bishop of Norwich, to see his foundation finished according to his wishes. This same William Bateman in 1350 founded his own college, Trinity, designed primarily for the study of civil and canon law.[55] As Bishop Fuller so quaintly describes Bateman: " He was one of a very stout spirit, and very well skilled in civil and canon law (and we may presume the common law, too because a Norfolk-man) . . ." [56] Corpus Christi College was the first college to be founded by a gild (two, in fact, Corpus Christi and the Blessed Virgin Mary) in all of England. Sometimes known as S. Benet's College, Corpus Christi College was designed and endowed for the education of the clergy; at least, according to the declared motive of its founders, it was to fill up the ranks which had been depleted by the ravages of the plague.[57] The foundation was only a small one, since it provided for but two scholars. As the revenues of

[52] Mullinger, op. cit., p. 252; Rashdall, Universities of Europe in the Middle Ages, III, 304.
[53] Mullinger, op. cit., p. 239; Rashdall, Universities of Europe in the Middle Ages, III, 305.
[54] Mullinger, op. cit., p. 240.
[55] Ibid., p. 242; Rashdall, Universities of Europe in the Middle Ages, III, 309.
[56] Fuller, op. cit., p. 74.
[57] Rashdall, Universities of Europe in the Middle Ages, III, 311.

the college increased so the number of the scholars were to increase.[58]

The personal actions of the students during the fourteenth century had not improved to any great extent. Bitterness and antagonism still remained between the Town and Gown, and occasionally the smouldering resentment burst into flames, slaughter and spoliation being meted out by both parties.[59] Because of this resentment, a group of Oxford students and masters, disgusted by the homicides, crimes, and robberies, withdrew from Oxford in 1334-35 and seceded to Stamford, where they proceeded to establish a new university. From Oxford's appeal to Edward III, a proclamation was issued stating that no universities were allowed except at Oxford and Cambridge,[60] but it is interesting to note that even in the fifteenth century the candidate for an M. A. had to swear not to teach or read at Stamford.[61] Drastic action on the part of the universities against the scholars was sometimes necessary: they were fined or suspended for bearing arms within certain limits; for insulting one another; for causing false imprisonment; and ordered to recant if found guilty of heresy.[62] Slowly but surely the university took over or shared privileges that had been within the jurisdiction of the town: the authority in assize and assay of bread and beer: the power of convening lay people before the chancellor; all causes concerning contracts involving a clerk; and the cognizance of the chancellor in all personal actions where a clerk was the party of one part.[63]

On the whole, the fourteenth century had been one of brilliance and renown for the universities, but after the death of Wycliffe there appeared a downward proclivity in their fortunes.

[58] *Ibid.*, 311-312.
[59] *Mun. Acad.*, I, 113-117, 190, 202, 224-225; *Documents*, I, 3, 6, 27; *Privileges*, I, 10, 13, 14, 18, 22, 23, 24.
[60] *Educational Charters*, pp. 286-289.
[61] *Mun. Acad.*, II, 374-376; *Statuta Antiqua Universitatis Oxoniensis* (edited by Strickland Gibson; Oxford: Clarendon Press, 1931), p. 20. Hereafter referred to as *Statuta Antiqua.*
[62] *Mun. Acad.*, I, 91-94, 119-120, 122-125, 203, 209-212; *Privileges*, I, 10, 16, 17.
[63] *Mun. Acad.*, I, 78-81, 159, 173-180; *Documents*, I, 4, 28; *Privileges*, I, 12, 15, 18.

Cambridge and Oxford in the Fifteenth Century

The opening years of the fifteenth century were ones of dark foreboding to the universities. Ever since the last years of Wycliffe's life, ecclesiastical authorities had been attempting to stamp out the heretical tendencies that had cropped up with Wycliffe's attacks on the doctrine of Transubstantiation and the abuses of power and property owned by the ecclesiasts. Arundel, Archbishop of Canterbury and Chancellor to the King, was possessed with an almost fanatical zeal to root out all traces of Lollardy, and in this determination he was enthusiastically supported by Henry IV. Henry expressed his opposition to the Lollards as early as 1400 by passing a statute against them to this intent:

. . . That none within the said realm, or any other dominions, subject to his royal majesty, presume to preach openly or privily, without the licence of the diocesan of the same place first required and obtained, curates in their own churches, and persons hitherto privileged, and other of the canon law granted, only except. Nor that none from henceforth any thing preach, hold, teach or instruct openly or privily, or make or write any book contrary to the Catholic faith or determination of the holy church, nor of such sect and wicked doctrine and opinions shall make any conventicles, or in any wise hold or exercise schools. And also that none from henceforth in any wise favour such preacher, or maker of any such and like conventicles, or holding or exercising schools, or making or writing such books, or so teaching, informing or exciting the people, nor any of them maintain or any wise sustain. And that all and singular having such books, or any writings of such wicked doctrines and opinions shall . . . cause to be delivered all such books and writings to the diocesan of the same place within xl. days, from the time of the proclamation of this ordinance and statute. And if any person or persons, of whatsoever kind, estate, or condition that he or they be, from henceforth do or attempt against the royal ordinance and statute aforesaid . . . then the diocesan of the same place in his diocese, such person or persons in this behalf defamed or evidently suspected and every of them, may by the authority of the said ordinance and statute cause to be arrested, and under safe custody in his prisons to be detained, till he or they of the articles laid to him or them in this behalf, do canonically purge him or themselves, . . . so that the said diocesan by himself or his commissaries do openly and judicialy proceed against such persons so arrested, and remaining under his safe custody to all effect of the law, and determine that same business according to the canonical decrees within three months after the said arrest, any lawful impediment ceasing . . .[64]

---

[64] *Statutes-at-Large of England and Great Britain* (Cambridge: University Press, 1762-), II, 416-417. Hereafter referred to as *Statutes-at-Large*.

Backed by the Crown, Arundel was determined to break up these heresies, and he earned the undying hatred of the universities by asserting his authority as archbishop in visiting them. This proposed visitation was a blow aimed directly at the heart of the universities' privileges and independence of any ecclesiastical control except that of the Pope, and accordingly the plan met with a storm of protest. When, in 1411, the Archbishop deliberately disregarded the Papal Bull of Exemption granted by Boniface IX, exempting Oxford from the jurisdiction of all archbishops, bishops, and ordinaries, and proceeded with his visitation to Oxford, he was met with spirited resistance by the scholars, and not permitted to enter. Oriel, according to the historian of Oriel College,[65] seems to have been an active centre of resistance. An inquiry was held, probably after the settlement of 1411, and charges of misconduct were lodged against William Symon, Robert Dykes, and Thomas Wilton. A writ was issued on May 13, 1411, which commissioned the chancellor of Oxford or his commissary, and the king's kinsman, Master Richard Courtenay, to arrest Nicholas Panter, Thomas Wilton, John Clifton, Robert Burton, John Shakyl, William Veisy, Cerle Wyse, John Bernevile, and William Okely, and bring them before the king and his council with all speed.[66] Still another link in the chain of evidence that Oriel was the centre of resistance is reported by Riley, who says that he found

. . . A long parchment Roll, of three membranes sewed together, being a contemporary copy of Depositions taken, A. D. 1411, relative to riots in the University between the Northern and Southern Scholars, and resistance to the Visitation of the Archbishop of Canterbury; three Fellows of the College, Master William Symon, Robert Dukes, and Thomas Wyttone, by name, and John Rote, the chaplain of the College, being the parties principally concerned . . . They are here accused of being night-walkers, of collecting the scholars within Oriel in arms, of frequenting taverns, entering the College at ten, eleven, twelve at night, and, when they could not gain admission upon knocking at the gate, climbing over the College walls, and inducing strangers to do the same.[67]

---

[65] C. L. Shadwell, op. cit., p. 101.
[66] Great Britain Public Record Office, Calendar of the Patent Rolls (London: His Majesty's Stationery Office, 1903-1909), Henry IV (1408-1413), IV, 317-318. Hereafter referred to as Patent Rolls.
[67] Great Britain Historical Manuscripts Commission, Second Report

There was every reason in the world why Oxford should struggle so bitterly against this visitation. The English universities had been singularly free from ecclesiastical intervention in their academic affairs, and they prided themselves on their jealously guarded freedom of discussion on any Church doctrines or tenets or their outspoken opinions on any of the beliefs of the scholastic writers. Only a few years previous to the proposed visit, Arundel had succeeded in getting a series of constitutions against the teaching of Wycliffism in the schools or elsewhere passed at a convocation of the clergy held at St. Paul's in London, in which it was declared that:

. . . No Master of Arts or Grammar, should instruct his pupils upon any theological point, contrary to the determination of the Church, or expound any test of Scripture in other manner it had been of old expounded, or permit his pupils either publicly or privately, to dispute concerning the Catholic faith or the sacraments of the Church. Secondly, that no book or tract compiled by John Wiclif, or any one else in his time or since, to be compiled thereafter, shall be read or taught in the schools, hostels, or other places in the province, unless it should first be examined by the Universities of Oxford or Cambridge, or at least by twelve persons to be elected by each of these bodies, and afterwards expressly approved of by the Archbishop or his successors. . . . That whosoever shall read or teach any book or treatise contrary to the form aforesaid, should be punished as a sower of schism and favourer of heresy, according to the quality of his offence.[68]

Now a second blow was being aimed at their privileges and it was futile to try to ward it off. The type of prying that Oxford was being subjected to was probably based on questions that Arundel presented to Cambridge when, on a visit there in 1401, the chancellor and heads of the colleges of Cambridge were examined by him " singly, secretly, and *cum silentio* " :

  1. *In primis.* Whether the statutes and laudable customs of the University be observed by all therein?

of the Royal Commission on Historical Manuscripts (edited by Henry Thomas Riley; London: George Edward Eyre and William Spotteswood, 1871), Appendix, pp. 136-137.
  [68] Cooper, *op. cit.*, I, 151-152. Rashdall remarks, " It is characteristic circumstance that a New College man, John Wytenham, was at the head of the Delegacy for condemning Wycliffe's books in 1411, all the other Doctors being monks or friars." (" New College," *Colleges of Oxford*, p. 163). Wykeham and his college contributed to some extent in bringing about the suppression of Wycliffism.

2. *Item.* Whether there be any Scholars in the said University which refuse to obey the mandates and admonitions of the Chancellor?

3. *Item.* Whether there be any disturbers of peace and unity in the said University?

4. *Item.* Whether the common chests, with the money therein, and keys thereunto belonging, be carefully kept?

5. *Item.* Whether Masters, Bachelors and Doctors formally perform their exercises, and take their degrees according to their deserts?

6. *Item.* Whether there be any suspected of Lollardism or any other heretical pravity?

7. *Item.* Whether the Doctors dispute publicly in the Schools, how often, and when?

8. *Item.* Whether the number of Fellows be complete in Halls and Colleges, according to the will of the Founders?

9. *Item.* Whether any Scholars be defamed for any notorious crime, or do not profit in their studies, or hinder others from profiting therein?

10. *Item.* How the University is governed in victuals or any necessaries? [69]

No matter how valuable such an inquiry might be—certainly the questions on the whole were ones from which a good deal of practical information could be obtained—it lost its value, in the eyes of Oxford, because it was to have been made by one whose authority the scholars could not recognize.

Oxford's refusal to allow the Archbishop to enter the university angered the king, and he immediately ordered the chancellor and proctors to resign. The masters deliberately re-elected the officials and it was only through the intervention of the Prince of Wales that they were allowed to keep their positions.[70] Finally, Oxford was forced to recognize the Archbishop's right of visitation. To show her complete submission to the Archbishop and all he stood for, the university, in 1412, had this statute enrolled in the Chancellors' and Proctors' Book:

In order that the University may recover her former high reputation, which has been greatly damaged by the erroneous opinions held by some of her unnatural children, it is enacted that no Doctor, Master, Bachelor, or Scholar shall teach, defend or maintain any of the conclusions lately condemned at the Council of London, under pain of imprisonment and deprivation and his degree and of the greater excommunication. And, lest any should plead ignorance, all the aforementioned conclusions, along with this present statute, shall be written out and kept in a book in the library, so that anyone may take copies

[69] Fuller, *op. cit.*, pp. 93-95.

[70] Mallet, *op. cit.*, I, 239; and Rashdall, *Universities of Europe in the Middle Ages*, III, 133.

thereof. And all who graduate hereafter shall, on admission to their degree, make oath that they will not teach, defend, or maintain, publicly or privately, any of the said conclusions, not comfort another in so doing. And in order to the rooting out these tares from among the wheat, all governors of colleges and halls, shall, every year before All Hallows' Day, swear in the presence of the Chancellor, that they will not admit into their societies any Master, Bachelor, or Scholar, or even servant who is suspected of being a Lollard, under pain of losing his office and his academical degree, and the Chancellor, at his admission, shall swear that he will faithfully see that this statute is observed.[71]

So, at the end of the first fifteen years of the fifteenth century, the English universities had settled in a groove of passive submission to the king and his chancellor, and they were to remain there for many long years to come. Occasionally they plucked up enough courage to rebel against a policy of a bishop or archbishop, or to defy the king with respect to his wishes on the appointment of a minor official, but all these were matters of slight importance. Lollardy had a habit of cropping up in unexpected places, but Oxford, ever mindful of the crushing blow dealt her by Arundel, was quick to reply to any accusation, direct or otherwise, that she still might be harboring (as undoubtedly she was, regardless of her denials) any such heretical teachings. When Edward IV's letter on the repression of heresy was read in convocation, Oxford answered it by saying:

. . . search was immediately made for all such works of Wyclif and Pecok as could be found, and they were committed to the flames with the approbation of all; and if any further copies should be discovered they shall likewise be burnt . . .[72]

---

[71] *Mun. Acad.*, I, 269-270. Marginal notes. Cf. also *Statuta Antiqua*, pp. 221-222.

[72] *Epistolae Academica Oxoniensis* (edited by Henry Anstey; Oxford: Clarendon Press, for the Oxford Historical Society, 1898), II, 411-412. Hereafter referred to as *Epist. Acad.* Marginal notes. Cooper, *op. cit.*, I, 153-154, cites an example of this renunciation at Cambridge: "On the 22nd of February [1412/13] Peter Hirforde, Bachelor of Arts, in the new chapel of the University, before Eudo la Zouche, LL. D., Chancellor, and the venerable congregation of Masters, regent and non-regent, renounced the conclusions and opinions of Wycliffe, and took an oath that he would never teach, approve, or defend these conclusions, opinions, books, or treatises, but resist the same and all favoring them, in the schools or elsewhere, to the utmost of his power. This renunciation was attested by Richard Billingforde, D. D. William Someresham, D. D. John Judde, Doctor of Decrees, and others, and by Thomas de Burbye, clerk, of the diocese of York and notary by apostolic authority, who drew up a public instrument setting forth the proceedings."

One wonders if the " approbation " were given in the abstract, so to speak, upon the supposition that if any of the books were found they would be burned, or whether the burning actually took place in the presence of the masters. Probably the former method was the one followed, with the result that the books escaped the conflagration.

This question of heresy in the ranks of the masters was always a sore point with Oxford, and one on which she fought back with as much spirit as she dared. In 1438 one of her masters, a certain Phillip Norris, was falsely accused (or so Oxford claimed) of heretical teaching, and was banished, and excommunicated. The Lord Chancellor of England was reminded that such a cause should be tried by the chancellor of Oxford, otherwise it would be a violation of the university's privileges,[73] and an appeal was even sent to Henry VI, but no results were forthcoming. In retaliation, Oxford suspended Friar Musselwyk, who had excommunicated Master Norris without the chancellor's sanction. Immediately the Order complained to the king and to the Duke of Gloucester, who wrote the university for an explanation, probably reprimanding it for its high-handed measures, for we find the chancellor explaining that the Duke must have been misinformed as to the actual incident. However, pressure must have been brought to bear, because in the next letter to Gloucester, Oxford remitted the friar's penalty, only, it remarks glibly, " as a personal favour to you, not because it was unjust or precipitate." One condition was imposed: that the offender come to the university and ask pardon for his perjury and manifold offenses.[74] Whether the friar did so, and whether Master Norris returned to the university cleared of the charges lodged against him is not told. It may even be that in this case the irritation was not caused by the accusation of heresy but by the fact that the whole affair had been carried on outside the court of the chancellor of Oxford, an express violation of the rule that any case where one member was connected with the university was to be under the uni-

[73] *Epist. Acad.*, I, 157-161.
[74] *Ibid.*, I, 162-168.

versity's jurisdiction.[75] A few years later the university once more showed that she still possessed enough pride in her former freedom of action to defy the king's wish that Oxford readmit a master who had been banished for misconduct. Instead, a letter was sent to Henry VI, in which Oxford explained her position on the matter:

> . . . We would gladly allow him to return, if we could do so with safety, but his life has been such that his presence was a constant peril to our liberties and privileges, which he endeavoured to violate both by his own actions and abetting others. Pious and peaceable masters he has prosecuted upon false charges, and with insolence and contumaceous conduct refused to submit to the penance we inflicted. In short, his whole life here has been a continual strife and discord. Such a wicked and litigious man we deem unfit to reside in a quiet and studious society, and indeed neither does the Church nor God himself receive into favour an impenitent sinner. We have long waited expecting his submission, before writing this letter, and we doubt not that you will even thank us for what we have done; for it is certain that if we overlooked his offenses many others would be found to imitate him.[76]

Deprived of her more important privileges, Oxford occupied herself in protesting against petty infringements of her rights. For instance, she complained to George Neville, Bishop of Exeter and Lord Chancellor, that certain citizens had committed crimes against the university and had refused to be corrected. As the scribe writes:

> . . . They are determined to govern and not be governed; and, led by one of the principal citizens—well-known to you—they violate our privileges and endeavour to establish a precedent against them. We look for your help, especially when it shall be necessary to bring the matter before the King.[77]

A few years later Neville, then the Archbishop of York, received another letter asking his help in three things: in enforcing the privileges; in compelling the vicar of Abingdon to pay a donation to the new school; and to arbitrate in a feud

---

[75] Three other instances of this violation were protested against in letters sent by Oxford in 1466 and 1478 to the Archbishop of York and the Bishop of Lincoln. *Ibid.*, II, 378-380, 444-445. Even Pope Sixtus interfered by issuing a bull in 1476 condemning such practices, and ordering anyone who brought priests of any rank or condition before a secular court to be excommunicated, and not absolved except *in extremis. Mun Acad.*, I, 348-351.

[76] *Epist. Acad.*, I, 264-266. Marginal notes.

[77] *Ibid.*, II, 366.

between the doctors of medicine and civil law, " by which the peace of the University has been disturbed, and murder only by the mercy of God avoided." [78] Evidently Oxford was unable to control even her own scholars, for political and ecclesiastical authorities were bombarded with letters asking help in quelling the disturbances of peace as well as the threatened loss of her " vital privileges." [79] In despair, the university passed a statute in which a monetary fine was levied on all offenders of the peace, as, it mournfully signed, " there is no better way of punishing the disturbers of peace than by a pecuniary fine." [80] The pages of the *Acta Curiae Cancellarii* are filled with all sorts of crimes and misdemeanors of the scholars and their servants: carrying arms, stealing a servant boy, incontinence, adultery, violence of all sorts, refusal to appear when summoned, debts, contumacy, non-payment of rent, abduction of a girl, shooting, defamation of character, and " playing tennis." [81] Bachelors in the faculties of civil and canon law were overbearing and presumptuous; they insisted on calling themselves masters, and created such scenes that patrons were called on for aid.[82] Sometimes, however, Oxford felt that her scholars were unjustly accused of living in violence and refusing to pursue their studies,[83] and claimed that some of the misdemeanors of which the scholars were said to be guilty were in reality committed by pseudo-scholars called " Chamberdekyns." In order to combat this false slander (and also to curb the true scholars), it was decreed c. 1410 that all scholars must reside in some college or hall, under pain of imprisonment or banishment, and that no

---

[78] *Ibid.*, II, 383-384. Cf. also the feud at Cambridge between the regents and non-regents and the graduate scholars of civil and canon law. Great Britain Public Record Office, *Calendar of the Close Rolls* (London: His Majesty's Stationery Office, 1929-), Henry V (1413-1419), I, 147. Hereafter referred to as *Close Rolls*.

[79] *Epist. Acad.*, I, 96-97, 108-110, 116-117, 118-124, 126-128.

[80] *Mun. Acad.*, I, 304-306. " *Non aptiore medio quam poena pecunaria . . .*"

[81] *Ibid.*, II, 505-608. Cf. also *Close Rolls*, Henry IV (1402-1405), II, 67; Henry V (1413-1419), II, 218; *Patent Rolls*, Henry IV (1401-1405), II, 341; Cooper, *op. cit.*, I, 218.

[82] *Epist. Acad.*, I, 115-116, 130-135.

[83] *Ibid.*, pp. 48-49.

townsmen, without special leave from the chancellor, should permit a student to live in his home.[84] This enactment may have helped to quell the disturbances a little, but the times were too turbulent and allegiances too varied for it to have had much effect. Many of these outbreaks were due to the over-zealous patriotism of the non-English clerks. The reigns of both Henry IV and Henry V, and occasionally Henry VI and Edward IV had been fraught with Scottish, Irish, and Welsh rebellions, and the clerks of those nationalities were reported to have assembled unlawfully at night for the purpose of rebellion; consequently they were arrested, whenever possible, by the proper authorities and punished.[85] However, as troublesome as some of the non-English clerks were, not all of them were so ebullient, and, when a statute was enacted in 1422 compelling Irishmen to return to Ireland upon pain of forfeiture of possessions, and imprisonment, graduates in the schools and scholars were among those exempted, if they could find surety for their good conduct and did not become principal of a hall or hostel. In addition, they had to bring to the chancellor of the universities letters testimonial signed by the lieutenant or justices of Ireland.[86]

The turbulence in the universities was but a reflection of the confusion and violence that was reigning in England during the first fifty years of the fifteenth century. Pestilence and famines, feuds and private wars, lawlessness of the nobility, extortion and oppression, depleted reserves and resources (due, in some measure, to the wars with France as well as to these private feudal wars) produced a poverty throughout England which affected the well-being of the universities. Over and over again Cambridge and Oxford complained that economic distress was causing a decrease in the number of scholars and a loss of prestige. In 1438 Oxford dispatched a letter to the Archbishop of Canterbury and other members of the Council then sitting at London:

[84] *Statuta Antiqua*, p. 208.
[85] *Patent Rolls*, Henry IV (1401-1405), II, 132; (1405-1408), III, 482.
[86] *Statutes-at-Large*, III, 74-75.

4

The University is like Rachel mourning her lost children. Her beauty is gone for very trouble. Once she was famous in the world; students flocked to her from almost every nation; then she abounded with men learned in every art and science, her schools were not dilapidated nor the halls and inns empty. Now alas! the nation is so impoverished by war and scarcity both of food and money, and so slender is the reward of merit, that hardly do any now care to resort hither: scarce one thousand remain. Our doors are locked, our buildings in ruins. Those who still labour here until old age find no reward, for they see that ignorant and unlettered men are promoted while they are turned out of doors. But how shall they teach who have no knowledge? We beseech you, therefore, to consider what sort of labourers you send into the vineyard, and to encourage education by promoting graduates to benefice.[87]

This matter of the promotion of " ignorant and unlettered " men to valuable benefices and important positions was one concerning which the universities continually raised objections, declaring that it was not worth while for a scholar to attend the schools if he were not properly rewarded for his labors.[88] And indeed this lack of provision for scholars was an important item in cutting down attendance. As a result of such petitions made both in 1438 and again in 1439, the archbishop, with the concurrence of the synod, decreed that for ten years to come all patrons of ecclesiastical preferment should confer the benefices in their gift exclusively on graduates of the universities, and that vicars-general, commissaries, and officials should be chosen from graduates in civil and canon law.[89]

That lack of funds was a constant thorn in Oxford's flesh is shown in the many letters addressed to powerful patrons who might be in a position to help her. Oxford had been invited to send a deputation to the Council of Basle (later Ferrara) and because of her poverty had to appeal to the

---

[87] *Epist. Acad.*, I, 154-155. Marginal notes.

[88] *Ibid.*, I, 168-170, 184-187.

[89] Cooper, *op. cit.*, I, 187. The mere fact that such a decree was passed in the synod was no assurance that it would be carried out. Ten or more years previous to this two representatives from Cambridge and Oxford had, at a convocation, made eloquent protests on behalf of the scholars of the universities " that the worth of scholars in the universities might be rewarded, and preferment proportioned to their deserts." Fuller, *op. cit.*, pp. 101-102. As indicated, these impassioned pleas must have fallen on heedless ears, for the graduates were still unrequited.

Archbishop of Canterbury and the Convocation for aid.[90] Again, in 1445, Oxford appealed to the king, writing that " Master Gascoigne has resigned as Chancellor because of insufficient means," [91] and urged him to help them get Gascoigne back. When the members of the Benedectine order attending the university wanted the fee of six and eight pence (usually paid to the master whose lectures they attended) abolished, Oxford protested that " if this fee were abolished, the recent revival of learning here would receive a mortal blow." [92] The " recent revival of learning " may have reference to the aid given by the Duke of Bedford in 1432 that " gave an impulse " to the study of the seven liberal arts and the three philosophies,[93] and the exhibition and chests founded by the Archbishop of Canterbury.[94] The Duke of Gloucester, a steadfast friend in all the university's trials and tribulations, came to the rescue in 1433 by founding lectures in the arts and philosophy; two years later, however, there were complaints that due to the great misery to which the university was reduced, the lectures had ceased, and an appeal was sent forth the following year asking Gloucester to provide for their continued maintenance.[95]

That the universities were in poor financial straits at this time is not to be denied. However, three events occurred during the fifteenth century which showed that, in spite of such difficulties, these institutions of higher learning were at least holding their ground, and in some instances advancing: the foundation of at least seven new colleges at Cambridge and Oxford, a series of endowments made not only to the universities proper but to individual colleges, and a building program that was undertaken at the beginning of the century and successfully carried through regardless of barriers and financial upsets.

The first of these events took place for the most part under the patronage and protection of Henry VI, who was keenly and

[90] *Epist. Acad.*, I, 72-74, 153-154.
[91] *Ibid.*, I, 247-249.
[92] *Ibid.*, I, 76-79.
[93] *Ibid.*, I, 81-82.
[94] *Ibid.*, I, 74-75.
[95] *Ibid.*, I, 106-108, 139-140, 151-153.

profoundly interested in the furtherance of education. During the second quarter of the century six colleges were founded, three at Oxford and three at Cambridge. Richard Fleming, Bishop of Lincoln, had once been sympathetic with Wycliffism, but in later years had turned against the " swinish snouts " and proposed to supply a perpetual succession of enemies to Wycliffe's doctrines by building a college for theologians.[96] Fleming's proposal was to build the college out of his own money, but to endow it from already existing revenues; and therefore he begged and received permission from the king and Parliament, the Archbishop of Canterbury, the Mother-Church of Lincoln, the Archdeacon of Oxford, the Mayor and Corporation of London, and the parishioners of all three churches, to unite the three Oxford parish churches of All Saints', St. Mildred's, and St. Michael's, as well as the chantry of St. Anne's in All Saints' into a college, which was to be called the College of the Blessed Mary and All Saints, Lincoln.[97] Fleming's college was to consist of a warden or rector, and seven fellows who were to study theology, *omnium imperatorix et domina facultatum*, and by the time of the bishop's death in 1430/31, or a year or two later, the charter had been received, the buildings begun, twelve manuscripts had been given to its library by Thomas Gascoigne, a small annual revenue provided for, and a rector, William Chamberlayne, named. At Chamberlayne's death, Bishop William Grey nominated Dr. John Beke for rector, and his rectorship lasted from 1434 to 1460.[98] Mallet [99] credits John Beke with securing such powerful assistance for Lincoln that the building program progressed rather rapidly: the Archdeacon of Oxford gave money, John Forest, Canon of Lincoln and Dean of Wells, built the chapel, library, hall, and kitchen; even the neighbors helped, so that by 1461 the college was on its feet.

[96] *Registrum Collegii Exoniensis* (edited by Charles William Boase; Oxford: Clarendon Press, for the Oxford Historical Society, 1894), p. lxii; Andrew Clark, " Lincoln College," *The Colleges of Oxford*, p. 171-172; and Mallet, *op. cit.*, I, 349.

[97] Clark, *op. cit.*, p. 172; Mallet, *op. cit.*, I, 349; *Patent Rolls*, Henry VI (1422-1429), I, 455.

[98] Clark, *op. cit.*, pp. 173-174.   [99] *Op. cit.*, I, 349-350.

The founder of All Souls' College, Oxford, Henry Chichele, appointed Archbishop of Canterbury at Arundel's death, was a firm supporter of Henry V's policy of war and brought all his influence to bear on it. Although he was not able to cope with his political difficulties (he opposed both Cardinal Kemp and Cardinal Beaufort) during Henry VI's reign, he was a liberal and steadfast patron of Oxford, and did much in the way of foundations. Trained in New College, he was resolved to follow his old Master Wykeham in building a well-ordered and well-endowed house of learning.[100] His first attempt was a small college at St. Giles (later called St. Bernard), but in 1437 he handed this over to the Cistercian monks,

. . . to form of them a college of a prior and scholars, who, as soon as they be gathered in this manner, shall be incorporated and have a common seal; he [Chichele] having shown that for want of such an habitation such students have found it difficult to fulfil the observances and customs of their order, and that many have quitted the university for that reason or refused to go there, although elected. . . .[101]

Chichele then conceived the idea of an " academic foundation for the study and training " of clerks for the " increase of clergy in England." [102] He made all the plans, then turned the foundation over to his godson, Henry VI, who made him co-founder, " on account of the great cost which he (Chichele) has laid out and proposes to lay out on the same." Richard Andrew was nominated as warden, and Thomas Lavenham, Robert Stephenes, Robert Seborgh, William Overton, Thomas Eston, Richard Penwortham were chosen by the archbishop as scholars; the warden and his successors were allowed to choose and admit more scholars to the number of forty.[103] Rashdall [104] stresses the fact that All Souls was the first college founded at Oxford by a great ecclesiastical lawyer, and that the proportion of law students to theologians was naturally large (twenty-four artists or theologians, sixteen jurists). It is interesting to note that the souls of those to be prayed

[100] C. W. C. Oman, " All Souls College," *Colleges of Oxford*, p. 209.
[101] *Patent Rolls*, Henry VI (1436-1441), III, 45-46.
[102] *Ibid.*, Henry VI (1436-1441), III, 172-173.
[103] *Ibid.*
[104] *Universities in Europe in the Middle Ages*, III, 227.

for were those who fell in the French Wars: " Thomas, late Duke of Clarence, the dukes, earls, barons, knights, esquires, and subjects of the king's father and of the king, who have perished on service in France." [105] The fellows were to be trained in the rudiments of grammar and plain-song, to be of free condition and legitimate birth, of good character and conduct, of three years' standing in the university as students of arts, civil law, or both; the founder's kin was preferred first, then natives of places where the college had property, and finally poor and indigent scholars studying in Oxford, according to the counties to which they belonged. All those except the founder's kin were to have a year's probation before being admitted as full fellows. Masters of arts were expected to go on to the study of theology, and had to enter priests' orders within two years after their regency. Bachelors of civil law who turned to canon law were also to take orders, but those who became doctors of civil law need not become priests. As many as seven or eight fellows a year, however, vacated their fellowships because their appointment was not very valuable, and because the acceptance of the preferment outside of Oxford, or the absence of more than six months without the express leave of the college was sufficient to vacate the fellowship.[106] The suppression of alien priories (becoming so prevalent in this century) contributed largely to All Souls' endowments.

William Byngham, parson of the Church of St. Zachary, London, was so perturbed over the state of grammar schools and the neglect and scorn with which the degree of Master of Grammar was treated that he requested in 1439 licence from the king to found at Cambridge a college of a priest and twenty-four scholars to be called God's House, for the express purpose of educating the scholars to the degree of Master in Grammar and priests' orders, and then to send them throughout the country to schools which had become deserted.[107] In his petition to the king he remarks that he

---

[105] *Patent Rolls*, Henry IV (1436-1441), III, 172-173.
[106] Oman, *op. cit.*, p. 214.
[107] *Patent Rolls*, Henry VI (1436-1441), III, 295-296.

. . . founde of late over the est parte of the wey ledyng from Hampton to Coventre and so forth no ferther north yan Rypon, lxx Scoles, voide or mo yat were occupied all at ones within L. yeres passed, because yat yere is so grete scarstee of Maistres of Grammar . . .[108]

Since this was a college founded expressly for the purpose of training teachers, God's House may rightly be called the earliest Teachers College on record. Several years later, God's House was so close to the new college of St. Mary and St. Nicholas, Henry VI's pride and joy, that the building of the new college could not proceed without incorporating God's House, and Byngham, at the king's request, turned it over to him. In turn, God's House, with its founder and masters, William Lichfield, William Millington, William Gulle, Gilbert Worthyngton, John Cote, Professors in Theology, John Tilney, Doctor of Decrees, and John Horley, Bachelor of Theology, was moved to the parish of St. Andrew.[109] At the beginning of the sixteenth century it was merged with Christ's College, founded by Lady Margaret.[110]

The foundation *par excellence* of the fifteenth century was the sumptuous King's College, Cambridge, with its attendant Eton College, in Windsor. Founded by Henry VI, modelled almost slavishly on New College, Oxford,[111] and richly endowed with suppressed alien priories,[112] King's College rapidly grew to great proportions. Starting out in 1441 as the king's College of St. Mary and St. Nicholas (almost immediately spoken of as King's College), with one rector and twelve scholars, to be governed by such statutes and ordinances as might be set up by William, Bishop of Lincoln, William, Bishop of Salisbury, William Lyndewode, Keeper of the Privy Seal, John Somerseth, Chancellor of the Exchequer, and John Langton, Chancellor of Cambridge University,[113] it was re-

[108] *Documents*, III, 153-154.
[109] *Patent Rolls*, Henry VI (1441-1446), IV, 460.
[110] Mullinger, *op. cit.*, pp. 445-446; Rashdall, *Universities of Europe in the Middle Ages*, III, 314.
[111] H. C. Maxwell Lyte, *A History of Eton College* (London: Macmillan and Co., 1875), p. 16; and Mullinger, *op. cit.*, p. 307.
[112] The *Patent Rolls* are filled with the bestowal of suppressed priories not only on King's College, but other colleges as well. See below, pp.
[113] *Patent Rolls*, Henry VI (1436-1441), III, 521-523; and Cooper, *op. cit.*, I, 189.

founded and greatly enlarged, with the king taking it upon himself to alter the statutes, after having relieved the above-mentioned commission from their task.[114] William Millington was made the first provost, and the number of fellows increased to seventy. Henry also secured for the college bulls of exemption from the jurisdiction of the Archbishop of Canterbury, the Bishop and Archdeacon of Ely, and the chancellor of the university. An important step was taken when Cambridge itself granted the college freedom from its own jurisdiction except in scholastic matters.[115] The curriculum of this foundation was very precisely marked out, with theology, the arts, and philosophy the chief subjects; two masters of arts, of superior ability, could study civil law, four canon law, two medicine, and two astronomy.[116] After three years' probation, the provost and fellows were permitted to elect them to their number.[117]

Eton's growth was concomitant with King's. It consisted of a provost, twenty-five poor scholars (later raised to seventy), ten fellows, four clerks (later ten), six choristers (later sixteen), a schoolmaster (later aided by an usher), and thirteen " poor and infirm " boys.[118] The fellows, appointed for life, had to be masters or bachelors of divinity, or doctors of canon law and masters of arts, and had to swear that they would not hold to the opinions of Wycliffe or Pecock.[119] The schoolmaster, appointed by the proctors and the fellows, had to be of good character, skilled in grammar and teaching, unmarried, and, if possible, a master of arts; his duties were to instruct the scholars, choristers and any other boys in the school, and to punish them with moderation.[120] The scholars, " when sufficiently learned in grammar," were to be elected to King's College. Among other requirements, the scholars were to be boys of good character and decent life, poor and needy, with a competent knowledge of reading, Donatus, and

[114] *Documents*, I, 45.
[115] Cooper, *op. cit.*, I, 203-204.
[116] Mullinger, *op. cit.*, p. 308.
[117] *Ibid.* p. 309.
[118] Statutes II and LXIV of Eton College, translated and abridged, Appendix A of Lyte, *op. cit.*, p. 489.
[119] *Ibid.*, IX, XXIII, XXV, XXVII, LXII, and LXIII, p. 491.
[120] *Ibid.*, XIV, XXVIII, and XXIX, p. 493.

plain-song, be not less than eight years old nor more than twelve (unless they were particularly well-read, then seventeen was the limit). A larger number of scholars than the actual vacancies at King's College was elected, and the electors were told to disregard the " instances, prayers or requests of kings or queens, princes or prelates, nobles or gentlemen " and consider instead the proficiency of the boys in grammar.[121] June 3, 1446 saw the grant of monopoly to Eton for teaching grammar and the prohibition of other grammar schools in Windsor and in a radius of ten miles around Eton.[122] This monopoly was rather advantageous to education, in a way, because it discouraged grammar schools of perhaps two or three students, taught by poorly-prepared teachers, and thus permitted the boys in that section to come together under one competently-equipped master; disadvantageous, because some boys might not be fortunate enough to be chosen by Eton for such schooling.

The organization of Eton was aided by the presence of William of Waynflete, who had been master at Winchester for a number of years, and who was persuaded by the king, a great admirer of Waynflete, to come to Eton in the same capacity. The association that was the result of this close communion of the two schools which were soon to become famous as the Public Schools of England was fostered to the extent that in 1444 Eton and Winchester, and King's and New colleges, made a covenant to " assist and support one another mutually in all causes, trials, and difficulties through all future ages." [123]

It was on Eton that Edward IV's displeasure fell when he took over the reins of the kingdom from Henry VI in 1461. Jealous and resentful of the ruler he had deposed, and of all the affairs with which Henry had been connected, Edward wanted to discredit anything that might bring glory to his dangerous rival. At any rate, Edward's first plan was to suppress Eton entirely and to annex all its endowments to

[121] *Ibid.*, III, IV, VI, X, XV, XXVI, and XXIX, pp. 494-495.
[122] *Educational Charters*, pp. 413-415.
[123] Lyte, *op. cit.*, p. 22.

St. George's, Windsor.[124] A particularly bad time occurred: the almsmen were abolished, the number of scholars had considerably diminished, and for one whole year (1468) no stipend at all was received by the provost and fellows.[125] At this time there reappeared on the scene Clement Smith, who assumed the direction of the foundation. It was he who guided Eton on its precarious way, and by the time he left (in 1469) the king had been persuaded to abandon his plan of annexing Eton to St. George's.[126] There was still no permanent security for the foundation. Edward IV gave and took endowments indiscriminately; but in 1476 Cardinal Bourchier required the Chapter of Windsor " to abstain from any sort of molestation, under the pain of the greater excommunication." The year that Henry VI returned to the throne for a short time saw an endowment of a manor, a farm rent, and an advowson. But with Edward IV's seizure of the throne, once more bad luck set in. After the provost of Eton's death, the fellows, in defiance of the king's wishes, elected Thomas Barker as the new provost, but, fortunately, as far as avoiding the king's wrath, he refused the position, and at the next election the king's choice, Henry Bost, was selected.[127] Bost was also appointed for life as warden of King's Hall, at the death of Roger Rotheram.[128] Oddly enough, King's College did not seem to suffer from Edward IV's dislike of Eton; even though they were not given many additional endowments, at least they were granted some.[129] Thomas Rotheram, Archbishop of York, gave large sums of money to King's towards completion of the chapel, and left in his will one hundred pounds for the same purpose.[130] William Skelton was still another benefactor—he bequeathed his library to King's.

The other college that encountered a little opposition from Edward IV was Lincoln. However, it had picked a most inopportune time to ask for its charter—the year that Edward

[124] *Ibid.*, p. 62.   [126] *Ibid.*, p. 66.
[125] *Ibid.*, p. 65.   [127] Lyte, *op. cit.*, pp. 82-83.
[128] *Patent Rolls*, Edward IV and V, Richard III (1476-1485), p. 54.
[129] *Ibid.*, Edward IV (1461-1467), I, 74, 103.
[130] Charles Henry Cooper, *Memorials of Cambridge* (Cambridge: William Metcalfe, 1860), p. 212.

deposed Henry for the first time—so it was to be expected that a little persuasion would be necessary. Through the efforts of Bishop Neville, Edward granted Lincoln its confirming charter in 1461-2, and extended its rights to hold lands in mortmain.[131]

It is interesting to note that at this rather precarious time of the crowning of a new king and the deposing of an old one, Oxford was seemingly unperturbed, whether her individual colleges were or not. When Henry VI was restored to his throne in 1470, she immediately sent this letter to him:

When we heard that you had recovered the throne, we felt glad that you had been restored, as it was just that you should be, to your former dignity; and at the same time we rejoiced, because in you we have once more a monarch who is a true lover and defender of the Church and of this University. The happy circumstances too of your restitution, without bloodshed and beyond all human expectation, are undoubtedly the work of the divine hand . . .[132]

She was just as quick to write to Edward IV when he had deposed Henry VI for the second time:

Your former victories, though we have heard of them with great pleasure, did not give us the joy we feel on account of that you have recently obtained; for by it the civil war, which has well-nigh destroyed the kingdom, has been brought to an end, and a king at once most wise and successful restored, as by a miracle, to his throne. Henceforth, under your government we need fear no enemy, and can pass our lives in peace. We thank God, therefore, the giver of this and all other good gifts, that he has subdued your enemies under you and delivered you from such great perils; and relying upon the benevolence you have showed us in the past, we humbly beseech you to continue the same gracious favour in the future.[133]

And yet, the university must have been a little uneasy over the political situation, because, just before Edward was put off the throne, she sent a letter to Masters Thomas Bonifaunt and William Dudley:

That you, who are such good friends to us, have so high a place in the King's favour naturally gives us great pleasure. While, therefore, we thank you for your steady advocacy of our interests hitherto, we entreat you, if unfavourable statements are made to the King respecting the University, that you will contradict them; and inform

---

[131] Clark, *op. cit.*, p. 175; *Patent Rolls*, Edward IV and V, Richard III (1476-1485), pp. 115-116.

[132] *Epist. Acad.*, II, 391-392. Marginal notes.

[133] *Ibid.*, II, 395. Marginal notes.

us if it should seem desirable that we should write to his majesty. We believe we have done nothing to deserve his anger, and can fearlessly assert that, in all the recent troubles of the realm, the tranquility of the University was never greater; and we do not know a single instance of a scholar taking arms for either side. As we have been, so shall we continue to be, loyal subjects; nor indeed are we insensible of the value of the King's favour, and hope that you will so use your influence for us, that our mother the University may be proud of having produced such sons.[134]

On the whole, however, the universities had little to fear from Edward. If he was not overly-enthusiastic in his patronage, at least he did them no harm. His wife, Elizabeth Woodville, on the other hand, became interested in one of the fifteenth-century colleges, and showered favors on it to the extent that it called her co-foundress and changed its name for her benefit. This was the foundation that had started out in 1446 as the College of St. Bernard, in Cambridge, under a Richard Andrew, burgess.

The College of St. Bernard, consisting of a president and four fellows, was refounded on another site in 1447.[135] Margaret of Anjou, wife of Henry VI, became interested in the college and wrote to her husband asking his permission to be its foundress and patroness, since " In the whiche universite is no college founded by eny quene of England hider toward." Accordingly, in 1443, the old charter was revoked and licence was granted to found her College of St. Margaret and St. Bernard.[136] Andrew Doket was made the first president, and John Lawe, Alexander Forkelowe, Thomas Haywode, and John Carewey were the fellows. Statutes were not given the college until 1475, when Elizabeth Woodville, Edward's queen, became interested in it, and reserved to herself, the president, and five of the senior fellows the right to alter or do away with any of the provisions during her lifetime.[137] At the time of their election, the fellows were to be at least questionists in arts, or scholars in theology. After regency in arts, they were allowed to teach the liberal arts for three years, or

---

[134] *Ibid.*, II, 387. Marginal notes.
[135] *Documents*, I, 49; and Rashdall, *Universities of Europe in the Middle Ages*, III, 320.
[136] *Documents*, I, 50.
[137] Mullinger, *op. cit.*, p. 316. The name was shortened to Queens'.

they could continue studying in arts, or study the natural, moral, and metaphysical philosophy of Aristotle.[138] If the fellows decided to teach during those three years, the college paid them a small salary.[139] At the end of the three years, if a fellow had no desire to study theology, he was allowed to enter canon or civil law, but only with the consent of the master and majority of the fellows. The first break in the long line of clerks studying to become ecclesiastical lawyers seems to appear in these statutes. Public opinion was being turned against the excesses of these worldly clergy until even academic leaders were in favor of curtailing the study of law. In the case of Queens', only two were allowed to proceed to any faculty other than theology. An even more definite rule about the study of canon and civil law was laid down in St. Catherine's College Statutes.[140]

The last of the great colleges founded at Oxford in the fifteenth century was Magdalen, founded by William Patten, more commonly known as William of Waynflete. Waynflete was perhaps the most outstanding of all the founders or patrons of colleges because he was first and foremost an educator. Called from the mastership of Winchester to become the first head of Henry VI's great foundation, Eton, he became interested, as he became wealthier,[141] in creating a college of his own, and in 1448 he obtained from the king a license to found a hall for a president and fifty scholars (later curtailed to forty), to be called St. Mary Magdalen Hall, " a hall of learning of the sciences of sacred theology and philosophy." [142] John Hornley was chosen as the first president.[143] Eight years later Waynflete was made chancellor, and immediately after that promotion decided to change his foundation from a hall to a college. After securing permission from the king to do so, Waynflete bestowed greater endowments on it, and acquired for it the possessions of the Hospital of St. John the Baptist, with which, in 1458, it was united and the charter

---

[138] *Ibid.*, pp. 316-317.   [140] Vide below.
[139] *Ibid.*   [141] Mallet, *op. cit.*, I, 385.
[142] *Patent Rolls*, Henry VI (1446-1452), V, 152.
[143] H. A. Wilson, " Magdalen College," *Colleges of Oxford*, p. 235.

granted.[144] Twenty scholars were appointed, and all were either bachelors or masters of arts.

It was not until after the death of Henry VI (1471) that the work of building on Magdalen College was actually begun.[145] A valuable piece of inheritance came to it through Sir John Falstaf's will, even though the grant was unintentional. Sir John, in his will (1459), left property in the custody of John Paston, who was to found for him a college of seven monks or priests.[146] Much wrangling and confusion accompanied the granting of this licence, and after a few years Waynflete asked the king to appropriate the inheritance to his foundation, which the king did accordingly. Waynflete was fortunate in possessing the goodwill of both Edward IV and Richard III; both kings visited the foundation to see how things were progressing, Edward in 1481, and Richard in 1483.[147] By 1483 the statutes had been given to the college, and things were runing smoothly.[148] There were to be forty fellows, thirty poor scholars (called " Demies "), four chaplains, eight clerks, sixteen choristers, a schoolmaster, and an usher. The fellows were to be masters or bachelors of arts drawn from certain dioceses, if possible, with a year's probation before election to fellowship. A few might proceed to law and medicine but the majority were to proceed to theology. Fellows were liable to lose their places if they married, deserted their studies, turned monks, or succeeded to an inheritance or benefice of a certain value. The Demies were to be not younger than twelve, nor older than twenty-five, and were to study grammar, logic, and sophistics. This instruction was to be under the schoolmaster, and others besides the Demies could attend if they wished. When considered fit by the president and masters, the Demies could enter the university course in arts.[149] Provision was made for the teaching of

---

[144] *Ibid.*   [145] *Ibid.*, p. 236.
[146] *Paston Letters* (edited by James Gairdner; London: Chatto and Windus, 1904), III, 147-189.
[147] Wilson, *op. cit.*, p. 237.
[148] *Ibid.*, pp. 237-238; Mallet, *op. cit.*, I, 387-390; and Rashdall, *Universities of Europe in the Middle Ages*, III, 228-235.
[149] At least two or three were to apply themselves " so long to grammatical and poetical and other humane arts that they could not

moral and natural philosophy, and theology. Appointments of readers were expressly made for this, and the lectures were open to everyone, whether he were a member of the college or not. The choristers were to be taught singing by one of the chaplains or clerks or some other well-qualified person, who should also give them their elementary education.[150] Sons of noblemen and well-born persons (called *Commensales*, or " Commoners ") up to the number of twenty were allowed to stay at their own expense in the college, but they had to be in the charge of tutors, *sub tutela et regimine creditorum, vulgariter creancers nuncupatorum*. The remainder of Waynflete's rules on behavior, dress, disputations, etc., followed along the lines laid down by Wykeham. Waynflete reserved the right to add to or revise the statutes if he should see fit.

Too much stress cannot be laid upon the importance of the grammar schools attached to the colleges of Oxford and Cambridge, two of which, Eton and Magdalen School, came into existence in the fifteenth century. Since just as much care and attention was paid to these schools as was paid to the statutes of the colleges, they became centres of importance because they were so well organized. Many famous schoolmasters and textbook writers of the late fifteenth and early sixteenth century received their training in these schools and were well-prepared to carry out later and more modern ideas of teaching. Anwykyll, Stanbridge, Colet, and Lily are but a few who received their first experience in secondary education in these Public Schools.

The last college founded in the period in which our interest has been centered was St. Catherine's College, which attempted to prevent entirely its fellows from studying law. It has already been pointed out that there was a tendency in academic circles to swing away from the excesses of a mundane and worldly life indulged in by many priests. Political plums in the way of ecclesiastical preferments in high courtly positions, accumulation of vast estates and wealth, utter lack

only profit themselves but be able to instruct and educate others."
Robert Spencer Stanier, *Magdalen School* (Oxford: The Clarendon Press, for the Oxford Historical Society, 1940), pp. 22-23.
[150] *Ibid.*, p. 26.

of regard toward divine will and plan, and complete negligence of the duties inherent in their selection as a man of God, had finally become so great and so offensive that, in order to reform such blatant faults, founders of new colleges in the universities were beginning to prohibit the studies that had led to such a situation. Mention has already been made of Queens' attempt to divert clerks from the study of law. At St. Catherine's, canon and civil law were entirely excluded from the course of study by its founder, Robert Wodelarke, and *all* the fellows were to pursue theology " in the exaltation of the Christian faith and the defence and furtherance of holy church by the sowing and administration of the word of God." [151] The purging of the ranks of the clergy was not to take place yet, but even at this time a few farsighted prelates were attempting to straighten them out.

In spite of the poverty which the universities declared was rampant on their campuses, and to which Oxford, particularly, was continually calling attention in the many letters sent to her patrons and former students, numerous and very generous bequests and endowments were made either to the individual colleges or to the universities as a whole. The older colleges were by no means neglected during the years that new colleges were springing up. Through the kindness of their benefactors and remembrances in wills, nearly all the colleges received incomes or licenses to purchase property of one sort or another that helped to alleviate the distress and want of their scholars. In Cambridge, Pembroke received a reversion of a yearly pension of twenty-eight pounds, an alien priory, an advowson and two chantries.[152] Michaelhouse received license to acquire lands, rents, and possessions to the value of twenty pounds yearly, and freedom from certain taxations for twenty years, as well as an appropriation of a church in mortmain, and an alien priory in return for two

---

[151] Mullinger, *op. cit.*, p. 318; *Patent Rolls*, Edward IV and Henry VI (1467-1477), p. 544.

[152] *Patent Rolls*, Henry VI (1436-1441), III, 377, 401; Edward IV, V, Richard III (1476-1485), p. 232; *Documents*, I, 42. The college claimed that her revenues had decreased to one-third their former amount because of the damage done by the tides, the sea, and the floods of fresh water.

tenements given to King's College.[153] King's College, known
more often as the "Royal College of St. Mary and St.
Nicholas," fared better than the others, since it was Henry
VI's favorite project: lands, rents, pensions amounting to
forty pounds yearly, the keeping and marriage of several
heirs with the increments therefrom, pardons of certain debts,
fines, etc.[154] Clare Hall complained that her income had fallen
from one hundred pounds to sixty pounds a year, and was
accordingly given an additional return of forty pounds and
several tenements to make up the deficit, as well as lands,
rents and reversions to the value of twenty pounds.[155] Trinity
received lands to the value of sixty pounds per year, the
Hospital of St. Margaret, and other privileges in return for
favors done to King's College.[156] God's House and Gonville
Hall also shared to some extent in these bestowals,[157] but
Queens' College, like King's, benefited because of royal favor,
this time queenly favor.[158] In Oxford, Merton was set free
from certain taxes and granted a manor, a fair and an advowson, etc.; [159] All Souls' College was given certain manors and
lordships in Kent and Sussex, advowsons, alien priories, and
exemptions from taxes; [160] Oriel, in addition to rents, advow-

[153] *Patent Rolls*, Henry IV (1401-1405), II, 114; Henry VI (1436-
1441), III, 542; Henry VI (1441-1446), IV, 160; (1452-1461), VI,
514; *Documents*, I, 42.
[154] *Patent Rolls*, Henry VI (1436-1441), III, 427, 507, 557; Henry
VI (1441-1446), IV, 111-112, 181, 269, 279, 323, 329, 358, 390, 409;
Henry VI (1446-1452), V, 57, 127, 128, 143, 205, 210, 257, 336, 428,
450, 475; Henry VI (1452-1461), VI, 23, 82, 466, 476, 502, 531;
Edward IV, Henry VI (1467-1477), p. 240; *Close Rolls*, Henry VI
(1441-1447), IV, 102-103; *Documents*, I, 38, 39.
[155] *Patent Rolls*, Henry VI (1441-1446), IV, 435, 457-458; Edward
IV, Henry VI (1467-1477), p. 538.
[156] *Patent Rolls*, Henry VI (1436-1441), III, 437; (1441-1446), IV,
415, 434; Edward IV (1461-1467), p. 118; Edward IV, V, Richard III
(1476-1485), p. 46.
[157] *Patent Rolls*, Henry VI (1441-1446), IV, 98; (1446-1452), V,
103; (1452-1461), VI, 434; Edward IV (1461-1467), pp. 217-218;
Edward IV, Henry VI (1467-1477), pp. 130-131; Edward IV, V,
Richard III (1467-1485), pp. 71, 259.
[158] *Patent Rolls*, Edward IV (1461-1467), p. 495; Edward IV,
Henry VI (1467-1477), p. 394; Edward IV, V, Richard III (1476-
1485), pp. 34, 423, 477; Cooper, *Annals of Cambridge*, I, 210.
[159] *Patent Rolls*, Henry VI (1441-1446), IV, 286, 449-450; (1446-
1452), V, 56, 524.
[160] *Patent Rolls*, Henry VI (1436-1441), III, 231, 261, 341, 394, 437,
563; (1441-1446), IV, 141, 407; (1446-1452), V, 278-279.

sons, and fees, was the legatee of one thousand pounds from
John Frank, Master of the Rolls, for the support of four
additional fellows, while John Carpenter, one-time provost,
left possessions to support another fellow, and William Smith,
Bishop of Lincoln, founded another fellowship for his own
diocese.[161] University College, Great Hall, New College,
Magdalen College, Queen's, and Lincoln were all recipients
of bestowals in one way or another.[162] Individual gifts to the
universities were numerous and generous, and the following
bequests are but a few of the more outstanding gifts. Joan
Danvers, widow of William Danvers, esquire, gave to Oxford
the sum of one hundred pounds for the relief of poor scholars,
thus starting c. 1457 the " Danvers Chest." [163] Henry Brother
of South Hinksey assigned thirty shillings for the support of
John Kantewelle, scholar of Heren Hall.[164] William Alnwick,
dying in 1449, left a will bequeathing money for the exhibition
of poor scholars of the dioceses of Lincoln and Norwich,
studying either at Oxford or Cambridge.[165] Henry Chichele,
Archbishop of Canterbury, gave the sum of two hundred
marks for helping out poor students,[166] while John, Duke of
Exeter, founded the Exeter Chest with one hundred marks,
and Hugh Freen a chest of two hundred pounds.[167] Henry
Beaufort, dying in 1447, left one thousand pounds to each
of the colleges of Eton and King's; Thomas Bourchier, Archbishop of Canterbury, at his death in 1486, left one hundred
and twenty-five pounds for the support of poor scholars at

[161] *Ibid.*, Henry IV (1408-1413), IV, 190-191; Henry VI (1436-
1441), III, 396, 497, 540; Edward IV (1461-1467), p. 27; Edward IV,
V, Richard III (1476-1485), pp. 306-307; Shadwell, *op. cit.*, pp.
104-105.
[162] *Patent Rolls*, Henry IV (1401-1405), II, 112, 376-377; Henry VI
(1436-1441), III, 516, 571; (1441-1446), IV, 185, 192, 411-412; (1446-
1452), VI, 324, 343; Edward IV (1461-1467), p. 54; Edward IV,
Henry VI (1467-1477), pp. 63-64, 557-558; Edward IV, Edward V,
Richard III (1476-1485), pp. 48, 53, 143, 378; Henry VII (1485-
1494), I, 256; (1494-1509), II, 64; *Close Rolls*, Henry VI (1429-
1435), II, 31; *Epist. Acad.*, I, 219-222.
[163] *Mun. Acad.*, I, 336-343.
[164] *Ibid.*, II, 516.
[165] Cooper, *Annals of Cambridge*, I, 204.
[166] *Epist. Acad.*, I, 83-89; *Mun. Acad.*, I, 291-299.
[167] *Epist. Acad.*, I, 205-208; II, 593-594.

Cambridge; Elizabeth Clere gave Cambridge two hundred marks for the restoration of the Cambridge chests, and Roger Drury, of Hawsted, left in his will one hundred marks to maintain a student in divinity at Cambridge for ten years.[168]

While it is impossible to calculate the actual amount of money entrusted to the colleges and universities in these enumerations, it seems likely that these bequests and appropriations were almost more than enough to help counteract the economic and financial depression which had been making itself felt on the campuses. Not only were contributions made by wealthy and influential prelates, but they were also given by the " little fellows " whose interest in the support of education had been awakened by its very evident need. The records are cluttered with hundreds of these unknown benefactors. Truly the English universities were rich in neighborly goodwill, if not in actual cash.

The third proof that poverty was not as great as the universities liked to imagine was the generous contributions made by individuals on behalf of the building program begun in the fifteenth century. St. Mary's Church and the schools in School Street were old and dilapidated; a new library was needed to house the generous bequests of books that were being made to the universities. Therefore St. Mary's Church must be rebuilt; a whole new divinity school and law school were planned for Oxford, and philosophy and law schools for Cambridge. The new libraries were to be built on these new schools. Oxford started a campaign entirely modern in spirit for money to complete the buildings: she set herself the task of canvassing all her wealthy friends, former graduates, persons of high estate, and well-to-do members of the middle class for money to build its new schools of theology and divinity. It even approached its sporadic enemies, the regulars, promising them the free use of the schools should their assistance be forthcoming, although the bargain was not always kept.[169] Some of the people thus approached were the Dean and Chapter of Salisbury, the Order of St.

[168] Cooper, *Annals of Cambridge*, I, 198, 232, 235, 243.
[169] *Epist. Acad.*, I, 20-22, 26-27, 242-243.

Augustine, the Master of St. Thomas' Hospital, London, the Bishop of Durham, the Order of St. Benedict, the executors of Cardinal Beaufort's estate, the executor of Master Gidney's estate, Master Thomas Lesurs, the Dean of St. Pauls' Dr. Fitzjames, Sir Reginald Bray, Dr. William Sutton, and St. Alban's.[170] Cambridge was a little less subtle in her approach: Laurence Booth, chancellor, caused a collection to be made for the building of the philosophy and civil law schools, from those who broke their word in taking their degrees, those who hired chairs of canon and civil law, from every religious person of the Order of Begging Friars, from rich persons, and from bishops and prelates.[171] Two bequests, one of one hundred pounds, and the other one hundred marks, were also received by Cambridge, the first from Thomas Beaufort in 1426 for poor students, and the other from Richard Billingsford in 1432.[172]

A most generous contribution was made by the executors of Cardinal Beaufort's estate when they gave Oxford five hundred marks for the erection of new schools provided that trustees be found who would undertake to erect the buildings within five years, or refund the money. No one could be found that was willing to risk it until Gilbert Kymer, Chancellor, and Master Holcote agreed to undertake the task, the university having promised to indemnify them for any loss they might sustain. In connection with this same project, graces were granted to those who gave money for the buildings, and indulgences from the Pope and bishops.[173] When Bishop Kempe of London was appealed to for aid in completing the school of divinity,[174] he responded immediately. What a flurry of excitement there must have been when Oxford found out that the Bishop had wanted or intended to send money to her at once, but through some mistake no agent of the university

---

[170] *Ibid.*, I, 24-27, 28, 41-42, 52-53, 55-56, 242-243, 266-268, 275-279, 613, 621, 630.

[171] Fuller, *op. cit.*, p. 124; *Grace Book A* (edited by Stanley M. Leathes; Cambridge: University Press, for the Cambridge Antiquarian Society, 1897), I, 13.

[172] Cooper, *Annals of Cambridge*, I, 177 and 184.

[173] *Mun. Acad.*, II, 567-574.

[174] *Epist. Acad.*, II, 429-430.

had approached him for it![175] That matter was soon reme-
died, it is needless to say.[176] The sum granted was one
thousand marks, two hundred then and the same amount
every year on the Feast of All Saints. If any remained when
the school of theology was finished, the remainder was to be
placed in the Kempe chest and used for the support of poor
scholars.[177] In 1481 an invitation was extended to the Bishop
to visit the university, so that he might see for himself the
workmen: " Industrious as bees, some carry the stones,
others polish them, some carve out the statues, others place
them in their niches."[178] Not only was a new school of
canon law to be built, but one for civil law; however, the civil
law was to be " on the ground, and Canon Law over it, if we
can find the requisite funds."[179] The Bishop of London was
urged to invite the Bishops of Ely, Norwich, and Bath and
Wells to aid, for " your wishes will have weight."[180] So by
dint of hard work, cajoling, follow-ups of estates left without
any special disposition, and constant badgering of prominent
people, the universities, by the end of the fifteenth century,
were ready to hold classes in their new buildings and to move
their ever-growing libraries into their new quarters.[181] Not a
bad accomplishment for such hard times!

This, then, is the picture of the fifteenth-century university
presented to us: a university shorn of most of her vital privileges, marked by petty dissensions and quarrels within her
ranks, yet expanding and growing. It was still a force to be
reckoned with, however, and it was still the intellectual centre
of that great ecclesiastical body, the Church.

The Career of a University Student

When a young man decided to enter upon the lengthy and
somewhat arduous career of a university student, his first
and immediate task was to present himself to a regent master

---

[175] *Ibid.*, II, 435.
[176] *Ibid.*, II, 436.
[177] *Ibid.*, II, 437-441.
[178] *Ibid.*, II, 470-471.
[179] *Ibid.*, II, 479-480.
[180] *Ibid.*, II, 481-482.
[181] The Divinity School of Oxford was completed by 1488, and St.
Mary's by 1495. *Epist. Acad.*, II, 547-548, 630-631.

for enrolment, and settle in his place of residence, in one of the colleges, if he had been appointed as one of its fellows, or one of the many halls which flourished in the environs of Cambridge and Oxford, the principal of which must be a graduate, either a bachelor or master.[182] Generally speaking, the student's academic life was divided into three periods of opponency, determination, and inception, each period with certain definite regulations and requisites.[183] The first period, commonly called opponency, embraced all the studies which led up to determination, the second period, or the entrance into the state of bachelorhood. During the first part of opponency, the student, after having chosen a master under whom to study, was known as *sophista generalis*; [184] during the latter part of the period he was called *questionist*, and allowed to pass off his responsions, in which he answered publicly the questions posed him by the masters. The first step in determining was the securing of the testimony of several [185] masters as to the candidate's fitness not only in knowledge, but also in morals, age, stature, and personal appearance.[186] If there were any doubt or disagreement as to the determiner's appearance or stature, it was settled by the opinion of a majority of the regents of the university.[187] After being admitted to determine, the candidate had to dispute with the masters of the faculty in which he was determin-

---

[182] *Statuta Antiqua*, pp. 208, 226. In 1462 there were some sixty odd halls in Oxford. *Mun. Acad.*, II, 687-692. Halls varied in size and character: some were rented as private houses; some were rented by grammar masters and used as boarding houses for boys too young to be undergraduates; and some contained graduate as well as undergraduate students. *Registrum Cancellarii Oxoniensis* (edited by Herbert E. Salter; Oxford: Clarendon Press, for the Oxford Historical Society, 1932), I, xxix.

[183] Many of the requirements, listed under the various faculties on the following pages, could be dispensed with by applying to the Congregation of Regents for a dispensation. Usually, although not always, a fine was paid for such a grace. The university records are full of these transactions.

[184] *Mun. Acad.*, I, 242. The one who opposed was the one who spoke first, who laid down the thesis; he who spoke second was the respondent. The *replicator* summed up and awarded praise or blame.

[185] The number varied from faculty to faculty.

[186] *Mun. Acad.*, I, 246.

[187] *Ibid.*; *Statuta Antiqua*, p. 203.

ing.[188] Those who determined for themselves [189] began before dinner on the first Wednesday, Thursday, or Friday, or, at the very latest, the first Monday in Lent. All disputations had to be completed when compline rang at St. Frideswyde's. Logic was disputed every day, with the exception of Friday, when it was grammar's turn. On the first and last day of determination, " questions " were disputed. Those scholars who determined for others could enter the schools a little later, the Monday and Tuesday after Mid-Lent being the dead-line. Every determiner had to obey his master, who could correct and stop him if he disputed on things " other than logic, or if he used arguments which were irrelevant or sophistical." The master was also bound to send the names of the disobedient determiners to the chancellor, who, with the proctors, punished them.[190] Evidently the greater the number of listeners who attended the disputations of these determiners, the more creditable the showing. If the logical acumen and the intellectual ability of the disputer did not offer great enough attraction to draw a crowd, more forcible means were employed. Innocent bystanders in the streets, unfortunately in the vicinity when a determination was taking place, were bodily seized and dragged in, literally " kidnapped " to take part in the ceremony. This man-handling, rough-arm technique must have been vociferously disapproved of, because a statute appeared, threatening excommunication and imprisonment to anyone compelling passers-by to enter the schools unwillingly.[191] Bribery, too, must have reared its ugly head at this crucial time, for we read " in order that the

[188] In the early part of the fifteenth century it was enacted that bachelors at Oxford must determine only in the thirty-two schools in School Street, and not in private homes or churches. *Mun. Acad.*, I, 239-240.

[189] Determiners could determine not only *pro se* but *pro aliis*. The advantage in determining *pro aliis* seems to have been the cutting down of the period between determination and inception from three years to two, even though an additional book had to be read (if the determiner had not already determined for himself). *Mun. Acad.*, I, 243-245; II, 416-417. This determining *pro aliis* seems to have applied only to richer students bearing the expenses of poor students at the time of determination.

[190] *Mun. Acad.*, I, 246.

[191] *Ibid.*, II, 411; *Statuta Antiqua*, p. 25.

good character of Masters of Arts be not blackened by the crime of vain ambition or illicit profit, the Masters shall accept neither money, capes, robes, boots, rings, nor any other valuables from determiners." [192] Upon admittance to determination, the bachelor celebrated his attainment with carousing and feasting, even though the ceremonies had taken place during the Holy Season of Lent. This celebration and riotous conduct must have gone to great extremes, because an early statute appeared, prohibiting such convivial meetings.[193] This was later repealed.[194] Evidently the bachelor gave a banquet soon after being awarded his degree, because William Paston writes to John Paston:

> And yf ye wyl know what day I was maad Baschyler, I was maad on Fryday was sevynyth, and I mad my fest on the Munday after. I was promysyd venyson a geyn my fest of my Lady Harcort, and of a noder man to, but I was deseyvyd of both; but my gestes hewld them plesyd with such mete as they had, blyssyd be God, Hoo have yow in Hys kepying, Amen.[195]

After determination at least three more years of intensive study had to be undertaken in order to become a master in the faculties of arts, or to proceed to theology, medicine, civil and canon law. Occasionally a student, after receiving a bachelor's degree, dropped out and went to law school, or the Inns of Chancery. Edmund Alyard, in a letter to Margaret Paston, mentioned this possibility with regard to her son, Walter Paston:

> As for your son Water, his labor and lernyng hathe be, and is, yn the Faculte of Art, and is well sped there yn, and may be Bacheler at soche tyme as shall lyke yow, and then to go to lawe. I kan thynk it to his preferrying, but it is not good he know it on to the tyme he shal chaunge; and as I conceyve ther shal non have that exhibeshyon to the Faculte of Lawe. Therfore meve ze the executores that at soche tyme as he shal leve it, ye may put a nother yn his place, soche as shal lyke you to prefer. If he shal go to lawe, and be made Bacheler of Arts be fore, and ye wolle have hym hom this yere, then may he be Bacheler at Mydsomor, and be with yow yn the vacacion, and go to lawe at Mihelmas . . .[196]

Ordinarily, however, the bachelor proceeded to the third period in his career, inception, or the degree of master. The

---

[192] *Mun. Acad.*, II, 454.
[193] *Ibid.*, II, 453-454.
[194] *Ibid.*, II, 455.
[195] *The Paston Letters*, VI, 14.
[196] *Ibid.*, VI 11-12.

ceremony of receiving the licence to incept was somewhat similar to that of determination: first, the bachelor being presented by his master to the chancellor and the proctors, with the required number of masters swearing as to his intellectual and moral fitness, and then the candidate giving his own oath. This oath, the latter part of the fifteenth century, was ten-fold:

1. To observe the statutes of the university.
2. Not to disturb the peace.
3. Not to recognize any other university besides Oxford and Cambridge.
4. Not to foment disturbances between the different societies at Oxford.
5. Not to lecture or read at Stamford.
6. To provide himself with suitable dress and wear it while at the university.
7. To use the library books carefully.
8. Not to hold the doctrines condemned at the Council of London.
9. Not to hold the opinions of William Russell.
10. To pray for the Duke of Gloucester.[197]

This oath was, in the majority of cases, merely a lip-oath. All one has to do is to look over the Acts of the Chancellor's Court to realize that all but one part was broken innumerable times. The section that escaped was the one for the Duke of Gloucester's soul. He was always faithfully remembered. At the conclusion of the oath (which the inceptor made kneeling in the presence of the others), the chancellor, holding a Bible on which the inceptor placed his hand, bestowed on him the licence of master:

Ad honorem Domini nostri JESU CHRISTI . . . et ad profectum sacrosanctae matris Ecclesiae et studii, auctoritate mea et totius Universitatis, do tibi licentiam incipiendi in tali facultate, legendi, et disputandi, et omnia faciendi quae ad statum Magistri in eadem facultate pertinent, cum ea compleveris quae ad talem pertinent solemnitatem. In nomine Patris, et Filii, et Spiritus Sancti. Amen.[198]

The third and final period in a university student's life began with this licence. The inceptor was now bound to incept within a year after receiving this licence;[199] in other

---

[197] *Mun. Acad.*, II, 374-376. Marginal notes. *Statuta Antiqua*, pp. 20, 35, 58, 222, 229.
[198] *Mun. Acad.*, II, 383.
[199] A licentiate failing to incept within a year from this date had to pay a fine and get a new licence. *Ibid.*, II, 377.

words, to lecture in the schools, or to conduct a series of readings for at least a year in addition to the one in which he incepted.[200]

During this time he was called a regent master, and followed a prescribed method of teaching.

> . . . in lecturing, the Masters shall read the text; then if the matter require it, they shall explain it, fully and completely; and finally, they shall raise questions on it, but only if the questions arise naturally from the text, so that no prohibited science might be taught, or in such a way that no other faculty or the statutes of the colleges might be imperilled.[201]

At the conclusion of his two years' teaching, the master (or doctor—the terms were synonymous) could continue teaching at Oxford if he so desired, as a non-regent master;[202] continue on with his studies in another faculty; accept a benefice of a church and return to active life in the priesthood; or accept a political appointment of some kind. Concomitant, however, with his promise to incept within a year after receiving his licence, were some other requirements that the new master must have fulfilled. Among these were the conducting of a series of disputations in the forty days succeeding his inception;[203] the hiring of a hall in which to lecture;[204] the purchasing of suitable clothes with which to incept and lecture;[205] the provision of clothes for others;[206] the payment of twenty shillings and a pair of gloves to each bedel, or five additional shillings in place of the gloves; and the feasting of the regents.[207] The actual fees paid to the university for the taking of the bachelor and master of arts were comparatively small: half a week's commons for a bachelor, and a week's

---

[200] *Statuta Antiqua*, p. 54.

[201] *Mun. Acad.*, I, 288.

[202] This could very well be lucrative, since every student had to pay the masters for attendance at classes; the " collection " was levied at the end of the term (the price varied with the subject, canon law being the highest) and every master was obliged to collect his salary. This seemingly unnecessary rule was made to protect poor masters, for if wealthy masters disdained the payments, scholars might flock to them and receive their education for nothing, while poor masters would languish for want of pupils. *Ibid.*, II, 427-428.

[203] *Ibid.*, II, 423; *Statuta Antiqua*, p. 39.

[204] *Mun. Acad.*, II, 415; *Statuta Antiqua*, p. 32.

[205] *Mun. Acad.*, II, 434.

[206] *Ibid.*, II, 434-435.   [207] *Ibid.*, I, 324, 354.

commons for a master at Oxford, and a full commons for each at Cambridge.[208] The fee for the degree of doctor was much higher, with Oxford charging more than Cambridge.[209] Anstey [210] has figured out the expenses of a scholar at the university for a year, as follows:

	£	s.	d.
Lectures, for four terms at 2s. the term...	0	8	0
Rent of room..........................	0	10	0
Weekly commons for 38 weeks from Oct. 9th to July 7th at 10 d. a week.....	1	11	8
Servants for same time.................	0	1	4
	2	11	0

These figures, as can readily be seen, do not include any extra fees for books, taking of degrees, and other expenses. Many of the students, of course, were fellows of a college or members of an order, and had their expenses paid; others, if cash were scarce, received licences from the university to eke out their existence by begging, or worked as servants, or borrowed money from the chests on some valuable possession, which, if it were not redeemed at the stated time, might be sold to someone else, or benefited by bequests and allowances.

Teaching or lecturing to the students at Oxford or Cambridge during a school year of three terms was characterized by the adjectives *ordinary, extraordinary,* and *cursory.* Ordinary lectures were those lectures given in the morning hours, from nine o'clock until noon, and were reserved to doctors, while extraordinary lectures were those given in the afternoon, from one o'clock until five. Originally this distinction of time arose because of a difference between what were considered the more essential and the less essential of the Law-texts.[211]

[208] *Medieval Archives of the University of Oxford* (edited by Herbert E. Salter; Oxford: Clarendon Press, for the Oxford Historical Society, 1920), II, 275.

[209] *Ibid.,* II, 274.

[210] *Mun. Acad.,* Introduction, I, xcviii.

[211] The Ordinary books of the Civil Law were the first part of the Pandects technically known as the *Digestum Vetus* and the Code: the extraordinary books were the two remaining parts of the Pandects known respectively as the *Infortiatum and the Digestum Novum,* together with the collection of smaller textbooks known as the

The term *cursory* has been the subject of much discussion among the scholars of medieval education, resulting in comparative disagreement. Anstey says,

> What these '*cursory*' lectures were we can only conjecture, probably they were more what we should call lectures while the '*ordinary*' lectures were actual *lessons*; in the cursory lecture the master was the sole performer, in the ordinary the scholar was heard his lesson.[212]

Dean Peacock takes a somewhat similar view:

> A distinction is made in the statutes of all universities between those who read *ordinarie et cursorie*, though it is not very easy to discover in what the precise difference consisted: it is probable, however, that whilst *cursory lectures* were confined to the reading of the simple text of the author, with the customary glosses upon it, the ordinary lectures included such additional comments on the text, as the knowledge and researches of the reader enabled him to supply. The *ordinary lectures* would thus appear to have required higher qualifications than the *cursory lectures*,—a view of their character which is confirmed by a statute of the university of Paris, ordering that ' Nullus magister qui leget *ordinarie* lectiones suas debet finire cursorie.' [213]

Mullinger, in his *The University of Cambridge*, takes exception to the first two explanations of cursory lectures. He observes that cursory lectures were nearly identical with extraordinary lectures. It is from this angle that Mullinger sees it:

> In support of this view, and also to show that the original use of the terms *ordinary* and *cursory* had no reference to any special *mode of lecturing*, I would offer the following considerations:— (1) The meaning I have assigned to these terms harmonises with the etymology; but if *ordinarie* be supposed to have reference to a *peculiar method of lecturing*, what sense is to be assigned to the expression *extraordinarie*? (2) In the few early college statutes that relate to *college lectures*, no such distinction is recognised; yet some of these statutes specify not only the subjects but the authors to be treated. On the other hand, the view indicated by M. Thurot,—that the cursory lecture was an extra lecture, given in most instances by a bachelor, whose own course of study was still incomplete, and upon a subject which formed part of that course,—derives considerable support from the following facts:— (a) *Cursory* readers had, in some instances, their course of reading

Volumen or *Volumen Parvum*, which included the *Institutiones* and the *Authentica* (i. e., the Latin translation of Justinian's Novels), the Lombard *Liber Feudorum*, and a detached fragment of the Code known as *Tres Libri*. Rashdall, *Universities of Europe in the Middle Ages*, I, 206.

[212] *Mun. Acad.*, I, lxix.

[213] George Peacock, *Observations on the Statutes of the University of Cambridge* (London: John W. Parker, 1841), Appendix A, pp. xliv-xlv.

assigned to them by the reader in *ordinary*. Thus in statute 100 (*Documents*, I, 365-66) *De cursorie legentibus in jure canonico*, we find the cursory reader required to swear *se lecturum per duos terminos infra biennium in lectura sibi assignanda per ordinarie legentem*. That is, according to Mr. Anstey's theory, the lecturer engaged upon the more elementary part of the instruction determined what should be read by the lecturer who taught the more advanced pupils! (β) Those *incepting* either in medicine, in civil or canon law, or in divinity, are required to have previously lectured *cursorily* in their respective subjects before admission to the degrees of D. M., D. C. L., J. U. D., or D. D. (see statutes 119, 120, 122, 124, *Documents*, I 375-377) ; but to have lectured *ordinarily* is never made a prerequisite: for before a lecturer could be deputed to deliver an ordinary lecture, he must have passed through the *whole course* of the faculty he represented. (γ) Among other statutes of our own university we find the following: *Item nullus baccalaureus in artibus aliquem textum publice legat ante anni suae determinationis completum* (Statute 142, *Documents*, I, 385). This statute is entitled *De artistis cursorie legentibus*; if therefore the title is to be taken in conjunction with the statute, it is difficult not to infer that lecturing by bachelors was what was usually understood by *cursory* lectures; an inference which derives confirmation from the following statute among those which Mr. Anstey has so ably edited: ' Item, ordinatum est, quod quilibet *Magister* legens *ordinarie* metaphysicam, eam legat per terminum anni et majorem partem ad minus alterius termini immediate sequentis, nec cesset a lectura illa donec illam rite compleverit, nisi in casu quo fidem fecerit coram Cancellario et Procuratoribus, quod non poterit commode et absque damno dictam continuare lecturam, in quo casu, facta fide, cassare poterit licenter, dum tamen Magister alius regens fuerit continuaturus et completurus lecturam: quod si *Magister alius* tunc in ea non legerit, poterit licenter per *Bachilarium* aliquem compleri quod dimittitur de lectura, et valebit pro forma in casu praemisso *cursoria lectura*, non obstante ordinatione priore.' *Munimenta Academica*, p. 423. It remains to examine the evidence for Mr. Anstey's theory contained in the following statute, on which he lays considerable stress : ' Cum statutum fuerit ab antiquo quod Magistri tenentes scholas grammaticales *positivae informationi* Scholarium suorum, ex debito juramenti vel fidei praestitae, summopere intendere debeant et vacare, quidem tamen eorum lucro et cupiditati inhiantes ac propriae salutis immemores, praedicto statute contempto, *lectiones cursorias*, quas vocant audientiam abusive, in doctrinae Scholarium suorum evidens detrimentum legere praesumpserunt; propter quod Cancellarius, utilitati eorundem Scholarium et praecipue juniorum volens prospicere, ut tenetur, dictam audientiam, quam non tantum frivolam sed damnosam profectui dictorum juniorum reputat, suspendendo statuit quod, quioumque scholas grammaticales deinceps tenere voluerit, sub poena privationis a regimine scholarum, ac sub poena incarcerationis ab libitum Cancellarii subeundae, ab *hujusmodi* lectura cursoria desistant, ita quod nec in scholis suis, nec alibi in Universitate hujusmodi cursus legant, nec legi faciant per quoscunque, sed aliis onmibus praetermissis, instructioni positivae Scholarium suorum intendant diligentius et insudent. Alii vero a Magistris scholas tenentibus, qui idonei fuerint reputati, in locis distantibus a scholis illis, si voluerint, hujusmodi cursus legant, *prout antiquitus fieri consuevit*.' (*Munimenta Academica*, pp. 86, 87.) This statute is referred to by Mr. Anstey as ' one forbidding *cursory* lectures except under certain restrictions.' ' The most remarkable part of the statute is,' he adds, ' that it complains that teachers led by hope of gain indulged their scholars with *cursory* lectures, so that it would really seem that it was not uncommon for the boys to bribe the master to excuse them their parsing!' (Intro., p. lxix.) The whole of this criticism, so far as it applies to the question before us, falls to the ground, if we observe that it is not *cursory lectures* that are the subject of animadversions, but a *certain mode of delivering them*: this appears to be beyond doubt if we carefully note the expressions italicised: and finally the title of the statute, *Quomodo legi debent lectiones cursoriae in scholis grammaticalibus*, evidently signifies that cursory lectures in grammar are to observe a certain method, not that cursory lectures are to be discontinued. In fact, in another statute, which seems to have escaped Mr Anstey's notice, it is expressly required that *cursory lectures* in *grammar* shall be given. (*Mun. Acad.*, 438-39.) [214]

Rashdall, in *Universities of Europe in the Middle Ages*, distinguishes the lectures in this way:

The distinction continued to be primarily one of time: ordinary lectures were those delivered at the hours reserved originally for masters and always for the authorised teachers of the faculty; extraordinary or cursory lectures might be delivered (except on certain holidays) at any time at which no ordinary lectures were going on, by either master or bachelor (footnote 3: Mr. Mullinger is mistaken in supposing that cursory lectures were *only* given by bachelors, and ignoring the fundamental distinction of time.) . . . But though an 'extraordinary' lecture meant originally nothing more than a lecture delivered out of the close time reserved for the more formal lectures prescribed by the faculty, it is probable that the term 'cursory' came in time to suggest also the more rapid and less formal *manner* of going over a book usually adopted at these times as opposed to the more elaborate and exhaustive analysis and exposition, characteristic of the ordinary lectures.[215]

Dean Rashdall cites several authorities for his interpretation, among which are Bulaeus, III. 82: *Chart.* Part 1, No. 20: The expression in the Paris Statute of 1215 that certain books are to be read 'ordinarie et non ad cursum' can hardly refer only to the time of the lectures; Bulaeus, V, 646, in a Statute of 1460: 'desides, ignavi, *cursores* et discholi omni penitus Scholasticâ disciplinâ carentes,' which seems to indicate that the word carried with it the idea of rapid, superficial treatment; and Hautz, *Gesch. d. Un. Heid.* II, p. 335: The 'Cursor' at Heidelberg swore '*non extense sed cursorie* legere litteram dividendo et exponendo.' [216]

---

[214] Mullinger, *op. cit.*, Appendix E, pp. 646-648.
[215] Rashdall, *Universities of Europe in the Middle Ages*, I, 434.
[216] *Ibid.*, I, 434, n. 3.

Mallet, in his *History of the University of Oxford*, adheres to Rashdall in his explanation:

And at Oxford, which adopted the Paris tradition, cursory lectures, with their greater freedom as to time and place and the standing of the lecturer, came to mean something lighter and quicker in their methods, less exhaustive, it may be, in their treatment, at any rate less formal and elaborate, than the ordinary lecture of the Schools.[217]

Strickland Gibson, in his Introduction to *Statuta Antiqua Universitatis Oxoniensis*,[218] has followed Anstey's interpretation of the statute [219] to which Mullinger takes exception when he (Gibson) remarks,

Teaching [in the grammar schools] *was to be of a precise character; cursory lectures* (that is lectures which consisted of a running commentary on a text) *being strictly forbidden.*

After having carefully considered the preceding statements and the statutes mentioned, one important truth emerges: that is, that, regardless of the fact that very early in the history of the medieval university there *may* have been some distinction between the terms *extraordinary* and *cursory*, with the passage of time that slight distinction was lost, and that by the fifteenth century *extraordinary* and *cursory* were practically synonymous, and meant a rapid, informal, and by no means elaborate or critical, survey of a subject, confined neither to bachelor or doctor, but employed at times by both.

Courses of Study in Fifteenth-Century Universities

It is difficult to draw any conclusions or make any comparison between the various curricula of Oxford and Cambridge, because of the confusion of the records and the scarcity of material. The courses themselves are indistinct and hazy, and, in many cases, repetitious. There was, on the whole, little difference in the requirements: in civil law, at Cambridge, five years' previous study was necessary for an M. A. to become a bachelor, and seven years' study for one who was not a graduate in arts; in Oxford, four and six years' work, respectively, were the conditions. In medicine, Cambridge

[217] *Op. cit.*, I, 185.
[218] P. lxxxv.   [219] *Mun. Acad.*, I, 86-87.

would allow only a graduate in arts to incept, and he had to spend five years in study before incepting. At Oxford, that regulation was non-existent; however, if one were not a graduate in arts, two years were added to the six required for the inception of an M. A. In arts, Cambridge insisted on determination before inception; this was unnecesary at Oxford, if the candidate had heard arts for eight years previous to his inception. The great similarity or the lack of dissimilarity in the curricula of the faculties of the two universities was due, probably, to two reasons: first, that the student body was composed almost entirely of men in orders, or of men preparing to take orders, and second, that both universities were modelled to a great extent on the same pattern—the University of Paris.

Greater number of students attended Oxford, not because of any difference in the type of studies offered, but rather because of its more illustrious history and the greater fame of its teachers. However, as Oxford grew in disfavor because of its proclivity towards heretical tendencies, Cambridge grew in size and popularity. But even at the end of the fifteenth century, despite all its drawbacks, Oxford University was still the leading English university.

Arts (Oxford)

The first great requirement for a student to be admitted to his bachelor's degree (*ad lecturam alicuius libri facultatis artium*) was to have spent at least four years in the study of the arts.[220] During the course of those four years [221] the candidate (1) must have been a *sophista generalis* at least a year before responding to the question, " *parvisum interim frequentantes, et se ibidem disputando, arguendo, et respondendo doctrinaliter exercentes;* " [222] (2) must have heard *lectionatim* four books on logic—Porphyry's *Isagogue*, Gil-

---

[220] *Mun. Acad.*, II, 410.

[221] *Ibid.*, I, 242-243; and II, 413-414; *Statuta Antiqua*, p. 220.

[222] *Mun. Acad.*, II, 412. The question to be disputed must have been proclaimed in the schools at least three days before the actual disputation.

bert de la Porree's *Sex Principia*, Aristotle's *Sophisti Elenchi*, and Donatus' *Barbarismus*; (3) must have heard and recited *Algorismus Integrorum* (a work on Arithmetic or Algebra), *Computus Ecclesiasticus* (the method of finding Easter), and *Tractatus de Sphaera* (an astronomical work by a thirteenth-century Scotsman, John Holywood (Johannes de Sacro Bosco); (4) must have heard cursory from bachelors in the schools all the books of the Old and New Logic [223] with the exception of the fourth book of Boethius' *Topica*, Priscian's *De Constructionibus*, and Donatus' *Barbarismus*; (5) must have heard Aristotle's *Ethica*; (6) must have heard Boethius' *Ars Metrica*; (7) must have heard Priscian *in majore*, or Aristotle's *Politica*, or ten books of *De Animalibus*, counting the books *De Progressu et Motu Animalium*; (8) must have heard Aristotle's *De Coelo et Mundo*; and (9) must have heard Aristotle's *Meteora*.

Three years had to elapse between determination and inception, with the addition of the following to the course of study: [224] (1) Grammar (for one term): Priscian, either *major* or *minor*; (2) Rhetoric (for three terms): the *Rhetoric* of Aristotle, or the fourth book of Boethius' *Topica*, or Tullius' (Cicero) *Nova Rhetorica*, or Ovid's *Metamorphoses*, or the poetry of Virgil; (3) Logic (for three terms): Aristotle's *De Interpretatione*, or the first three books of the *Topica* of Boethius, or the books of Aristotle's *Priora* or *Topica*; (4) Arithmetic (for one term): Boethius; (5) Music (for one term): Boethius; (6) Geometry (for two terms): Euclid, or Vitellio's *Perspectiva*, or Alhaçen; (7) Astronomy (for two terms): *Theorica Planetarum* or Ptolemy's *Almagesta*; (8) Natural Philosophy (for three terms): Aristotle's *Physica,* or *De Coelo et Mundo*, or *De Proprietatibus Ele--mentorum*, or *Meteora*, or *De Vegetabilibus et Plantis*, or *De Anima*, or *De Animalibus*, or any of the small books;

---

[223] The Old Logic: Porphyry's *Isagogue*, the *Categoriae* and *De Interpretatione* of Aristotle, the Logical works of Boethius, the *Sex Principia* of Gilbert de la Porree; the New Logic: *Priora Analytica*, *Topica*, *Sophisti Elenchi, Posteriora Analytica.* Hastings Rashdall, *Universities in Europe in the Middle Ages*, III, 153.
[224] *Mun. Acad.*, I, 286-287; *Statuta Antiqua*, pp. 234-235.

(9) Moral Philosophy (for three terms) : Aristotle's *Ethica* or *Economica*, or *Politica*; and (10) Metaphysics (for three terms) : Aristotle's *Metaphysica*.

Inceptors must have responded at least twice, have given a public lecture on any book of Aristotle, and have been provided with schools wherein to lecture during their regency. If the candidate had not determined, then he must have heard the arts for at least eight years previous to his inception.[225] In order to secure the regular study of the seven sciences and the three philosophies, inceptors in arts had to swear on admission that they would lecture on these courses (for which they received fees) ; if there were twenty inceptors, the first two (in rank) would lecture on metaphysics, the next two on moral philosophy, etc., with the junior inceptors lecturing on grammar. If, for some legitimate reason, an inceptor could not lecture, he had to supply a substitute.[226]

Arts (Cambridge)

No student could be admitted to respond to the question in arts unless he had stood as a *sophista generalis* for two years, or at least for one whole year (the sons of lords excepted). He must have heard two *sophismata generalia*, and responded twice.[227]

No one could determine before his fifth year of study. Previous to this, the determiner must have heard *ordinarie* the book of Terence for two years, logic for one year, and natural and metaphysical philosophy for one year (if they should happen to have been read at the time).[228] After determination, no bachelor of arts could lecture publicly on any text until the completion of his year of determination.[229]

A candidate could not incept unless he had previously determined. In addition, he must have studied continuously at Cambridge or elsewhere in a university in the same faculty for three years; must have heard the books of Aristotle on

---

[225] *Mun. Acad.*, II, 414 and 416-417; *Statuta Antiqua*, p. 33.
[226] *Mun. Acad.*, I, 272-274; *Statuta Antiqua*, p. 263.
[227] *Documents*, I, 382.
[228] *Ibid.*, I, 384-385.   [229] *Ibid.*, I, 385.

philosophy for three years, in the schools; and must have heard mathematics for three years, one year having been devoted to arithmetic and music, the second to geometry and perspective, and the third to astronomy. He must also have opposed and responded to three masters of arts. Lastly, five masters were required to swear *de scientia*, and seven other *de credulitate*, as to his moral as well as intellectual fitness. (This was done by the scrutiny and examination of the chancellor and proctors.) [230]

Canon Law (Oxford)

In order to become a bachelor of canon law it was necessary for the candidate to have heard civil law for five years; to have heard the *Decretals* [231] twice; to have heard the *Decretum* [232] for two years; to possess all the volumes (with glosses) of either laws; and to have lectured on the second and fifth book of the *Decretals*.[233]

The exercises previous to inception in canon law were: to have read *extraordinarie* two or three causes, or the tractate *De Simonia*, or *De Consecratione*, or *De Poenitentia*; [234] to have opposed in all the schools, to have responded to the questions of the masters, once, at least, in each individual school; and to have lectured for each master.

Those who wished to incept in canon law and were not regents in civil law must have heard civil law for at least three years; the Bible for two years; canon law for three years; and the *Decretals* in their entirety; and to have lectured for each regent.[235]

[230] *Ibid.*, I, 360, 382.
[231] *Decretales* (a code), consisting of the Decrees of Pope Gregory IX in five books, published *circa* 1230; the Sixth Decretal of Pope Boniface VIII in five books, published *circa* 1298; and the Constitutions of Pope Clement V in five books, published by Pope John XXII, *circa* 1317. *Documents*, I, 367, n. 2.
[232] *Decretum Gratiani* (a textbook), a collection made *circa* 1151 by Gratian, an Italian Monk, of the opinions of the ancient Latin fathers, the Decrees of General Councils, and the Decretal Epistles and Bulls of the Holy See. *Ibid.*
[233] *Mun. Acad.*, II, 398; *Statuta Antiqua*, p. 46.
[234] Parts of the *Decretum*. Rashdall, *Universities of Europe in the Middle Ages*, III, 157.
[235] *Mun. Acad.*, II, 399; *Statuta Antiqua*, p. 47.

After inception, the graduate had to lecture for the usual two years.[236]

Canon Law (Cambridge)

To become a bachelor of canon law a graduate must have heard civil law *ordinarie* for three years, a non-graduate for five years; the *Decretals* for another three years; and the *Decretum* for two (if lectures on that subject were being given at the time)!. Should the state of priesthood have kept him from hearing civil law, canon law could be offered instead. No one was permitted to lecture *cursorie* unless, in addition to having had all this preparation, he had given oath that, under penalty of a fine, he would lecture for two terms out of six (two years) on a lecture that was assigned to him by an " ordinary " lecturer.[237]

A total of five years' study in civil law (two years more after determination) was necessary for inception in canon law, and three years in addition to this five had to be spent on the *Decretum*, with emphasis on the *Tractatus de Simonia, De Matrimonia, De Poenitentia* and *De Consecratione* (since these had to be heard twice), and two years on the Bible. The inceptor also had to have lectured *cursorie* on one of the above-mentioned tracts, and one book of the *Decretals*, other than the fourth. The final requirements were the usual public opponencies and responses, and the testimony as to the candidate's fitness (*all* the doctors in canon law had to depose *de scientia*).[238]

If a doctor of canon law, graduated either from Cambridge or Oxford, should want to lecture on the *Decretals*, he was allowed to do so without any examination. If he were not a graduate in canon law, then he must have had such a doctor depose as to his fitness in morals and knowledge. If he were a graduate in civil law, he must have heard ordinarily from a lecturer the *Decretals* for two years and the *Decretum* for one, if he wished to lecture on the *Decretals*; if a non-graduate in civil law, but a graduate in arts, he had to have

---

[236] *Statuta Antiqua*, p. 47.
[237] *Documents*, I, 365-366.   [238] *Ibid.*, I, 376-377.

heard civil law for four years; a non-graduate in civil law and arts, for six years. Whether he were a graduate in arts or not, he must have heard in ordinary lecture the *Decretals* for four years and the *Decretum* for one. (The years of *Decretals and Decretum* must have been different from those of civil law.) A graduate in civil law must have previously lectured on the *Decretals* for two terms, while a whole year's lecture was demanded from a non-graduate in civil law.[239]

Civil Law (Oxford)

For a master of arts to be admitted *ad lecturam libelli Institutionum* [240] (in other words, to become a B. C. L.), he must have attended lectures in civil law for four years; the time was six years if he were not a graduate in arts.[241]

To incept in civil law, the bachelor must have lectured on *Libellum Institutionum*, or *Corpus Authenticorum*, or three extraordinary books of the Codex; *Digestum Novum*; [242] and *Infortiatum*. He must have opposed and responded in each school, and have given an ordinary lecture for each regent-master.[243]

One peculiarity noticed about the books in civil and canon law is that they had to be owned by the students, or at least be borrowed and used exclusively by them during the years of their study.[244]

---

[239] *Ibid.*, I, 367-369.

[240] *Institutiones* in four Books, on the elements of Roman Law, published by Justinian. *Documents*, I, 364, n. 1.

[241] *Mun. Acad.*, II, 402; *Statuta Antiqua*, p. 43.

[242] A division of the *Digesta* or *Pandectae*, published by Justinian, *in quinquaginta libris continentibus opiniones Jurisperitorum in ordinem redactas*. The other two parts are *Digestum Vetus* and *Infortiatum*. *Documents*, I, 364, n. 1.

[243] *Mun. Acad.*, II, 403-404; *Statuta Antiqua*, pp. 44, 45.

[244] *Mun. Acad.*, II, 402-403; *Statuta Antiqua*, pp. 43-44. See also the model letter of Thomas Sampson, late fourteenth century letter teacher, asking for money to defray the cost of a copy of the *Corpus Juris Canonici*. *Formularies Which Bear on the History of Oxford* (edited by H. E. Salter, W. A. Pantin, H. G. Richardson; Oxford: Clarendon Press, for the Oxford Historical Society, 1942), II, 366. Hereafter referred to as *Oxford Formularies*.

Civil Law (Cambridge)

To determine as bachelor, a graduate in arts must have heard *ordinarie, extraordinarie,* and *cursorie* for five years, and seven years if he were a non-graduate. He must also have commenced to lecture on the *Institutiones* within a year from his licence, and have lectured on and finished these four *libellos,* i. e., the text and glosses, within a year and a term from the start of the lecture.[245] Those bachelors lecturing *cursorie* must have shown evidence that they possessed or had borrowed all the volumes of civil law while they were lecturing and, in addition, that they had the two ordinary volumes, too.[246]

The requirements for inception were: if a graduate in arts, to have heard civil law for eight years, if a non-graduate, ten years; to have heard at least twice the " ordinary " books (*Digestum Vetus*), and once the " extraordinary " books (*Digestum Novum* and *Infortiatum*) ; to have lectured *cursorie* on the *Digestum Novum* or the *Infortiatum,* and on the *Institutiones*; and to have publicly opposed and responded to all the masters in the faculty of civil law, or in their absence, to the regent canonists. All the masters in civil law must have sworn *de scientia* as to the candidate's moral and mental fitness.[247]

Medicine (Oxford)

In order to practice medicine in Oxford, a master of arts must have had four years of study in that subject, and have been examined by regent masters on the actual practice of medicine. If not a graduate, the scholar could not attempt to practice in the city of Oxford unless he had heard medicine for eight years and had been duly examined. Anyone attempting to do so without having fulfilled these requirements could not proceed further in the university, nor enjoy its privileges until he was reconciled and had been reinstated, although what was necessary for such reinstatement is found nowhere.[248]

[245] *Documents,* I, 364-365.
[246] *Ibid.,* I, 364.   [247] *Ibid.,* I, 375-376.
[248] *Mun. Acad.,* II, 406-407; *Statuta Antiqua,* p. 41.

In order to incept, six years' study was required for an M. A., and eight years for a non-M. A. These studies were divided into two groups, one on the theory of medicine, the other on the practice of medicine. For the former, the texts used were *Liber Tegni*,[249] or *Aphorisms*;[250] for the latter, the texts were *Regimenta Acutorum*,[251] or *Liber Febrium*,[252] or *Antidotarium* of Nicolaus.[253]

The inceptors must also have responded two years previous to inception to questions posed them by the regents, lectured for two years, and disputed for forty consecutive days.[254]

Medicine (Cambridge)

To be a graduate in arts was the first requirement for incepting in medicine.[255] The five years study in medicine necessary to become a regent included hearing once *Johannicius*,[256] Philaretus' *Pulsibus*, Theophilus *De Urinis*,[257] some book of Isaac, and the *Antidotarium* of Nicolaus, and hearing twice the *Liber Tegni*, or *Liber Prognosticorum*,[258] *Liber Aphorismorum*, and *Liber de Regimine Acutorum*. The other requirements were to have read *cursorie* at least one book

[249] A medical work of Galen, translated from the Arabic by Constantine; and with the comment of Haly by Gerard. Rashdall, *Universities of Europe in the Middle Ages*, II, ii, 781. Original edition.

[250] A medical work of Hippocrates (with commentary of Galen translated into Latin, according to Constantinus Africanus). From Arabic by Constantine at Monte Cassino—eleventh century. *Ibid.*

[251] A work of Hippocrates, from the Arabic by Gerard, at Toledo (some MSS attribute to Constantine). *Ibid.*, 782.

[252] Work of Isaac Judaeus, written in Arabic. From Arabic by Constantine—eleventh century. *Ibid.*, 781.

[253] Probably of Nicolaus, Praepositus of Salerno—twelfth century. Latin original. *Ibid.*

[254] *Mun. Acad.*, II, 406-409; *Statuta Antiqua*, pp. 39, 40-42, 231.

[255] *Documents*, I, 362-363, 376; and Fuller, *op. cit.*, p. 102.

[256] 'Regimenti.' This must mean the *Ysagogue in Medicinam*, the only work of Joann, translated. Early translation from Arabic. Name of translator not given. Rashdall, *Universities of Europe in the Middle Ages*, II, ii, 781. Original edition.

[257] Theophili Protospatharii de Urinis (Greek Christian writer of the seventh century A. D.; Philaretus is believed to be the same man). Old translations: traditional; not known to have passed through Arabic. *Ibid.*

[258] *Prognostics* of Aratus, a meteorological poem said to be founded on *Meteorologica* of Aristotle. No record of any Arabic translation. It is said there were Latin translations made from the Greek. *Ibid.*

on theory and one on practice, to have opposed and responded, to have the testimony of all the masters in medicine regarding theory as well as practice, and to have practiced medicine for two years.[259] No one could practice medicine within the limits of the university until he had graduated in medicine, or until he had been licenced *ad legendum*.

Theology (Oxford)

" Because greater maturity is fitting for professors of Holy Scriptures," graduates in arts had to spend five years in the study of theology before they were allowed to oppose; non-graduates in arts had to study philosophy for eight years, and theology for six or seven years more. An additional two years were required for responsions.[260] Only at the end of that time (seven years for arts candidates and nine years for non-arts candidates) were the scholars admitted *ad lecturam libri sententiarum*.[261] Within a year following the degree of B. D. a sermon had to be preached.[262]

For inception, the bachelor must have heard the Bible for three years; have lectured in the schools of theology on some book of the Bible or the Sentences; have preached a sermon at St. Mary's Church; have made eight responsions; and opposed publicly in the schools.[263]

Theology (Cambridge)

The course in theology required ten years to complete.[264] The candidate must have heard lectures on the Bible for two years previous to inception, and have lectured cursorily on " some book of the canonical Scriptures " for one year,

[259] Earlier in the same statute the time limit for practice is *one* year.
[260] *Mun. Acad.*, II, 389-390; *Statuta Antiqua*, pp. 48-49. Dr. Salter, in the introduction of *Registrum Annalium Collegii Mertonensis* (Oxford: Clarendon Press, for the Oxford Historical Society, 1923) holds that only one responsion and one opponency were necessary for a B. D.   P. xxvii.
[261] Peter Lombard's *Book of the Sentences* and the Bible were the backbone of the course in theology.
[262] *Mun. Acad.*, II, 396-397.
[263] *Ibid.*, II, 391, 394-395; *Statuta Antiqua*, pp. 50, 179.
[264] *Documents*, I, 377.

or at least ten days out of every term. He must also have lectured on all the books of the *Sentences*, and could not be licenced until three years had passed after the completion of these lectures. (This was later modified to permit the licencing of a bachelor of theology in the third term of the year after his lectures on the *Sentences*, provided that he had completed the required exercises in opposing, responding, lecturing, and preaching.) [265] No one could be admitted to oppose before his fifth year, and Statute 107,[266] contrary to the proviso in Statute 124,[267] that one must have been a graduate in arts to follow theology, seems to imply that nongraduates were permitted to enter that faculty, since provision was made to allow a non-graduate to oppose after his seventh year. The final requirement for a Master of Theology was to preach his sermon *ad Clerum*.

Grammar (Oxford)

Few scholars attended the faculty of grammar, admittedly known as the "inferior" faculty (often not even dignified by even the title of faculty), and consequently not many teachers of grammar schools were properly qualified. Evidently the superior faculties of arts, medicine, law, and theology offered too much attraction in the way of later remuneration and ecclesiastical attainment, so that consequently the grammar faculty was neglected.

The requirements of a grammar master were few.[268] No master could be licenced in grammar until he had been examined in versifying and *dictamen*,[269] and approved by the chancellor. Thereupon, thus licenced, he swore that he would teach diligently and faithfully his boys, attend to their morals, and punish any transgressor properly. The only requirements of an inceptor in grammar was that he be found *habilis* and *idoneus*, and that he promise to continue his lecturing for two years following his inception. The books

---

[265] *Ibid.*, I, 378.   [266] *Ibid.*, I, 369.   [267] *Ibid.*, I, 377.
[268] *Mun. Acad.*, II, 436-442; *Statuta Antiqua*, pp. 169-174.
[269] The art of composing speeches and letters. Some splendid examples of fifteenth century model letters are shown in *Oxford Formularies*, II, 431-450.

used in the lecturing or reading were Priscian and Donatus; Ovid's *De Arte Amandi* and Pamphilus were forbidden because of their illicit allurements. Upon receiving his licence to teach and being installed in a grammar school, the master in grammar immediately set his students to copy and compose verses and epistles in both English and French, as well as in Latin.

. . . tenentur singulis quindenis versus dare, et literas compositas verbis decentibus non ampullosis aut sesquipedalibus, et clausulis succintis, decoris, metaphoris manifestis, et, quantum possint, sententia refertis, quos versus et quas literas debent recipitentes in proximo die feriato vel ante in pergameno scribere, et inde sequenti die, cum ad Scholas venerint, Magistro suo corde tenus reddere et scripturam suam offere.[270]

Regent masters in grammar were under the authority of two superintendents, Masters of Arts, who were appointed yearly to inspect the grammar schools weekly, and who were paid a regular salary in addition to dividing the sum of money paid annually to the university by the grammar masters for the privilege of teaching.[271] Non-graduate teachers in the schools (of whom there were quite a few, indicating paucity of numbers in residence at the university for study in that subject) were under the authority not only of the two superintendent masters but also of the regent grammar masters.[272]

Grammar (Cambridge)

The exercises for inception in grammar were:[273] three public disputations in grammar, with bachelors and masters of the faculty acting as opponents; thirteen lectures on Priscian's *De Constructionibus*, the first of which was to be *solennis*; the presentation of the candidate to the proctors by a master of grammar who had incepted at Cambridge, or by a " Master of Glomery ";[274] the recommendations as to morals, stature, etc., by three masters appointed by the university; the promise to incept within a year after admission, under

[270] *Mun. Acad.*, II, 437-438.
[271] *Statuta Antiqua*, pp. 22, 121, 173.
[272] *Ibid.*, pp. lxxxvi-lxxxvii.
[273] *Documents*, I, 374.
[274] Superintendent of grammar schools in Cambridge.

penalty of one mark, unless he should incept in another faculty. After inception, the regent master had to lecture for a year on Priscian *major*, and during this time had to hold three *Convenite* (general conventions at the beginning of each term), in which he had to discuss or explain, after the fashion of Priscian in his *Twelve Verses of Virgil*, poetic verses. During his regency, the master had to carry the crucifix in all general processions, or appoint a substitute, suitable in the eyes of the proctor, to do it for him.

Matthew Stokys, a bedel in the University of Cambridge in the early sixteenth century, has left us an account of the ceremony of the inception of a master of grammar:

The Enteryng of a Master in Gramer

The Bedyll shall sett the Masters of Gramer to the Fathers place at vij of the Clocke, or betwene vii or eyght, Than the Father shal be brought to Saynt Mary Chyrch to the Masse begynyng at viijth of the Clocke: he shall cume behynde, & hys eldyst sonne nexte hym on hys ryght honde, lyke as is sayde afore of the Inceptours in Arte. When Masse is done, fyrst shall begynne the acte in Gramer. The Father shall have hys Sete made before the Stage for Physyke, and shall sytt alofte under the Stage for Physyke. The Proctour shall say, Incipiatis. When the Father hath arguyde as shall plese the Proctour, the Bedyll in Arte shall bring the Master of Gramer to the Vice-chauncelar, delyveryng hym a Palmer wyth a Rodde, whych the Vycechauncelar shall gyve to the seyde Master in Gramer, & so create hym Master. Then shall the Bedell purvay for every Master in Gramer a shrewde Boy, whom the master in Gramer shall bete openlye in the Scolys, & the master in Gramer shall give the Boye a Grote for hys Labour, & another Grote to hym that provydeth the Rode and the Palmer &c. de singulis. And thus endythe the Acte in that Facultye.[275]

In addition to these formally recognized masters of grammar, there were other teachers under the control of the regent masters and the superintendents, who also gave instruction in grammar as well as in writing, French, the drafting of deeds, and the art of keeping lay courts and pleading in the English manner,[276] to which flocked numbers of young men interested not in being trained as scholars, but as men of business, particularly that of the management of an agri-

---

[275] Extracts from Matthew Stokys Esquire Bedel His Book, found in Appendix A of George Peacock's *Observations on the Statutes of the University of Cambridge*, p. xxxvii. Peacock says this method was also followed at Oxford.

[276] *Statuta Antiqua*, pp. 169, 240.

cultural estate.[277] William of Kingsmill is an example of one of these fifteenth-century teachers in Oxford. William, scrivener, flourished around 1415 to 1430, and his courses at Oxford included such elements of instruction as rhymes for teaching children elementary French; dialogues for teaching French conversation to travellers and merchants; French numerals, days of the week, etc.; *Tractatus* on French spelling; letter-writing; treatise on French conjugation; treatise on drafting charters; and the art of pleading in French, with examples.[278] Kingsmill, a successor to Thomas Sampson, an outstanding *dictator* at Oxford in the fourteenth century, stated that his audience would be composed of clerks and laymen whose vocation would be to draw up charters and other muniments in accordance with the common law and custom of England:

Quia pium et necessarium est informare tam plures clericos [clericulos] quam alios idoneos, in cognicione et composicione cartarum et aliorum munimentorum minime eruditos, qui huiusmodi artificium proponunt exercere secundum communem legem et regni Anglie consuetudinem, ego igitur Willelmus Kingesmylle, non solum propter stipendium in hac parte michi promissum, sed motus pietate, ac propter vestram utilitatem qui societati mee adherere velitis, ac propter Dei amorem, de forma et composicione cartarum et [aliorum] munimentorum antedictorum, secundum parum scire meum et intellectum, ad usum et modum modernorum breuiter tractare propono.[279]

And money is not the only reason for his teaching—the love and piety of God and the good of those who wish to belong to his society are included among his motives!

Other fifteenth-century teachers of such courses at the universities were John of Bromley, William of Horbury, and Simon O. This latter teacher wrote a treatise on *dictamen* sometime in the early fifteen hundreds, as well as another on conveyancing. " The general form of his exposition," says Dr. Richardson, who has made a thorough study of these teachers, " suggests the lecture-room and the methods of a teacher who

---

[277] Henry Gerald Richardson, " Business Training in Medieval Oxford," *American Historical Review*, XLVI (Jan., 1941), 269.
[278] M. Dominica Legge, " William of Kingsmill—A Fifteenth-Century Teacher of French in Oxford," *Studies in French Language and Medieval Literature Presented to Mildred K. Pope* (Manchester University Press, 1939), pp. 241-242.
[279] Cited in *Oxford Formularies*, II, 340, n. 1.

makes additions to his notes in the course of his teaching and never puts them into literary shape." [280]

That these business teachers with their many students were numerous enough to require special attention from the university administration as early as 1350, is seen in the statute that required masters in grammar to be examined as to their competence in *dictamen* before they could be licensed.[281] However, such instruction seems to have declined by the end of the fifteenth century. French as a means of correspondence among educated Englishmen fell into disuse; the rise of the collegiate system in the universities and the development of the legal schools probably contributed in part to its decline.[282] The number of grammar schools in the environs of both Cambridge and Oxford had also decreased to such an extent by the close of the century that at Cambridge they sometimes failed to appoint a Master of Glomery,[283] while at Oxford it was decided in 1492 that, since the superintendents of the grammar schools now had no work to do but still received a salary, they should be made superintendents of the disputations at the Austin Friars.[284] The establishment of some free schools may have helped to empty the old grammar schools.[285]

The Organization of the University

The administrative head of the university, the chancellor, was usually chosen from the doctors of theology and canon law, and was elected biennially at Oxford by the regents.[286] At Cambridge, the election was held by all the regents in arts, if there were as many as twelve at the time, and if there were fewer than twelve, the non-regents were permitted to vote.[287] On his election, he took an oath to defend his

[280] Henry Gerald Richardson, "An Oxford Teacher of the Fifteenth Century," *John Rylands Library*, Bulletin XXIII (1939), 436, 442.
[281] *Statuta Antiqua*, p. 120.
[282] Henry Gerald Richardson, "Business Training in Medieval Oxford," *op. cit.*, p. 274.
[283] *Grace Book* I, xxxvii.
[284] *Mun. Acad.*, I, 363.
[285] *Medieval Archives of the University of Oxford*, II, 285.
[286] *Statuta Antiqua*, pp. lxxii, 64, 146-147.
[287] *Documents*, I, 309.

university and to put down rebellions, and to observe faithfully all the statutes, privileges,[288] customs, liberties, and laws
of the university.[289] As head of the university, the chancellor
had control of the assize of bread and ale, and the assaying
of weights and measures.[290] He also acted as the representa-
tive of the university in dealings with the town, particularly
with regard to the letting of halls, the cession of debts, and
the engagement of servants by the scholars.[291] He was pro-
tector of the morals of the students, and thus held power of
banishment and äbjuration, and other penalties, such as
penance, fines, and the pillory. With regard to fines, the
university retained one third, the proctors one-third, and
the chancellor the remaining third.[292] The imposing of fines
for all sorts of disturbances was a very effective means of
increasing the chancellor's revenues, particularly during the
periods of political unrest, which was reflected in the conduct
of the scholars and their retinue.[293] The chancellor was also
head of the court which settled civil disputes, in which matters
he was assisted by an official called *ebdomadarius*,[294] and held
sole archdiaconal jurisdiction over doctors, masters, scholars,
and their servants.[295] When it was necessary for the chancellor to be away for any length of time, he appointed an
assistant to take his place during his absence, and to help him
in his duties.[296] When during the fifteenth century the office
of chancellorship became a non-resident one, sometimes of a
short period of time, and occasionally of a long period, this
assistant, given the title of vice-chancellor, assumed the chan-

---

[288] For two summaries of the privileges of Oxford prevalent c.
1485-1500, see Appendix III, pp. 352-370, of *Medieval Archives*, I.
[289] *Mun. Acad.*, I, 309-310; II, 488-489; *Statuta Antiqua*, p. 245.
[290] *Registrum Cancellarii Oxoniensis*, I, xv; *Mun. Acad.* I, 159-167.
[291] *Registrum Cancellarii Oxoniensis*, I, xiv; *Mun. Acad.* I, 279.
[292] *Registrum Cancellarii Oxoniensis*, I, xviii-xix, 221, 398, 400, 402;
II, 101, 156, 160, 161, 181, 208; *Mun. Acad.*, II, 500, 540; *Statuta
Antiqua*, pp. 81, 641-642; *Medieval Archives*, I, 247-252.
[293] See *Statuta Antiqua*, p. 204, for a table of fines for offenses, set
up in 1410.
[294] *Registrum Cancellarii Oxoniensis*, II, 284.
[295] *Statuta Antiqua*, p. lxxi; *Medieval Archives*, I, 243-247.
[296] At Cambridge, should the chancellor have to be away for more
than fifteen days, the power of naming his deputy passed to the congregation of regents. *Grace Book A*, I, xxxii; *Documents*, I, 311.

cellor's responsibilities. High birth, wealth, and political or ecclesiastical power eventually became the reasons for the selection of a chancellor, as these names indicate: Gilbert Kymer, Thomas Bourchier, John Carpenter, John Norton, Richard Northeram, William Grey, Thomas Gascoigne, John Kexby, Henry Sever, Robert Thwaytes, George Neville, and Thomas Chandler, Richard Billingsford, Guido la Zouche, John and Henry Rykinghale, John Holbroke, Nicholas Swaffham, Thomas Rotheram, Thomas, Bishop of Lincoln, and John, Bishop of Salisbury.[297] Should the chancellor die or resign, which happened frequently, and an immediate election was impossible, a *cancellarius natus*, usually a senior theologian, took over his duties.[298]

The administrative officers next in order of importance were the two proctors, usually representing the northern and southern factions, and elected by the faculty of arts. To them was entrusted all the public business of the university, the superintendence of elections, the regulation of academic business, the administering of oaths, and the management of finances.[299] Proctors held their office for one year and were ineligible for re-election.[300]

The bedels, six in number at Oxford, two at Cambridge, were elected at the same time and in the same manner as the chancellor, and were the " superior servants " or the " masters of ceremonies " of the university.[301] They had to be present at inceptions, feasts, and funerals, gave notice of disputations, and assisted the proctors in collecting fees and fines. They were elected for one year and could be re-elected. Payment was provided for them by the university.

[297] One of Oxford's letters reveals that Gilbert Kymer, clerk to Humphrey, Duke of Gloucester, was elected chancellor so that he might tell the university what the Duke's wishes were. *Epist. Acad.*, I, 255-256.

[298] Salter has discovered that there were as many as eight of these *cancellarii nati* during the years 1437 and 1453. *Registrum Cancellarii Oxoniensis*, I, xlii.

[299] *Statuta Antiqua*, pp. lxxv-lxxvi; *Documents*, p. 340; Mallet, *op. cit.*, I, 175. For a detailed list of their duties, see *Statuta Antiqua*, pp. 197-198.

[300] *Mun. Acad.* I, 81.

[301] *Statuta Antiqua*, p. lxxvii; *Mun. Acad.* I, 362 and II, 494-495, 496; *Grace Book A*, p. xxxvii. At Oxford, there were two for each of the faculties of theology, civil law, and arts.

The legislative power lay in the hands of the assembly of regents and non-regents (*Congregatio Magna*), but the faculty of arts reserved to themselves the right to deliberate on all matters before they were finally settled in Convocation.[302] This *Congregatio Magna* was the chief legislative assembly, and had the power to enact, repeal, and amend the statutes, while the regents alone (*Congregatio Regentium* or *Minor*) dealt with the graces, studies, and other administrative matters.[303] Voting was by the faculties. In *Statuta Antiqua*, there is, a form in use around 1480-1488 which gives us a very good idea of how legislation was carried on at Oxford.[304] First, at one p. m. a bell rang to call together the regents of the faculty of arts for the purpose of discussing the resolutions to be presented in a day or so to *Congregatio Magna*. After a few days the *Congregatio Magna* met, and elected four scrutators, who were presented with the resolutions in writing from the chancellor. The next day the non-regents received the resolutions, while the regents grouped themselves into their proper faculties and carried on discussions in their accustomed places. On the fifth day, the various faculties voted and the resolutions were declared carried or lost. The senior scrutator announced the votes of the non-regents, the chancellor or senior theologian the votes of the theologians, the senior proctor those of the artists, and so on. After the chancellor announced the results, the Congregation was dismissed. Then it was the duty of the chancellor and the proctors to enter these acts in their registers within fifteen days.

In January, 1456, an attempt was made to reform these statutes, but evidently nothing came of it.[305] The faculty of arts (Black Congregation) declared that the statutes relating to appeals and the formal disputations of theologians had lost their power because they were conflicting and hazy. The appointment of a committee to reform these statutes, or to add, reject, or re-enact them was recommended. A few

---

[302] *Mun. Acad.*, I, 117, 331-332; II, 491; *Grace Book A*, p. xxxiii.
[303] *Statuta Antiqua*, pp. xxiii, xxv; *Grace Book A*, p. xxxiii.
[304] *Statuta Antiqua*, pp. xxx, 291-293.
[305] *Statuta Antiqua*, p. xlvi.

days later eight masters were elected, but that seemed to end the matter.

There were two additional administrative offices, one of which was characteristic only to Cambridge. The first was the office of scrutator, who acted as officers of the non-regent house, taking the notes and declaring the results,[306] while the other was the office of taxor.[307] Two regents were appointed by their associates to tax or fix the rents of hostels and houses occupied by the students (the taxors worked with a committee of townsmen), to assist the proctor in making assize of bread and beer, and in other affairs relating to the regulation of markets.

These, then, made up the administrative agents of the university in the Middle Ages. Almost the only changes that occurred in the various offices during the fifteenth century was the tendency of the chancellorship to become more of an honorary and permanent position, while the vice-chancellorship assumed the duties formerly performed by the chancellor, and the appearance of the office of registrar for the first time in 1448, according to Strickland Gibson.[308]

The Library

One of the most outstanding features of fifteenth-century education was the generous gifts of books to the universities by men who had slowly and carefully built up collections that students and masters were only too eager to have available for study. Because of the great amount of work attached to the copying of books, the time consumed in such copying, and the expense of the materials used in the process, books were very costly, and highly prized by anyone fortunate enough to possess them.[309] Scholars copied *verbatim* texts delivered by the masters, who in turn had received their information in

[306] *Grace Book A*, p. xxxvii.
[307] *Ibid.*, p. xxxvi-xxxvii; Peacock, *op. cit.*, pp. 25-26. This latter was distinctive of Cambridge.
[308] *Statuta Antiqua*, p. xx.
[309] The rise of the printing press in the last quarter of the century helped to ease this situation, although many of the printed books were not found in clerical hands.

7

exactly the same manner. A few of the more important scholastic books owned by the colleges or the universities were made available to the students by being placed in one room in stalls, chained to the desks so that they could not be lost or stolen. The authorities realized very early the importance of the proper care of books entrusted to them, and in 1412 at Oxford composed the following set of rules and regulations to be strictly followed:

Since, by the blessing of God there has come to be a library in the university, the careless management of which would cause great evils, the University ordained that a Chaplain in holy orders should be elected to have charge . . .[310] In order that the books may not be injured by the multitude of readers, nor students disturbed by throngs of visitors, it is decreed that no one shall be allowed to read in the library but graduates and religious who have studied philosophy eight years. . . . No Bachelor who is not a Master may read in the library except in the dress of his degree. For the safer custody of the books, all now resident, who are allowed to use the library, shall make oath . . that when they go to read they will use the books properly, making no erasures or blots therein, nor otherwise injuring the folios. All graduates at their admission, shall, along with the other oaths, take the following oath: ' Item, Tu jurabis, quod cum ad librariam Universitatis communem acceseris, libros ibi contentos, et quos insprexeris, modo honesto et pacifico pertractabis, nulli librorum hujusmodi, per turpitudinem aut rasuras abolitionemve quaternorum seu foliorum, praejudicium inferendo.' That the librarian may not be overtaxed on the one hand by being all day in the library, nor the readers inconvenienced by his inattention on the other hand, it is ordered that the hours during which the library shall be open, shall be from nine to eleven before noon, and from one to four afternoon, except on Sundays and on the days when the masses of the University are celebrated, and that constant residence may not injure his health, the librarian shall be allowed a month's absence during the long vacation. The library shall be closed at all other times . . . unless for the admission thereto of some stranger of eminence, and on the occasion of such visits, it shall be opened, if required, from sunrise to sunset, if the visitor be a distinguished person and not accompanied by a disorderly crowd. Also, the Chancellor of the University may at any time during daylight, visit the library; . . . A large and conspicuous board shall be suspended in the library, on which shall be inscribed in fair writing the names of all books in the library, with the names of the donors. The books and the windows and the doors of the library shall be closed every night. The oftener a gift is seen the more it is remembered; therefore, within three days after the gift, every book shall be presented to congregation, and within fifteen days, shall be chained down in the library. . . . That the Chaplain may never plead ignorance of his duties, all these statutes concerning the library shall be read to him at his election, and he

---

[310] In Cambridge he received forty shillings, according to *Grace Book A*, p. 40. See also pp. 10, 84, 90, 107, 122 for similar library rules and regulations at Cambridge.

shall swear to observe them. And all who hold office in the University generally shall swear to observe the statutes relating to their several duties.[311]

One of the most important and generous benefactors to Oxford in this matter of books was Humphrey, Duke of Gloucester. Altogether, Oxford received a total of about two hundred and sixty-four volumes, for which the university was most appreciative.[312]

Humphrey's bequests were a little slow in arriving and Oxford had to write to several prominent men (Waynflete, Somerset, the Marquess of Suffolk, Lord Say) to hurry things up a bit, until eventually the university got possession of them.[313] That Oxford was always on the lookout for books for its library is evinced in the letters sent in 1449 to several executors of the Bishop of Chichester's estate, asking them to " grant a handsome donation of the books of the late Bishop of Chichester; who, as we learn from those who were intimate with them, always intended to give them to us. . . ."[314]

In order to safeguard this precious collection, a new register was made in which the names of the volumes were entered, and the books were forbidden to be removed from the library except for repair and unless the Duke wished to borrow them; masters actually lecturing in those subjects could borrow them under an indenture, or principals of halls, under certain conditions, and the librarian had to give an account of them yearly.[315] Oxford was outspoken in its gratitude and suggested to the Duke the possibility of moving his books into the new school just being built:

By your magnificent donation, from having been well-nigh without books, this University has become richer than any other in these

---

[311] *Mun. Acad.*, I, 261-268. Marginal notes. The individual colleges had their own libraries, and their own rules, similar to the university ones. Cf. G. R. Driver, " Magdalen College Library," *Oxford Bibliographical Society, Proceedings and Papers*, II (1927-1930), 145-200.
[312] *Epist. Acad.*, I, 177-184, 197-199, 204-205, 232, 237, 244-246; *Mun. Acad.*, II, 758-772. For a very valuable account of Humphrey's interest in the classics, see Robert Weiss, *Humanism in England during the Fifteenth Century* (Oxford: Basil Blackwell, 1941).
[313] *Epist. Acad.*, I, 258-262.
[314] *Ibid.*, I, 281-282.
[315] *Mun. Acad.*, I, 326-330.

treasures; so that we scarcely know where to bestow them. What-
ever has been written that is worth reading is now accessible here to
all comers. Here the Greek and Latin tongues in their original
majesty, for so many centuries consigned to oblivion, by your instru-
mentality see the light again; and here too are being placed most
elegant works dedicated, as no doubt many others will hereafter be,
to your name. Hither flock from every land men of industry un-
wearied and of acutest intellect. We wish you could behold with what
greediness and thirst for knowledge the troops of students hang over
your books; and hear how they encourage and stimulate each other.
The gift is a noble action of a noble mind; and no prince, however
great his learning, his love of literature, his patronage of scholars,
could have devised one more in harmony with his own cultured taste.
Our words are too feeble to express our thanks, and we wish for a
permanent memorial of your generosity. If we could place your
books in a suitable chamber, separate from others, the crowding of
the readers might be avoided; and for this purpose we would offer
the new school now in building. The situation is retired and quiet, and
we venture to suggest that the new library should be called by
your name. Will your boundless charity excuse this presumptuous
suggestion? [316]

Another munificent gift of books was made late in the
century by Master Richard Lichfeld, Doctor of Laws, who in
1489 gave one hundred and twenty-eight volumes to Ox-
ford.[317] Other miscellaneous gifts included a copy of Josephus'
Antiquities and *Wars of the Jews*, by Thomas Knoll, a citizen
of London,[318] and "sundry books" left by Henry V and
Master Richard Brown (alias Cordone).[319] When this same
Richard Brown died, he had in his possession these theological
and legal books: *Diversi tractatus Lincolniae, Catholicon,
Hugo de Vienna super libris Regum usque Job, Sermones
Jordani (de temporali et Sanctorum), Petrus de Crescentiis,
Jeronymus in Epistolas, Lathbury super Threnis, Decretals,
Sextus,* and *Clementines.*[320] A copy of Alexander Neckham's
De naturisrerum and other books came to Oxford from J.
Somerset;[321] the Duchess of Suffolk was liberal with her
books as well as her money;[322] and the Abbot of St.

---

[316] *Epist. Acad.*, I, 244-246. Marginal notes.

[317] *Mun. Acad.*, I, 357. *Register of the University of Oxford* (edited
by Charles William Boase; Oxford: Clarendon Press, for the Oxford
Historical Society, 1885), I, 10-11; *Epist. Acad.*, II, 559-560. This
latter reference gives the number as one hundred and thirty-two.

[318] *Epist. Acad.*, I, 229-230.

[319] *Ibid.*, pp. 151-153, 279-280.

[320] *Mun. Acad.*, II, 639-657.

[321] *Epist. Acad.*, I, 220, 309-310, 313-314.

[322] *Ibid.*, p. 326.

Alban's, John Wethampsted, presented the university with *Propinarium*.[323]

The individual colleges of Oxford benefited to a great extent in the gifts of books made to them by former students and friends. For example, Master William Gascoigne and Master William Chamberlayne made a covenant in 1432 by which, in return for certain books given by Chamberlayne to Lincoln College, certain anthems were to be sung in honor of St. Anne in All Saints' Church on certain days.[324] Master Thomas Barker also made an agreement with the college (1488) in which the college loaned him four volumes of the books of the " Doctor Subtilis " he had already given to the library, and after his death the books were to be chained in the library for the use of the students.[325] The Second Report of the Manuscript Commission also includes this item:

> In folio 15 b an Inventory begins of all the books in the Library of the College, date probably about 1500. The names also of those who gave the volumes are in many instances added, and the books are enumerated desk by desk. Among them is this item:—' Also, on the second side of the same desk, Waldene against Wyclyf, the gift of the Founder (Richard Flemyng, Bishop of Lincoln). . . .' As to Chronicles, the following are mentioned:—' Also, the Chronicle of Ivo of Chartres, the gift of Master Thomas Gascoigne. . . .' Also the Chronicle which begins with ' Cornelius', given by the same. Also the Policronicon, with a table (tabula), the gift of William Lane. . . . Also Boccace (Boccasius) on Illustrious Men and Eminent Women, the gift of Robert Flemyng. In the second part of the same (the fourth desk) a little book of the Chronicles of Mariacus (an error for Manianus) Scotus.' The works of the Doctor Subtilis (Duns Scotus) are very numerous in this list.[326]

Magdalen College was the recipient of a magnificent gift of eight hundred volumes from its founder, William of Waynflete, as well as jewels and books from Thomas Ingledew and a scholar by the name of Rushall.[327]

---

[323] *Ibid.*, II, 373-374.
[324] *Second Report of the Historical Manuscript Commission*, Appendix, p. 130.
[325] *Ibid.*
[326] *Ibid.* According to the Catalogue of 1474, there were one hundred and thirty-five chained books on seven desks, and, in 1476, thirty-five additional books called the " common choice " books, from which the rector could choose one, and after him the fellows one each, until all the books were taken out. Clark, *op. cit.*, p. 183.
[327] G. R. Driven, *op. cit.*, p. 145.

An investigation of the wills left by the scholars of Oxford at their death, of indentures, and of inventories, throws additional light on the kinds of books that were in use at the universities during the fifteenth century.[328]   James Hedyan, Bachelor of Canon and Civil Law, had, as might be expected, a *Digest* (the *Infortiatum*), a book of *Decretals* (*cum codice*), the book *Sextus*, and a book of Sophistry.[329]   Master John Moreton, who died in 1451, left a *Trifolium, Jacobus Fortunensis super teḡ. Gal., De praxi amici tui, Tabula de simplicibus*, and *Liber de Attonone*.[330]   Thomas Spray's will, executed in 1455, revealed a *Liber sermonum Magdalenae* and *Manipulus curatorum*,[331] while David Turnour's showed *logicales libros* and *libros vocatos* 'primers.' Master Rolph Dreff of Broadgates Hall had a *Bible, Januensis super sermonibus Dominicalibus, Liber Clementinarum cum glossa ordinata*, two *Digests, Portiforium, Repertorium, Casuarius super Digest, Casuarius super decimo libro decretalium, Jurnell*, and *Prima pars* Rabani.[332]   Master Henry Calday owned *De potentia Dei et malo, Commentator super libros propheticorum, Petrus paludis, Psalterium glossatum*, a book of the *Homilies of Pope Gregory*, two *Fortiatum, Digestus Vetus, Sextus, Martialis*, Plato's *in Timaeo, Codex*, two *De diversis contentis, Casus Bernardi*, Priscian's *in majore*, Anselm's *Cur deus homo, De communi glossa secundum Mattheum, Doctrinalis, Epistolae Senecae ad Lucilium*, Hugo de Victore *de* ———, *Clementinus*, and *Decretales*;[333] and John Lashowe who died intestate (1455) possessed *Liber grammaticalis Ugucionis,* " *Chartuary,*" *Liber Sequentiarum glossatus, Liber sermonum,, Liber de regulis grammaticalibus*.[334]

The library of Cambridge University was in much the same state as Oxford, with many and generous gifts bestowed on

---

[328] Cf. also the list of books in the Warden's study in *Registrum Annalium Collegii Mertonensis*, pp. 13-15, 79-80, 143-144, 168, 198, 235; the books mentioned in *Registrum Cancellarii Oxoniensis*, Appendix IV, 367-371; and *The Dean's Register of Oriel* (edited by G. C. Richards and H. E. Salter; Oxford: The Clarendon Press, for the Oxford Historical Society, 1926), pp. 1-2.

[329] *Mun. Acad.*, II, 546.
[330] *Ibid.*, II, 614.
[331] *Ibid.*, II, 660.
[332] *Ibid.*, II, 582-583.
[333] *Ibid.*, II, 610-611.
[334] *Ibid.*, II, 663.

her and her colleges. Dr Richard Holme left a bequest of books in or before 1424, which are contained in the one of two catalogues of books made public by Henry Bradshaw.[335] Other donors found in this list were Aylmer, Nicholas Ive, John Preston, John Church, Jacob Matissal, Thomas Paxton, John Water, William Hollere, John Holbroke, Christopher Kirkby, Richard Langley, Nicholas Upton, Robert Alney, Robert Teye, Richard Blynneforth, Hugo Paris, John Croucher, John Scot, John Wraughby, John Smith, John Teasdale, Richard Kendall, John Thornell, John Aldewyck, Thomas de Castro Bernardi, John Paris, Walter Crome, John Thorp, Thomas King and Thomas Thurkyll. The second list, as its title indicates, was made in 1473, and contains an account of the library as it was just before Chancellor Rotheram made his contributions to it—funds to complete the new building, as well as valuable books to enrich it.[336] In the first list, the books are classed according to subjects; in the second, they are grouped according to the stalls they occupied, which in turn were according to subject matter.

According to a catalogue of 1418, we find the following among the books which Peterhouse was fortunate enough to possess: *Posteriora, Priora, Topica*, and *Elenchi* of Aristotle; texts of Porphyry; William of Heytesbury's *Sophismata*; Boethius; *Philosophia* of Albertus Magnus; Ockham's *Summa*; commentaries of Kilwardby and St. Thomas; *Summa* of Peter Hispanus; William Brito's *Quaestiones*; eighteen volumes of Aristotelian texts on natural and moral philosophy, and metaphysics; commentaries of Averroes, Aquinas, Egidius Romanus, Walter Burley, Durandus and Peter de Alvernia; John Dumbleton's *Summa*; works in agriculture and veterinary medicine of Palladius and Columella; works of Seneca and Pliny *De animalibus*; works of Capella and Isidore; Priscian; *Dictionary* of Hugucis; John de Janua's *Catholicon*; Brito's *Summa de expositione verborum Bibliae*;

[335] *The Collected Papers of Henry Bradshaw* (Cambridge: University Press, 1889), pp. 16-54.
[336] Cooper, *Annals of Cambridge*, I, 221; see also *Grace Book A*, pp. 130, 136, 187; and *Grace Book B* (edited by Mary Bateson; Cambridge: University Press, 1903), Part I, 64.

De grammatica of Bacon; *Doctrinale Puerorum* of Alexander; Guido della Colonne's *History of the Trojan War; Pharaoh's Dream* by John Lemouicenses; *Practica sive Usus Dictaminis* of Laurence Aquilegiensis; three copies each of *Cynus super Codicem, Parvem Volumen, Digestum, Vetus, Digestum Infortiatum, Digestum Novum,* and *Codex; Liber Sextus; Extravagants* and *Clementines;* commentaries of Paulus, Johannes Andreae, William de Monte Lauduns, William de Mandagots, Henry of Susa; *Constitutions* of Otho and Ottobon; *Liber taxarum omnium beneficium Angliae; Summa Ostiensis;* Guido de Baysis' *Rosarium; Speculum Juris,* or *Speculum Judiciale* of William Durand; thirteen volumes of medicine, including Galen, *Breviary* of Constantine, Johannicius' *Isagogue,* Nicolaus' *Antidotarium,* Theophilus' *De urinis,* and *Isaac;* works of Chrysostom, Augustine, Ambrose, Jerome, Gregory, Isidore, Bernard, Anselm, Stephen Langton, Lyra, Hugo de St. Victor, Euclid; Ptolemy; Bacon's *De multiplicatione specierum cum perspective ejusdem; Historia Scholastica* of Peter Comestor, four Bibles, a glossed *Gospel of St. John;* tractate on *Epistles of St. Paul;* Grosseteste's *De oculo morali;* two copies of *Magister Historiarum;* six Psalters; nine copies of Peter Lombard's *Sentences;* Aquinas' *Summa;* the *Quaestiones* of Henry of Ghent; and the *Super Sententias* of John Bokyngham; works of Cassiodorus, Valerius Maximus, Sallust, Vegetius, Frontinus, Quintilian, Macrobius Seneca, Priscian, Hugucio, Alexander de Villa Dei, Ovid, Statius, and Lucan.[337]

Thomas Markaunt, fellow of Corpus Christi College, bequeathed to the library in 1432 seventy-six volumes,[338] valued at one hundred pounds,[339] while John Tytleshall, who died in 1446, was another donor.[340] Pembroke College was the recipient of many highly-valued manuscripts from such masters

---

[337] T. A. Walker, "English and Scottish Education. Universities and Public Schools to the Time of Colet," *The Cambridge History of English Literature,* II (1932), 362-366.

[338] Montague Rhodes James, *A Descriptive Catalogue of the Manuscripts in the Library of Corpus Christi College, Cambridge* (Cambridge: University Press, 1912), I, xi.

[339] Cooper, *Memorials of Cambridge,* p. 148.

[340] James, *op. cit.,* pp. xi, 533.

as Lavenham, Sudbury, Somerset, Clench, Langton, West-haugh, Woodcock, Damlet, Sawnders, Stukley, Greene, Wright, Cokkaram, and Gawyn.[341] William Skelton, who died c. 1471, left his library to King's;[342] and a valuable manuscript Bible, in three volumes, was presented in 1448 to Queens' by Marmaduke Lumley, the Bishop of London, and the Chancellor of Cambridge.[343] Thomas Stoyll made a bequest of books to Clare College, c. 1466, and took precautions to have them chained there.[344] The earliest college register of St. Catherine's contains a Latin list of " Books, the gift of Robert Wodelarke, the first founder of this College, chained in the Library." Among them are: *Lincolniensis* [Grosseteste] *de Oculo Morali*; Franciscus Petrarcha *de Remediis utriusque Fortunae*; Stephen Langton's *Super Ecclesiastem*; *Distinctiones Holcoti super Sapientia*[m] ; Policronica; Boccasius' *In Anglicis de Viris Illustribus*; *Historiae Cronicales Angliae, Franciae, et aliarum regionum*; several works of Aristotle; and many treatises of Thomas Aquinas and Duns Scotus. Three of the works of Aquinas were given by a Master Nelson, along with *The Epistle of Ieronime*, the gift of John Fisher, Bishop of Rochester.[345]

One has only to glance at the titles to these volumes to see that the subject of fifteenth-century England collegiate texts was heavy. The preponderance of writings of the Church Fathers, legal works, glosses on the Bible as well as on the writings of the Scholastics indicates the narrowness and rigidity with which the reading habits of students were bound and fettered. Weighty curricula were well fortified by weighty tomes. The humanistic era, which was just beginning to take root in England, was evidenced in the medieval libraries by a few sporadic gifts of manuscripts and books which the

[341] Montague Rhodes James, *A Descriptive Catalogue of the Manuscripts in the Library of Pembroke College, Cambridge* (Cambridge: University Press, 1905).
[342] Cooper, *Memorials of Cambridge*, p. 212.
[343] *Ibid.*, p. 298.
[344] *Second Report of the Historical Manuscript Commission*, Appendix, pp. 110-116.
[345] *Fourth Report of the Historical Manuscripts Commission*, Appendix, pp. 421-428.

classical scholars left either to their own college's library, or to the university library. For example, Robert Fleming, the Dean of Lincoln, gave Lincoln's library thirty-eight manuscripts, mostly classical authors, such as Terence, Virgil, Caesar, Horace, Plautus, Quintilian, Juvenal, Cicero, and Aulus Gellius.[346] Such men as William Grey, John Tiptoft, John Free, John Gunthorpe, Richard Bole, Thomas Chandler, William Selling and Richard Fleming were the leaders in this new school of thought, who, after studying at an English university, had travelled to Italy to carry further their scholarly pursuits.[347] Mallet [348] says that John Free was " perhaps the most celebrated English author of his day." At any rate, he graduated from Balliol in 1450, became a Doctor of Medicine in Padua, was a lawyer of some importance, a poet, and a Greek scholar.[349] John Tiptoft, widely read and widely travelled, collected many manuscripts and left them, valued at five hundred marks, to Oxford.[350] William Grey returned from Italy with many manuscripts. Mullinger says that

. . . some of them of authors that had never before crossed the channel, and all of them well calculated to impart to the few scholars to be found among his countrymen a notion of the movement in progress in the Transalpine universities.[351]

His collection, in addition to the traditional theological books, included the letters of Petrarch, orations of Poggio, Aretino, and Guarino, a new translation of Plato's *Timaeus*, one of *Euthyphron*, the *Institutions* of Lactantius, versions of the *Golden Verses of Pythagoras*, additional orations of Cicero and Quintilian, some discourses of Seneca, and Jerome's *Letter to Pammachius*.[352] Grey had been proctor in Rome

---

[346] Clark, *op. cit.*, p. 176. Weiss, *op. cit.*, p. 100, n. 4, says that until Fleming's gift, Lincoln College possessed no classical or humanistic texts.

[347] C. L. Kingsford, *Prejudice and Promise in XVth Century England* (Oxford: Clarendon Press, 1925), pp. 45-46; Weiss, *op. cit.*, chapters VI and VII.

[348] *Op. cit.*, I, 343.   [349] Mullinger, *op. cit.*, p. 397.

[350] *Epist. Acad.*, II, 389-390; Reginald Poole, " Balliol College," *The Colleges of Oxford*, p. 38. Cambridge was a recipient, also. Weiss, *op. cit.*, p. 118.

[351] *Op. cit.*, p. 397.

[352] *Ibid.* See Weiss, *op. cit.*, pp. 92-94 for further titles. Richard Bole, Grey's secretary, was also a donor to Balliol.

for Henry VI, and when he was recalled in 1454 to be Bishop of Ely, he wanted his books kept in his old college, Balliol.[353] About two hundred in number, including a *printed* copy of Josephus, they were preserved in a new building erected especially for that purpose.[354] John Gunthorpe, who accompanied Free to Farrara to listen to Guarino, collected manuscripts which he gave to both Cambridge and Oxford.[355]

These donations of books to the universities and colleges of England stimulated in the scholar an interest in neoclassicism that was furthered, particularly in Oxford, by the humanistic interests and leaning of such men as William Chandler,[356] John Farley,[357] Stefano Surigone,[358] John Anwykyll,[359] and William Grocyn.[360] In Cambridge, however, according to Weiss,[361] the university library's only humanistic work was Petrarch's *De Remediis*; Peterhouse had Petrarch's *Letters*; St. Catharine's, two copies of *De Remediis*, Bruni's *Ethics*, and Decembrio's *Republic*; and Pembroke's, one copy of Bruni's *Letters*. King's College had the only valuable collection of Renaissance texts, which included Bruni's *Ethics* and *Phaedrus*, some Latinized Plutarch's *Lives*, Decembrio's Latin text of Plato's *Republic*, Poggio's *De Avaritia*, and Beccaria's translation of St. Athanasius. Cambridge, too, lacked such a roster of " New Learners " as Oxford had, but it was not entirely devoid of such influences. Two Italians, Lorenzo da Savona and Caius Auberinus, were instrumental in the late 1470's and early 1480's in arousing the attention of men of letters to the new standards of taste in polite letters, while John Doget, a member of King's College,

---

[353] Poole, *op. cit.*, p. 37. Cf. also William H. Woodward, *Studies in Education* (Cambridge: University Press, 1906), p. 107.

[354] Poole, *op. cit.*, p. 37.

[355] Mallet, *op. cit.*, I, 343; and Poole, *op. cit.*, p. 39.

[356] Chancellor of Oxford, 1457-1461, 1472-1479.

[357] Registrar of Oxford, 1458-1464.

[358] An Italian scholar who taught Latin eloquence at Oxford between 1454 and 1471.

[359] Grammar Master at Magdalen College School, about 1481, and author of *Compendium Totius Gramaticae*, a union of modern and medieval grammatical systems.

[360] Neo-classicist, and Reader in Divinity at Magdalen College, 1483-1488.

[361] *Op. cit.*, p. 161.

Cambridge, in the 1450's, revealed his classical interests in his commentary on Plato's *Phaedo*.[362]

These liberalizing strains were indicative of the stirring of a new era in England. With the ascension of Henry VII to the throne in 1485, the Middle Ages may be said to have come to a close. New forces were at work. The printing press, set up in England by William Caxton, meant an increase in the number of books available, with an accompanying decrease in cost. An economic and industrial expansion was taking place; new worlds were being discovered. In a few years England was to break away from the Roman Catholic Church and to create her own branch. Such illustrious persons as Erasmus, Colet, More, Grocyn, Linacre and Luther had appeared on the horizon; the English Renaissance had begun. Philosophy and theology were still enthroned in the universities, but the humanities were successfully clamoring for their rightful place in the currimulum. A new day was dawning, but it must be remembered that " Every period of time has three elements: the dying past, the flourishing present, and the promising future." All ages have their roots in the past.

[362] *Ibid*, p. 165.

CHAPTER III

SCHOOLS

The fifteenth century was, as has been so often noted, a century of transition, politically, economically, socially, and educationally. This is especially true with regard to secondary formal education, that system of training set up by the Church to take care of providing boys and young men to enter the priesthood or monastic orders, and the training of youngsters to take part not only in the recitation of prayers and the like, but also in carrying on the singing of the Mass. For hundreds of years education had been solely for the Church; but now a new middle class was demanding a new education. The merchants and artisans were not planning to have their children enter the ministry nor intending to have them clothe themselves with the mantle of monasticism. Even the laboring class, the villeins, were asserting their right to send their children to school. Although such had been done illegally for a number of years, this was made legally possible for them by the statute of 1406 which declared, among other things,

. . . that every man or woman, of what estate or condition that he be, shall be free to set their son or daughter to take learning at any manner of school that pleaseth them within the Realm.[1]

While a curriculum better suited to the needs of the people did not fully materialize until the sixteenth century and later, there were a few attempts at revision made in the latter half of the fifteenth century. The most notable of these were the College of Acaster, founded by Robert Stillington, Bishop of Bath and Wells, and Jesus College at Rotherham, founded by Thomas Rotherham, Archbishop of York, the chantry school of William Chamber of Aldwincle, and the courses in business training given on university soil. The first two

---

[1] *Statutes-at-Large* of England and Great Britain (Cambridge: University Press, 1762 —), II, 472.

of these included in their set-up a writing school, the masters of which were to be " learned and skilled in the art of writing and accounts "; the third foundation, Aldwincle Chantry, was to be a spelling and reading school for six poor boys, while the fourth trained young men to manage large estates. These, to be sure, were but the beginnings of a new conception of education, but nevertheless they had their roots in the period in which we are interested.

New schools were springing up; not many, perhaps, considering the size of England, the small number of students provided for, and the span of time encompassed in this study, but enough to refute such a statement that " the grossest ignorance prevailed among the people [in London] in general." [2] Old schools, too, were not neglected; on the contrary, they were often re-endowed, rebuilt, or repaired.[3] A determined effort to replace schoolmasters killed off by the ravages of the Black Death was made by William Bingham through the foundation of a Cambridge college, " God's House," for the training of teachers for grammar schools.

Probably the most important trend in schools in the fifteenth century was the direction toward lay control, as opposed to the ecclesiastical administration exercised by the secular and monastic authorities. Such agencies as the chantries, stipendiaries, gilds, and foundations by wealthy individuals, such as Eton and others, were responsible for this tendency. More and more individuals were becoming interested in education, not only members of the clergy, but merchants, burgesses, and lords, many of whom were beginning to make over part of their possessions toward the endowment of schools. The school-masters were still in holy orders, although even that, too, in a few instances, was also opposed; but they were not necessarily attached to a cathedral or monastic establishment, and consequently were free from their jurisdiction. These cathedral chapters especially were

[2] Nicholas Carlisle, *A Concise Description of the Endowed Grammar Schools in England and Wales* (London: Baldwin, Cradock, and Joy, 1818), I, xxii.

[3] For example: Stratford-on-Avon, St. Peter's, York, Beverly, Ripon, Pontefract, Howedon, etc.

jealous of this threat to their hitherto undisputed sway over, and monopoly of, the schools. The break-down of this mon- opolistic control was aided by the favorable decisions with regard to the Gloucester School case of 1410 and the petition and sanction of the parsons of four London churches in 1447 to establish permanent schools in their parishes in addition to the cathedral grammar schools which had been established there for years. Thus was started the breach that was to widen until the whole system of ecclesiastical control was to collapse during the Reformation.

We find in the fifteenth century then, the seeds of a chang- ing educational system characterized by the expansion of schools, a tendency to break away from the rigidity of the ecclesiastical system, and a trend toward lay control.

From the very earliest times, education had been considered the sole responsibility of the Church, and for almost six hundred years the only advanced teaching institutions in Western Europe were the grammar schools, attached to the cathedrals, monasteries, and collegiate churches, out of which came practically all those who attained to leadership in the service of the Church.[4] It was urged by the Lateran Council in 1179 that in every cathedral church there should be a master provided with a benefice to teach the clerks of the church and the poor scholars, freely, and punishment was threatened if anyone sold a license to teach.[5] This was reiter- ated again in England by the Council of London in 1200,[6] and in 1215, when Pope Innocent III ordered that not only should there be a grammar school in every cathedral, but a theological school in every metropolitical (archiepiscopal) church.[7]

The studies taught in the more important grammar schools of the early middle ages were those known as the seven liberal arts. The knowledge embraced in these studies represented

[4] Ellwood P. Cubberley, *The History of Education* (N. Y.: Hough- ton Mifflin Co., 1920), p. 153.
[5] Arthur F. Leach, *Educational Charters and Documents* (Cam- bridge: University Press, 1911), p. 122. Hereafter referred to as *Educational Charters*.
[6] *Ibid.*, p. 138.
[7] *Ibid.*, pp. 142-145.

the body of knowledge that had been saved from oblivion by the Church throughout the centuries. These seven arts comprised grammar, rhetoric, and logic, commonly called the trivium, and arithmetic, geometry, music, and astronomy, known as the quadrivium. Not all these subjects were taught by all the cathedral and collegiate grammar schools, particularly after the universities came into existence. After the rise of the universities the grammar schools concentrated their energies in part on preparing their students for this higher type of education. The grammar schools were also freed from the burden of teaching their pupils the fundamentals of music and reading by the growth of song schools,[8] and with this alleviation from above and below, they soon froze into the mold that was not to melt until the end of the fifteenth century. During this time, then, we find three types of schools attached to the great churches: the theological school (until the universities took it over) under the chancellor, who was ordinarily required to be a master in theology, or a doctor of divinity; the grammar school, under the grammar schoolmaster, usually required to be a master of arts,[9] appointed by the chancellor; and the song or music school under the song schoolmaster, appointed by the precentor or taught by him, and for whom no special qualification was necessary.[10]

There is little information available to help us pierce the cloud of darkness that hangs over the curriculum in a grammar school of fifteenth-century England. We know that the textbooks which the masters used were composed by Donatus and Priscian;[11] in fact, Donatus' text on grammar was so popular and so all-inclusive that grammar school students were familiarly known as Donatists,[12] and the word Donatus

---

[8] Schools that attached themselves to the church to prepare boys to take part in the services of the Church, especially the musical part, and which came in time to serve the function of elementary schools.

[9] This was not always the case. At Oxford in the fifteenth century non-graduates were pressed into service because of a lack of properly qualified masters.

[10] Arthur F. Leach, *The Schools of Medieval England* (N. Y.: The Macmillan Company, 1915), p. 158.

[11] *Vide* Course of Study for Grammar, pp. 79-81.

[12] ". . . we decree and direct to be inviolably observed that the present master and his successors shall have the Donatists. . ." *Educational Charters*, p. 275.

or Donat came to be a well-understood synonym for a Latin grammar book.[13] That the content was slim and the methods of teaching poor, either from indifference or lack of preparation on the part of the schoolmasters, even in the fourteenth century, is seen in a letter written in 1357 by Bishop Grandisson to the Diocese of Exeter:

. . . they [masters or teachers] . . . observe a form and order of teaching which are preposterous and useless . . . in that as soon as their scholars have learnt to read or say even very imperfectly the Lord's Prayer, with the Hail Mary and the Creed, also Matins and the Hours of the Blessed Virgin, and the like, which are necessary for faith and the safety of their souls, though they do not know how to construe or understand any of the things before-mentioned, or to decline or parse any of the words in them, they make them pass on prematurely to learn other school books of poetry or in metre . . .[14]

The remedy is:

We commission and command each of you to enjoin on all masters or teachers of boys, presiding over Grammar Schools . . . that they shall not make the boys whom they receive to learn grammar only to read Latin, as hitherto, but leaving everything else make them construe and understand the Lord's Prayer . . . etc.; and decline the words there and parse them before they let them go on to other books. . .[15]

Unfortunately there is no clue here as to what these books are, except that they are in verse; perhaps either Priscian's *Twelve Verses of Virgil* or the *Doctrinale* of Alexander de Villa Dei, a rhyming version of Priscian, was meant. Ovid and Virgil were sometimes taught the students, but parts of both poets were avoided because of their " illicit allurements." *Disticha de moribus ad filium Dionysii Catonis*, a collection of moral sayings, also was sometimes presented to the grammar students.[16] The books were construed in French and English, as well as in Latin.[17]

Such paucity of materials makes it difficult to draw any but

---

[13] W. Carew Hazlitt, *Schools, School-Books, and Schoolmasters* (London: J. W. Jarvis and Son, 1888), p. 47.
[14] *Educational Charters*, pp. 314-317.
[15] *Ibid.*
[16] Hastings Rashdall, *Universities of Europe in the Middle Ages* (new edition, edited by F. M. Powicke and A. B. Emden; Oxford: Clarendon Press, 1936), III, 351-352.
[17] *Munimenta Academica* (edited by Henry Anstey; London: Longmans, Green, Reader, and Dyer, 1868), II, 437-438.

the simplest conclusions concerning the materials and methods
of the grammar schools of the fifteenth century. The study of
Latin grammar—since it was considered the gateway to all
knowledge—was the backbone of the course, and Donatus
and Priscian the authorities used; a few classical authors
were sampled from time to time. By the first quarter of the
sixteenth century, when the humanistic trends were beginning to be fixed, such classical writers as Terence, Cicero,
Horace, and Lucan were added to the course, but the pro-
cedure of parsing and construing, memorizing rules and giving them back to the teacher must have been almost identical
with the methods used two or three centuries earlier.[18] For

[18] In the early part of the sixteenth century there appeared a small
volume of letters entitled *Epistolae Obscurorum Virorum*, thought
by many to have been composed by Erasmus, attacking with vitupera-
tive scorn the decadent Scholastics who still clung tenaciously to their
old methods and materials of teaching and study. As is the case with
any satirical writing, the faults were grossly exaggerated; yet from
these biting letters we can see that the new classical students were in
the main justified in their criticisms that many teachers would not
avail themselves of the new wealth of literature and the more advanced
ideas that were being presented to the army of students. Those who
refused to leave their precious Donatus and Alexander, and their
syllogistic reasoning, logical to the point of ridiculousness, were the
objects of such a letter as this: " One of those who sat at meat is a
poet, after the new fashion, and he is ever talking at the board about
Poetry, and he findeth much fault with the ancient fathers—*Alexander*,
and the *Graecist*, and *Verba Deponentalia* . . . Then quoth I, ' It
supriseth me that you pay such heed to these new-fangled grammarians, when you may find all things concerning feet, and the quanti-
ties of syllables, set forth metrically in the third part of *Alexander*,
not to speak of the Art of Scansion and the rest. . . .' . . . Then the
Curealist laughed loudly, jeering me, and asked me what I made of
the first syllable of ' Abacuc?' I replied, ' We must distinguish. For,
in so far as it is a proper name, the first syllable is indifferent, according to *Alexander*. . . . but in so far as it is asked what quantity the
first hath conformably to the quiddity of common nouns, then it hath
the first short; according to *Alexander*, who saith that *a* before *b* is
short—exceptions excepted.' Then he laughed me to scorn yet aagin
and said, ' Get thee gone, thou Cologne abecedarian, with thine *Alexander*, who was but a Parisian ass—and there are plenty more.' And
thus, shamefully reviling the good Alexander, he went his way."
Here is a sample of the letters that laugh at the philological mistakes
that many grammarians fell into: ". . . But forthwith he wrote a
lampoon against me, with many scurrilities therein, and vowed that I
was no sound grammarian, in that I had not rightly expounded certain
words when I treated of *Alexander*, his First Part, and of the book
De Modis significandi. Now therefore I will set down in due form
those words, that you may see that I have rightly expounded them

this reason, a time-table of " the ordre and use of teachyng gramer in the schole of Wynchester," although current in 1530, nevertheless is so similar to the manner of teaching grammar at an early day that it is quoted in some length. For, if we substitute Donatus and Priscian for " stanbridg accidens," [19] and remove Terence, Horace, and perhaps Cicero, keep Virgil, Aesop's Fables, Cato, Lucan, and Ovid, this time-table could easily be one typical of the fifteenth century.

Winchester Time-Table (VIIth and VIth Forms missing) [20]

Ovide metamorphoseos the thursday, Salust the fryday, with the vij forme. And at after none renderyng of ther rulys. The saterdaye lyke as the vij forme. The Sonday lykewyse.

The Vth forme.

They have the versyfycall rulys of Sulpice gevyn in ye mornying of one of the vi[th] forme & this Vth forme gevyth rulys to the fowrth; the which be preterita et supina of sulpice. Also iiij verses of ovide Metamorphoseos, the thursday salust iij fyrst dayes of the weke to be rendered on saterday in the mornyng. The latyne they have with ye fowrthe forme. There constructyons is throwgh owte ye weke unto

according to all the vocabularies, and I can moreover cite canonical writers, even in Theology. First, I maintain the ' seria ' sometimes meaneth a pot, and in that case is derived from *Syria* as being first made in that country; or from ' serius ' because useful and necessary; or from ' series ' because pots stand in a row. . . . ' Mechanicus' means adulterous, and hence the ' mechanical arts ' are named, as being adulterine, when compared with the liberal arts, which are true-born. . . ."
And here is one last quotation to expose what qualifications a would-be-teacher considered were acceptable in the eyes of a rector looking for an assistant teacher: " You are well aware that, by God's Grace, I am competent; . . . I qualified for the Bachelor's degree, and I should have graduated at Michaelmas if I had had the money. [An indirect accusation, perhaps, that if a student were wealthy enough, he could get his degree regardless of his qualifications.] I know how to expound the Boys' Exercise-book to learners, and the *Opus Minus* (Part II.), and I know the art of Scansion as you taught it me, and *Peter of Spain* in all his works, and the *Parvulus* of Natural Philosophy. I am a singer, too, and am skilled in plain-song, and prick-song, and I have a bass voice withal, and can sing one note below contra-C." Not a very inspiring picture of a competent school-teacher! Excerpts from *Epistolae Obscurorum Virorum* (The Latin Text with an English Rendering, Notes, and an Historical Introduction by Francis Griffin Stokes; London: Chatto and Windus), 1925, pp. 465, 337-338, and 328.
[19] A Latin textbook composed by John Stanbridge, a graduate of New College in the 1480's. Hazlitt, *op. cit.*, p. 53.
[20] *Educational Charters*, pp. 448-450.

fryday Vergills Eglogs & an other, tullies epistles they make maters ageynst tewisdays. The Wedenysday make verses, the thursday epistles. The friday in the mornyng a part of there rulys to be examyned. Att the afternone renderyng of there rulys lernyd that weke. The saterday xij verses to be said withowte boke on the mornyng with the examynatyon of the same with renderyng of there latyns. After none construyth epistles. The Sonday as the other hie formys dothe.

The Fowrthe Forme.

After rules & verses geven of the vth forme they hath a verbe providyd ageyne vij of ye Clok when the Scholem[r] comyth in. And hase the verbe examyned among them with vulgares upon the same. And after they write the laten that one of them shall make by ye assygnyng of the master. And the master construyth to them a portyon of Terence. And at after none thei construe it & parce it by the Ussher. And after renderith rules & then there latyn. this contynewith tyll friday then they have a part of there rulys to be examyned. And at after none renderith of ye rulys lernyd that weke. The saterday in the Mornyng xij verses of ovide Metamorphoseos. At after none repetyng & examynyng there terence lernyd before. The sonday with other low holydayes, an englysh of an epistle to be made in latyn dyverse wayes & sometyme Tullies paradoxes to be construyd.

The Thred forme

hath for ther ruls Sulpice genders and his heteroclits declarid every day a portyon of the ussher, and hath throwgh the weke over nyght a verbe set up to be examyned in the mornyng, and makith vulgars upon yt. And after none they have a theme to be made in laten, the which Latyne one of the said forme at the pleasure of the master makith openlie dyverse ways. And after that they write the Masteris owne latyne. For their constructyons, uponne mondayes and Wedenysdayes, Aesopes fabells, Tuesdayes and Thursdays, Lucyans dialogs. The friday in the mornyng examynation of ther rules. At the after none renderyng, Saterday in the mornyng proper verses of meter of lilies makyng, And after that repetytyon of there latens with the examynatyon of the same. That Sonday a dialoge of lucyane or a fable of Esope to be seid withowt booke and construed.

The seconde Forme

lykewise throwh the weke hath a verbe sett up over nyght, and makith vulgaris on it, and dothe like at laten as the thrid forme. Ther rulys, Parvula of Stanbridge, and ij verses of his vocables. There constructyons Esopes fabuls throwh all the weke, save that on the saterday in the Mornyng they have iiij verses of Cato to be renderid withowte boke with the examynatyon of the same.

The Fyrst forme.

In the mornyng a part of standbridge accidens, and a verbe of the same accidens to be said withowte booke, and then a laten to be said at the after none; After that repetycyon of rules. The friday there Comparisons, with the verbe sum. es. fui. to be said; At the after none repetytyon of these rules. At Saterday repetytyon of there Cato. The Sonday a fabull of Aesope.

Also every Forme renderith a fortenyght every quarter for thyngs lernyd the quarter before.

Disputations in the grammar school were also favorite techniques of activities, and we find a sixteenth-century volume describing that custom:

> As for the meeting of the school-masters on festival days, at festival churches, and the disputing of their scholars logically, &tc., . . . the same was long since discontinued; but the arguing of the schoolboys about the principles of grammar hath been continued even till our time; for I myself, in my youth, have yearly seen, on the eve of St. Bartholomew the Apostle, the scholars of divers grammar schools repair unto the churchyard of St. Bartholomew, the priory in Smithfield, where upon a bank boarded about under a tree, some one scholar hath stepped up, and there hath opposed and answered, till he were by some better scholar overcome and put down; and then the overcomer taking the place, did like as the first; and in the end the best opposers and answerers had rewards, which I observed not but it made both good schoolmasters, and also good scholars, diligently against such times to prepare themselves for the obtaining of this garland. I remembered there repaired to these exercises, amongst others, the masters and scholars of the free schools of St. Paul's in London, of St. Peter's at Westminster, of St. Thomas Acon's Hospital and of St. Anthony's Hospital; whereof the last named commonly presented the best scholars, and had the prize in those days.[21]

One must remember, however, that not all the schools in England in the fifteenth century that are described as grammar schools were of the same quality in either size or curriculum. Many of the educational establishments did not possess more than a handful of students, and many of the priests who were called " scolemasters " should hardly be dignified with that title. The chantry priests who were compelled to teach school in addition to their churchly duties were not always properly qualified to do so, and their scholars learned no more than those who were taught in the song or almonry schools—the Psalter, the Lord's Prayer, the Hail Mary, etc. Sometimes the vernacular was the language used, instead of the Latin, particularly if the priest were especially illiterate.

When we consider that Latin was the language not only for all Church services and communications, but for political and administrative documents, it is easy to see why so much stress was laid on its acquisition. Professional men such as theologians, lawyers, and physicians, used it as a medium of

[21] John Stow, *A Survay of London* (edited by Henry Morley; London: George Rutledge and Sons, Ltd., 1890), p. 101.

expression, and ambassadors, secretaries, and travelers, as well as merchants and clerks, needed it, for there was no other language that could be used as such. It was no surprise, then, that the statutes of Trinity College, Cambridge, as well as others, laid down that Latin grammar should not be taught in the colleges, except to choristers, since it was assumed that Latin as a spoken language had been fairly well acquired by the student before matriculation.[22] To be educated, in the medieval sense of the term, meant, then, to be able to read and write Latin, and it is interesting to note that it has only been within the past twenty years that the same idea has been partially filtered from our modern conception of liberal education. There are still some, even a great number, if the truth be told, of the old classical school of thought, who think that a man or woman is still not quite " educated " unless he has a background, if not of Latin and Greek, at least of Latin. It is amazing that the Latin grammar school idea of education could cling so tenaciously that it has accompanied its adherents in crossing the ocean and is still existing, although with diminished fervor, after eight centuries. Its hold has been so great that perhaps we shall never see its end.

Freedom of the schools from the monopolistic control of cathedral chapters and monastic foundations was gradually creeping in during the later Middle Ages, and was to come to a climax in the first half of the sixteenth century. Evidence of this tendency cropped up at various intervals and in unexpected places. In 1410, in response to a demand for new schools, one Thomas More had set up a grammar school in Gloucester, close by the priory of Llanthony Abbey, an occurrence which immediately caused the prior and master of the authorized school to protest this " infringement " of their privilege. Their complaint was that since the new school had appeared, the Gloucester School could not charge its regular fee of three shillings a quarter, but were forced to accept only

[22] Foster Watson, *The Old Grammar Schools* (Cambridge: University Press, 1916), p. 10. This, of course was not always true, and the various colleges were usually equipped with a grammar master.

twelve pence, a great loss to them. Public opinion was in favor of an additional school, however, and the prior was reprimanded with these words: " The teaching of children is a virtuous and charitable thing, and beneficial to the people, and is not punishable." Further action was not taken, because it was decided that the teaching of children was a spiritual matter and consequently should have been tried in an ecclesiastical court rather than the King's Court.[23]

Any threat to their privileges was fought against bitterly by the three London schools, St. Paul, St. Martin-le-Grand, and St. Mary-le-Bow. These schools were successful in 1393 when the Archbishop of Canterbury, the Bishop of London, the Dean of St. Martin's-le-Grand, and the Chancellor of St. Paul's presented a petition to Richard II in Parliament to put down

> . . . certain strangers, feigning themselves Masters of Grammar, not sufficiently learned in that faculty, who, against law and custom, hold general Schools of Grammar, in deceit and fraud of children, to the great prejudice of your lieges and of the jurisdiction of Holy Church.[24]

The privileged schools were successful this time in preventing the flourishing of much-needed, additional schools, but with the advent of Henry VI to the throne they were not so fortunate. Henry VI, as has been noted, was extremely interested in schools, and his interest was not confined merely to the universities. It was to him that one of the most famous grammar schools of all times, Eton, was due, and it was he who was responsible finally for the break-down of this London monopoly when he assented to the founding of new grammar schools in London. The first step in this process was the founding of the school attached to St. Anthony's Hospital by John Carpenter in 1441, when he obtained from the Bishop of London the appropriation to the Hospital of the Church of St. Bennet Fink, the revenues to be applied to the upkeep of

> . . . a master or fit Informer in the faculty of grammar, . . . to keep a grammar school (regere scolas grammaticales) in the precinct of

---

[23] J. E. G. de Montmorency. *State Intervention in English Education* (Cambridge: University Press, 1902), pp. 241-242; and Leach, *The Schools of Medieval England*, pp. 237-238.

[24] Leach, *The Schools of Medieval England*, p. 264.

the hospital or some fit house close by, to teach, instruct, and inform gratis all boys and others whatsoever wishing to learn and become scholars (scolatizare).[25]

Between 1441 and 1446 still another foundation, that of St. Dunstan's must have taken place, for by that time (1446) we find a writ of privy seal mentioning five schools in London, St. Anthony's and " Saint Dunstan in the Est," in addition to the usual three. Other schools were being conducted more or less surreptiously in London, however, as the writ indicates:

> For asmoche as the right reverend fader in God Therchebisshopp of Canterbury and the reverend fader in God the bisshopp of London considering the great abusions that have been of long tyme withinne oure Citee of London that many and divers persones not sufficiently instruct in gramer presumynge to holde commune gramer scholes in greet deceipte aswel unto theire scolers as unto the frendes that fynde theim to scole have of theire greet wysdome sette and ordeigned. v. scholes of gramer and no moo withinne oure saide Citee; Oon withinne the chirche yerde of Saint Poule; an other withinne the collegiate Churches of Saint Martin; the thridde in the Bowe chirche; the iiij in the chirche of Saint Dunstan in the Est; the .v. in oure hospital of Saint Anthony withinne oure said Citee . . . Wherfore we wol and charge you . . . unto alle oure subgittes of oure said Citee that thei nor noon of thaim trouble nor empeche the maistres of the said Scoles in any wyse.[26]

Emboldened, perhaps, by this evident weakening in the London ecclesiastical coat of armor, or goaded by the still great need of more schools to take care of the ever-growing demand for education that had not been sufficiently met, the year after this writ appeared, four parsons of as many churches in London [27] presented a petition to Parliament asking for permission to set up and establish permanent grammar schools in their parishes. (Evidently these were the schools referred to in the writ.) Their petition is most interesting, since it gives a rather vivid picture of the somewhat lamentable state

---

[25] *Ibid.*, p. 261. In addition to the schoolmaster, there were an usher and twelve children, six of whom were choristers, and six grammar boys. A song school was also established in connection with the grammar school.

[26] *Educational Charters*, pp. 416-418.

[27] Master William Lichfield of Allhallows the Great; Master Gilbert of St. Andrew's, Holburn; Master John Cote of St. Peter's, Cornhill; and John Neel of the Hospital of St. Thomas of Acres.

of affairs in London in 1447 and recognizes the need for more schools:

... And for asmuche as to the Citee of London is the commune concours of this land, wherein is grete multitude of yonge peple, not oonly borne and brought forthe in the same Citee, but also of many other parties of this lond, som for lak of Scole maistres in thier oune Contree, for to be enformed of gramer there, and som for the grete almesse of Lordes, Merchauntz and the other . . .; Wherefore it were expedient, that in London were a sufficieant nombre of Scoles and good enfourmers in gramer, and not for the singuler availl of ii or iii persones, grevously to hurte the multitude of yonge peple of all this Lond; For where there is grete nombre of Lerners and fewe Techers, and all the Lerners be compelled to goo to the same fewe Techers, and to noon other, the Maisters wexen riche in money, and the Lerners pouere in connynge, as experience openly shewith, aynst all vertue and ordre of well puplik.[28]

This petition was granted with the proviso that " it be doone by thadvyse of the Ordinarie, otherelles of the Archebishope of Canterbury for the tyme beyng." Whether or not these schools were actually founded is a question; Leach [29] thinks not, as he has found no evidence of them. Stow,[30] however, mentions that these four grammar schools were ordered to be erected, and then comments that

... since the which time as divers schools by suppressing of religious houses, whereof they were members, in the reign of Henry VIII, have been decayed, so again have some others been newly erected, and founded for them; as namely Paul's School. . . .

implying that they were in existence at least a few years. It is more than likely that Leach is correct in his assumption that these schools were never realized; there is no record of them in the Chantry Certificates. Besides this, the archbishop and his ordinary would by no means be in favor of their erection, and were probably as lax as they might dare to be in carrying out the proposals. In addition to all this, two of the petitioners died within a year after presenting their appeal.[31] All these circumstances point to their non-erection, so that the victory over ecclesiastical jurisdiction was probably but a moral one.

[28] *Educational Charters*, pp. 418-420. Montmorency, *op. cit.*, pp. 46, 48-49.
[29] *Schools of Medieval England*, p. 267.
[30] *Op. cit.*, p. 100.
[31] Leach, *Schools of Medieval England*, p. 267.

Coincident with this attack on the traditional belief that education should be solely in the hands of, and under control of the Church, was the great impetus toward lay control, which had its origin in the latter part of the fourteenth century and which spread so rapidly in the fifteenth century that it clearly indicated the great interest in education that was being stimulated: the foundation and endowment of schools by chantries,[32] stipendiaries, and other independent sources. Just as a drop of water continually falling on a rock eventually washes it away, so the custom of individuals endowing chantries whose main purpose was the maintenance of a free school gradually wore down the idea that education belonged entirely in the realm of the Church, to be instigated, maintained, and controlled only by the earthly representatives of Christ. Endowments, however, were not only in the form of chantries, but even greater deviation from custom was seen in the creation of schools by wealthy and influential citizens who placed their management in the hands of agencies other than chantry or stipendary priests. Sporadic and few as these attempts were, in proportion to the usual type of educational endowments, to break away from the pattern of adherence to the old custom of entrusting schools to the Church, it was but a short step, once the process had been started, for municipal, commercial, and national participation in educational activities.

An early instance of lay interest in and lay control of schools is the Oswestry Grammar School, made possible by the feoffment of certain lands in 1405-06 by one David Holbeach, a Welsh lawyer. This school was entrusted to a " mixed body of laymen and clerics, and not part of, or dependent on, an ecclesiastical foundation, college, hospital, or chantry." [33] A quarter of a century later, a London grocer

---

[32] A chantry was a foundation established by wealthy individuals or groups of individuals such as gilds to provide money for the support of religious and charitable purposes. One or more priests were employed to say mass for the souls of the founders, and, in specific cases, to spend the remainder of the time in teaching. A stipendiary was very similar to a chantry, except that the devotions were in honor of the Blessed Virgin Mary.

[33] Leach, *op. cit.*, p. 235; Leach, *English Schools at the Reformation*

by the name of William Sevenoaks left at his death certain
revenues to the rector, vicar, and churchwardens of the
Sevenoaks Church in Kent County

> . . . to find and maintain forever one Master, an honest man, suffi-
> ciently advanced and expert in the science of grammar, B. A., *by no
> means in holy orders*, to keep a Grammar School in some convenient
> house within the said town of Sevenoaks . . . and to teach and instruct
> all poor boys whatsoever coming there for the sake of learning, taking
> nothing of them or their parents or friends for the teaching and
> instructing them. . .[34]

The phrase, " by no means in holy orders," seems to be a
point of departure from the almost universal practice of em-
ploying only teachers who were priests, clerks, or in some
kind of holy orders. That this was not an unheard of occurrence, although perhaps a rare one, is shown in the records
of St. Peter's, York, where during the fifteenth century, at
least three of the masters were not in holy orders and in Beverley, where *probably* the same was true.[35] A few years later,
in 1443, John Abbot, citizen and mercer of the city of London,
founded a school to teach " the little ones of the parish of the
Church of Farthinghoe . . . freely and gratis without taking
any pay or profit therefor," but he made the unprecedented
move of entrusting the whole foundation to the " masters or
wardens of the Mystery of Mercers of London." [36] This was
an innovation which, although not to become a common occurrence in the fifteenth century, nevertheless was followed by

(Westminster: Archibald Constable and Co., 1896), i, 56; ii, 187;
Carlisle, *op. cit.*, II, 365. Howard Staunton, *The Great Schools of
England* (new edition; London; Daldy, Isbister and Co., 1877), p. 508.
   [34] *Educational Charters*, p. 401; Leach, *Medieval Schools*, p. 244;
Carlisle, *op. cit.* I, 616, and Staunton, *op. cit.*, p. 523.
   [35] Gilbert Pinchbect, master of St. Peter's School, had a wife who
died in 1431; the second master, Roger Lewsay, too, was married, for
in 1465 his will was proved by his wife; the third master, John Ham-
mundson, constituted his wife Alice as executrix of his will. William
Harding, master of the Beverley Grammar School from 1436-56,
constantly served as one of the governors of the town, making it
probable that he, too, was a layman. Arthur F. Leach, *Early Yorkshire Schools* (London: J. B. Nichols and Sons, 1899), XXVII,
xxviii. Mr. Leach's statement that it is highly probable that in the
largest grammar schools it was the rule for the masters not to be in
holy orders seems to be unwarranted. On the contrary, his examples
seem to be examples of the exception to the rule that all teachers of
schools were frocked.
   [36] *Educational Charters*, pp. 414-417.

several other far-seeing patrons. One of these was Sir Edmund Shaa, goldsmith and alderman of London, who, in 1487, left a will providing for the maintenance of two priests, one of whom was to be a " discrete man, and conning in Gramer, and able of connyng to teche Gramer." He was to teach freely

. . . al maner person's children, and other that woll come to him to lerne, as well of the said towne of Stopforde, as of other townes therabout, the science of Gramer as ferre as lieth in him for to do, unto the time that they be convenably in strut in Gramer by him, after their capaciteys that God woll geve them.[37]

Even the good alderman and mayor of London was quick to recognize the law of individual differences and to allow for it in his foundation! The " presentement, nominacion, and admission " of the two priests was to be in the hands of Sir Edmund's gild, the Goldsmiths' Company of London. Two other gilds are reported as taking an active interest in the furtherance of education, one the Trinity Gild of Deddington, licenced in 1446, and the other, the Trinity Gild of Chipping Norton, licenced in 1451,[38] both of which demanded of their priests the duty of teaching any of the children of their members who so desired it. Another school whose supposed foundation in this century showed remarkable public interest was that of Lancaster, a grammar school founded by the mayor and burgesses of the town, and supported from the profits of the town's mill.[39]

The grammar school founded previous to the fifteenth century and supported by the Stratford-on-Avon Gild, was endowed in 1482 by Master Thomas Jolyffe, gild priest, when he gave lands to support a schoolmaster there. He stipulated that the Master Warden and Thomas Clopton, master of the gild, and their successors, were to have the power to name

---

[37] Carlisle, op. cit., I, 125. See also Leach, Schools of Medieval England, p. 245; and Howard Staunton, op. cit., p. 529.

[38] Leach, Schools of Medieval England, pp. 269-270.

[39] Leach, English Schools at the Reformation, ii, 123. Carlisle, op. cit., I, 665, says that the free school in mentioned in some books belonging to the corporation as early as the year 1495. If this was a fifteenth century foundation, it is a rather remarkable one in view of the fact that it was a recognition of community responsibility toward education.

the priest who was to teach grammar whenever a vacancy occurred.[40]

The earliest chantry-grammar school of which we have any statutes was that founded in 1384 by a woman, Lady Katherine of Berkley, widow of Sir Thomas Berkley.[41] Since, as she averred in her foundation deed and statutes, " grammar, which is the foundation of all liberal arts, is daily diminished and brought to naught by poverty and want of means," she bestowed certain lands and tenements on two chaplains, who were, in turn, to appoint a master to teach and govern all scholars coming to the school-house to be built by them, and two poor scholars, all of whose necessities, except clothing and shoes, were to be supplied by the revenues. These two poor scholars to be admitted were not to be any younger than ten years of age, and it is curious to note that they were allowed a period of *six years'* probation! If, within that time,

. . . any of them . . . shall be undisciplined and shall be unwilling to devote his time to learning, and shall after due warning and chastisement refuse to amend, they shall be expelled by the master under the supervision of the lord [of Wotton] or his steward, and others put in their places.[42]

We see here in this foundation all the requisities for a chantry school foundation: (1) The master, who is to be a priest and to celebrate Mass for the souls of the founder and the founder's kin, and who is also to teach, beyond the scholars provided for, anyone else coming to him for instruction in grammar, without exacting any fee from them for such instruction; (2) a certain number of scholars whose expenses are taken care of from the revenues; and (3) the person or persons in whose hands the management of affairs shall be. This formula was the basis for all chantry school foundations; with one or two exceptions, the only variations were the number of non-scholars to be provided for, and the persons to be in charge of the school's affairs. It is interesting to compare a chantry foundation of a little over a hundred years later, to see how closely this formula was followed. In

[40] *Educational Charters*, pp. 381-387.
[41] *Ibid.*, pp. xxxv-xxxvi, and 330-341.
[42] *Ibid.*, p. 341.

1489 one William Chamber of Aldwincle, Northampton founded a spelling and reading school, which foundation was to be known as Aldwincle Chantry.[43] The master was to be Sir John Seliman, chaplain, and he was to instruct in spelling and reading, as well as celebrate divine service every day; the scholars were to be six of the poorest boys of the town, to be taught " freely, without [the master] demanding or taking any remuneration from their parents or friends "; and the person or persons in control were to be the founder and his wife Elizabeth, and after their death, the rector of St. Peter's Church and the chaplain.

Other chantry or stipendiary schools founded or mentioned in records for the first time in the fifteenth century are as follows: the grammar schools at Bolton-upon-Derne (1400), Middleton (1412), Gosfelde, put in feoffment by Thomas Rolff, Esquire (1440), Thornton, re-endowed by John Barton, jr. in 1443, St. Mary, Wokingham (1445), Towcester (1447), Alnwick (1448), the chantries of the Blessed Virgin, St. Nicholas, and St. Michael, at Appleby [44] (1478), Newland (1445), Cawthorne (1455), Newbury (1466), Long Preston (1468), Naylor's Chantry at Bodmin (1474), Kingston up Hull (1482 or 1499), Long Melford (1484), Skipton-in-Craven (1492), and Crewherne, re-endowed by John Combe in 1499.[45] Chantry schools which are either song or reading schools, rather than grammar schools, or which are listed only as chantries without any description of their schools are: St. Mary's Chapel, Wosborough, Yorkshire (1418), Stourbridge (1430), Newland (1445), Long Preston (1468), Pritwell (1477), Wakefield (1478), and Thaxted (1480).[46]

[43] *Ibid.*, p. 435.
[44] In the Chantry Certificates, collected in Leach, *English Schools at the Reformation*, ii, 253, an indenture between the Mayor, bailiffs, and commonalty of Appleby and Sir Thomas Whynfell, chaplain, is this statement: " The said Thomas covenanted that he would keep . . . a sufficient grammar school . . . according to the ancient custom of the school aforesaid.", indicating that the school had existed prior to the date of 1478. Leach, *Schools of Medieval England*, pp. 268-269, and Staunton, *op. cit.*, p. 421, state it existed in 1453.
[45] See Chantry Certificates in Leach, *English Schools at the Reformation*.
[46] *Ibid.*

The foundation of colleges attached to churches and universities was one of the most common methods of making provisions for education in the Middle Ages, and the fifteenth century proved no exception. In nearly all of them, however, was the stipulation that at least one of the clerks or masters be a grammar master, and that in addition to teaching the clerks, choristers, poor boys, etc., included in the foundation, he must also instruct anyone who might come to him for that purpose. The statutes of such collegiate foundations as Tong (1410), Fotheringay (1412-1415), Stoke-by-Clare (1419), Higham Ferrers (1422), Wye (1432), Tattershall (1439), Eton (1440), Newport (1442), Magdalen (1448), Acaster (1480), and Rotheram (1483), all emphasize the belief in grammar as the gate to higher learning, " the first foundation for the understanding of other liberal arts and sciences."

When Acaster and Rotheram colleges were founded, still another addition to the usual curriculum was made, indicative of the demand, as yet in its infancy, for practical schooling. The College of Nether Acaster was the foundation of Robert Stillington, Bishop of Bath and Wells, who attached to it three schools,

> . . . three divers Masters and Informators in the faculties underwritten; that is to wit, one of them to teach grammar, another to teach Music and Song, and the third to teach to Write and all such thing as belonged to Scrivener Craft, to all manner of persons of whatsoever country they be within the Realm of England . . . severally, openly, and freely without exaction of money or other things of any of their such scholars and disciplines.[47]

Rotheram College had a similar set of schools:

> . . . we have determined to make such a spring flow there forever, in other words to establish a teacher of grammar there;
> And in the second place . . . we have thought fit to establish forever another fellow learned in song and six choristers or children of the chapel, that divine service may be more honorably celebrated;
> In the third place, because that county [Yorkshire] produced many youths endowed with the light and sharpness of ability, who do not all wish to attain the dignity and elevation of the priesthood, that these may be better fitted for the mechanical arts and other concerns of this world, we have ordained a third fellow, learned and skilled in the art of writing and accounts . . .[48]

---

[47] Quoted in Leach's *Schools of Medieval England*, p. 274.
[48] *Educational Charters*, p. 425.

This emphasis on writing and accounts, really a simple form of bookkeeping, was quite in keeping with the economic trends of the century. There must have been some sort of rudimentary teaching going on wherever there was a priest capable of doing so, who had nothing else to occupy his time but saying the Mass and the few prayers required daily by his chantry endowments. Certainly the business transactions of the commercial and municipal corporations required a rather specialized type of training. Probably the bit of arithmetic taught in the schools (there must have been some arithmetic, since it was one of the subjects of the quadrivium) degenerated, scholastically speaking, more or less into the somewhat simple reckoning necessary for the keeping of such accounts. But it was not until the founding of these "scrivener" schools that there was any definite recognition given to their need. One other school founded around this time—the Aldwincle Chantry mentioned on page   —paid especial attention to spelling, which certainly did not seem to have much effect on students, if the treatises of the time are any indication!

Attached to the cathedral churches and large non-cathedral churches were groups of boys whose major purpose was designated as participation in the musical services of the Mass; in other words, to become choir boys. As early as the seventh century such schools were to be found at Canterbury, York, and Rochester. Bede speaks of James, the deacon who "acted as master to many in church chanting after the Rome or Canterbury fashion," and of Theodoric ordaining a man named Putta who was "especially skilled in the art of church chanting, which he had learnt from the pupils of the blessed Pope Gregory." [49] The head of the musical department was usually called a *precentor*, and upon him devolved the task of teaching the boys the chants. It was but to be expected that the schools, in order to create some sort of understanding of the service, would take over the task of teaching the elements of religion and reading, the basis of which was the Creed, Psalter, Ave Maria, etc. These boys,

[49] *Ibid.*, p. 7.

in return for their services as choristers, were usually given
board, lodging, and instruction,[50] and it was only natural that
the more promising boys would be singled out for at least
some elementary education in reading and writing. That these
song schools should in no way be confused with the grammar
schools beside which they flourished is understood when one
glances at the school statutes, many of which deliberately set
the two apart as distinct foundations with separate qualifications. As early as 796 Alcuin recommended that the Archbishop of York keep the grammar, song, and writing schools
separate: " Let there be separate spheres for those who read
books, who serve singing, who are assigned to the writing
school." [51] The statutes of Rotheram and Acaster colleges,
discussed a few paragraphs back, reveal the separate functions
of grammar and song schools. Occasionally the two schools
were combined, probably in small communities where the
master could easily conduct both.[52]

The description *par excellence* of the song school is given
by Chaucer in his *Prioresses Tale*, where occurs the famous
line that has been used time and time again against the value
of the school: " ' I lerne song, I can but smal grammere.' "

> A litel schole of Cristen folk ther stood
> Doun at the ferther ende, in which ther were
> Children an heep, yemen of Cristen blood,
> That lerned in that schole yeer by yeer
> Swich maner doctrine as men used there,
> That is to seyn, to singen and to rede,
> As smale children doon in his childhede.

> Among these children was a widwes son,
> A litel clergeon, seven yeer of age,
> That day by day to scole was his wone,
> And eek also, wher-as he saugh th' image
> Of Cristes moder, hadde he in usage,
> As him was taught, to knele adoun and seye
> His *Ave Maria*, as he goeth by the weys.

> .   .   .   .

> This litel child, his litel book lerninge,
> As he sat in the school at his prymer,
> He *Alma redemptoris* herde singe,

---

[50] Cubberley, *op. cit.*, p. 151.
[51] *Educational Chapters*, p. 19.
[52] *Ibid.*, pp. 342-343; Leach, *Schools of Medieval England*, p. 239;
Leach, *English Schools at the Reformation*, ii, 217-220.

9

As children lerned hir antiphoner;
And, as he dorste, he drough him ner and ner,
And herkned ay the words and the note,
Til he the firste vers coude al by rote.

Noght wiste he what this Latin was to seye,
For he so yong and tendre was of age;
But on a day his felaw gan he preye
T'expounden him this song in his langage,
Or telle him why this song was in usage,
This preyde he him to construe and declare
Ful ofte tyme upon his knowes bare.

His felawe, which that elder was than he,
Answerde him thus: 'This song I have herd seye,
Was maked of our blisful lady free,
Hir to salue, and eek hir for to preye
To been our help and socour whan we deye.
I can no more expounde in this matere;
I lerne song, I can but smal grammere.'

'And is this song maked in reverence
Of Cristes moder?' seyde this innocent;
Now certes, I wol do my diligence
To conne it al, er Cristemasse is went,
Though that I for my prymer shal be shent,
And shal be beten thryes in an houre,
I wol it conne, our lady for to honoure.'

His felawe taughte him homward prively,
From day to day, til he coude it by rote,
And than he song it wel and boldely
Fro word to word, according with the note,
To scoleward and homward than he wente;
On Cristes moder set was his entente.

As I have seyd, thurgh-out the Jewerye
This litel child, as he cam to and fro
Ful merily than wold he singe, and crye
O Alma redemptoris ever-mo.
The swetnes hath his herte perced so
Of Cristes moder, that, to hir to preye,
He can not stinte of singing by the weye.

We find in this tale several salient characteristics that were typical of the song school: first, instruction in singing and in reading, in that order of importance; second, children as young as seven years old attended school; third, the school held primarily for choristers in some room or building probably near the church was open to boys of the town; fourth, the subjects studied were religious, and musical; fifth, the student seldom knew or understood little of what he learned; sixth, learning was rote work; seventh, discipline was severe; eighth, the student had some sort of book by which to memorize his prayers; and ninth, evidently no attempt was made by the song master to expound or explain what was taught. This accusation was general of all masters, song or grammar.[53]

The mention of a primer, the student's " litel book," is interesting. Ordinarily the students had no textbooks because they were much too scarce and too valuable for even an ordinary clerk to possess more than one or two. Instead, the teacher gave slowly and carefully to his students the material contained in the book on which he was lecturing; in fact, the student copied it practically verbatim. If the seven-year old boy who attended the song school had a " litel book," he certainly would not have been proficient enough in writing as yet to have copied it himself; *ergo*, he must have been provided with some kind of prepared text. This may have been his Latin prayers, the Creed, etc., written out for him by the master. The number of students was not large enough to preclude such a possibility, and these " litel books " could have been returned to the master after the student had passed beyond his care for the future use of other students. We know that many persons besides ecclesiasts in the fifteenth century possessed the ability to write. The letters of the Paston, Cely and Plumpton families include letters written not only by them but by all sorts and conditions of people. However, this skill was in all probability developed not so much in the song schools as in the grammar schools and in the writing schools, and in the little groups of children taught by the parish or chantry priest. It is difficult to classify and attribute education outside the grammar schools to any particular kind of school. The process was one of infiltration rather than, a definitely applied one. Even some of the chantry and stipendary foundations of so-called " free gramer scoles " must have degenerated very quickly into a smattering of reading and writing, especially in isolated parishes where the priest may not have been any too well-prepared himself, and where only two or three children gathered together to take advantage of such opportunities.[54] It was these imperfections that the collegiate

[53] See Bishop Grandisson's letter to the Diocese of Exeter, p. 103.
[54] Many of the schools were in the vernacular, because the priests were illiterate in Latin.

and monastic foundations of the fifteenth century were trying to erase when the founders insisted on a separate master of grammar, an M. A., or at least someone " discrete and connyng " in that art to teach those of the college deficient in that study, and, of course, anyone else who so desired to attend the school.

The song school, regardless of its faults, however, and as numerous as these faults were, nevertheless performed a funtion that no other institution did—it was the beginning of elementary education, and in many cases, freed the grammar school from this elementary requisite, leaving it free to develop its own peculiar system.[55] It was the grammar school, however, that formed the bulk of the formal education in the fifteenth century, and which came to be considered the English secondary school system. But other agencies besides these formal schools were at work in the leavening of the lump of ignorance and illiteracy of the general laity; instruction was given to the children of the upper classes not only in the grammar schools just discussed, but also in court and abbey schools, while the lower classes received a vocational training through the medium of the apprenticeship system of the gilds.

---

[55] A somewhat parallel growth similar to the song schools attached to cathedral and the larger parish churches sprang up in the fourteenth century around the monasteries. A movement had arisen in conjunction with the increased reverence and devotion to the Blessed Virgin Mary for the establishment of choristers in the chapels dedicated to her in the monasteries (Leach, *Schools of Medieval England*, p. 213). The Almoner, the monk in charge of alms, whose office was at the gate of the monastery, was the one to whom fell the care of housing and feeding the boys who sang in her honor, and the choristers were thereupon called almonry boys. As was the case of the chorister boys attached to the secular churches, it was but natural for provision to be made for them for their instruction. These boys were sent either to the grammar schools nearby or funds were appropriated for the appointment of a schoolmaster to come in and teach them (*Educational Charters*, pp. 296-315) ; consequently quite a number of them received at least a rudimentary education in reading and singing, if not a grammar school education. Examples of such almonry schools in the fifteenth century were those at Norwich, the Coventry Cathedral Priory, the Ely Cathedral Priory, and the Abbey of St. Augustine.
For a somewhat different point of view regarding the song school as the beginning of elementary education, see A. W. Parry, *Education in England in the Middle Ages* (London: University Tutorial Press, Ltd., 1920), pp. 71-73.

CHAPTER IV

CLASS EDUCATION

Education, in the medieval sense, was strictly class education, and the systems of instruction were clear-cut and definite to the point of being narrowly utilitarian, permitting very little leeway at first for the changing economical and social order of the fourteenth and fifteenth centuries. If we exclude those preparing for the priesthood, there were left two groups of youths to be trained for their station in life: the children of the upper class, who were destined to be the rulers; and the children of the lower stratum, the working class. The educational facilities for these two types of education were the castle, manor, and, in some cases, the monasteries, for the former group, and, on the whole, the system of gild apprenticeship for the latter.

Noble-born boys and girls were trained for social leadership and the management of the great estates to which they would eventually fall heir. Males and females received almost identical rearing, with the exception that the boys were educated for knighthood, while the girls were educated for marriage or the nunnery. The polite accomplishments of dancing, singing, playing a musical instrument, chess playing and composing poetry, with instruction in morals, manners, etiquette, and a little reading and writing, made up the bulk of their education. To these accomplishments were added military training and hunting for the boys. Such education for the nobility was called chivalric or knightly education, and since great changes in the manner of warfare and the type of soldiery were gradually eliminating the knightly system of fighting, chivalric education came to be a shallow, meaningless system of training that wasted many precious years of the child's life. It should be remembered, too, that the refinements and traits of gentility inculcated in the well-born held true only for members of their own class; towards their inferiors they exhibited none of the courtesy and gentleness in which they were instructed.

Chivalry, the system of ideals and practices considered suitable for a noble,[1] was introduced into England by William the Conqueror at the time of the Norman Conquest. Although chivalric principles and customs were known to some degree to the Anglo-Saxons,[2] they were revived, strengthened, and thoroughly established as a part of the national government by the imported aristocratic class of medieval France, a class " dominated by mounted warriors." Knights had arisen as a body of mounted troops when, during the ninth and tenth centuries, there was a need for local defense, and they held their estates from some over-lord, under the proviso that they render to him military service whenever called upon. Europe was governed, during the Middle Ages, by that class called " noble." A noble was distinguished by his membership in the knightly order and by his possession of an estate large enough to maintain himself as a fully armed, mounted soldier with an attendant.[3] In England, during the reigns of the first three Edwards, this estate varied in value from forty to fifty pounds *per annum*.[4] Knighthood, like feudalism, to which it became united, eventually came to be commuted in terms of money, if the knight so desired.

The manor and castle were the centre of feudal and chivalric activities. The household of such a manor included not only the lord and his immediate families, but an entourage of men-at-arms, a chaplain, servants, and quite a few young people being reared under his direction, for it was the custom of the gentry to send their children away from home either to a great secular or spiritual house, where they might be brought up in the knowledge of running a household of their own. Indeed, in the time of Henry VII, we find an Italian berating

---

[1] Sidney Painter, *Chivalric Ideas and Practices in Medieval France* (Baltimore: The Johns Hopkins Press, 1940), p. 1.

[2] Charles Mills, *The History of Chivalry* (London: Longman, Hurst, Rees, etc., 1825), I, 5, 9, and 11.

[3] Frederick Eby and Charles Flinn Arrowood, *The History and Philosophy of Education Ancient and Medieval* (Prentice-Hall, Inc., 1940), pp. 794-795.

[4] Mills, *op. cit.*, I, 386.

the callousness of the English for allowing their children to be sent away from their homes at the tender age of seven:

The want of affection in the English is strongly manifested towards their children; for, after having kept them at home till they arrive at the age of 7 or 9 years at the utmost, they put them out, both males and females, to hard service in the houses of other people, binding them generally for another 7 or 9 years. And these are called apprentices, and during that time they perform all the most menial offices; and few are born who are exempted from this fate, for everyone, however rich he may be, sends away his children into the houses of others, whilst he, in return, receives those of strangers into his own. And on inquiring their reason for this severity, they answered that they did it in order that their children might learn better manners. But I, for my part, believe that they do it because they like to enjoy all their comforts themselves, and that they are better served by strangers than they would be by their own children. Besides which the English being great epicures, and very avaricious by nature, indulge in most delicate fare themselves, and give their household the coarsest bread, and beer, and cold meat baked on Sunday for the week, which, however, they allow them in great abundance. That if they had their own children at home, they would be obliged to give them the same food they made use of for themselves. That if the English sent their children away from home to learn virtue and good manners, and took them back again when their apprenticeship was over, they might, perhaps be excused; but they never return, for the girls are settled by their patrons, and the boys make the best marriages they can, and assisted by their patrons, not by their fathers, they also open a house and strive diligently by this means to make some fortune for themselves; whence it proceeds that, having no hope of their paternal inheritance, that all become so greedy of gain that they feel no shame in asking, almost 'for the love of God,' for the smallest sums of money; and to this it may be attributed, that there is no injury that can be committed against the lower orders of the English, that may not be atoned for by money.[5]

Chivalric Education for Boys

The educational preparation of a knight was divided into three periods of approximately seven years each. During the first period, the child was kept at home until the age of seven, to learn religion, morals, common courtesy, respect to superiors, and obedience. It was recognized by all concerned that the formative years of infancy were best cared for by the mother, and it was she who took the initiative in this period. The second period began at the tender age of seven, or thereabouts, when the child was sent to the home of a nobleman,

[5] *A Relation of the Island of England* (translated from the Italian by Charlotta A. Sneyd; London: Nichols and Son, for the Camden Society, 1847), pp. 24-26.

usually the father's feudal superior, and placed under the supervision of the lord and lady of the castle. In the record book of the household of Henry Algernon Percy, Earl of Northumberland, in the first decade of the sixteenth century is found this notation:

Item, my Lordis Hansman iij Yonge Gentylemen in Housholde at their Frendis fyndynge ij = v [6]

When there were a number of young gentlemen gathered together at a powerful lord's castle, or at the king's court, where it was common practice for the heirs of baronies in the crown's wardship to be brought up with the royal children,[7] it was but natural for the group to form a school and be taught under a master. Sir John Fortescue, in charge of the education of Henry VI's son and heir, young Edward, says that in Henry VI's court " is the supreme academy for the nobles of the realm, and a school of vigor, prowess, and manners by which the realm is honored and will flourish . . ." [8] These manners and virtues, such as singing, exercising " in all kinds of harmony," dancing and other pastimes, were the commendable qualities requisite for noblemen.[9] The person or teacher in charge of these henchmen, as the young men were called, was known as the " Maister of Henxmen," and it was his duty

to shewe the schooles of urbanitie and nourture of England, to lerne them to ryde clenely and surely; to draw them also to justes; to lerne them were theyre harneys; to have all curtesy in wordes, dedes, and degrees; dilygently to kepe them in rules of goynges and sittings, after they be of honour. Moreover to teche them sondry languages, and othyr lerninges vertuous, to harping, to pype, sing, daunce, and with other honest and temperate behaviour and patience; and to kepe dayly and wekely with these children dew convenity, with corrections in theyre chambres, according to suche gentylmen; and eche of them be used to that thinge of vertue that he shall be moste apt to lerne, with remembraunce dayly of Goddes servyce accustumed. This maistyr sittith in the halle, next unto these Henxmen, at the same boarde,

[6] *The Regulations and Establishment of the Household of Henry Algernon Percy, the Fifth Earl of Northumberland, at His Castles of Wresill and Lekinfield* (London: Wm. Pickering, 1827), p. 40.

[7] F. Warre Cornish, *Chivalry* (London: Swan Sonnenschein and Co., Ltd., 1908), p. 59.

[8] Sir John Fortescue, *De Laudibus Legum Angliae* (edited by S. B. Chrimes; Cambridge: University Press, 1942), p. 110.

[9] *Ibid.*, p. 118.

to have his respecte unto theyre demeanynges, howe manerly they ete and drink, and to theyre communication and other formes curiall, after *the book of urbanitie.*[10]

This description gives in a nutshell exactly what the second period of preparation for knighthood required: riding, jousting, playing of the harp and pipe, singing, dancing, practicing their religion, learning languages, probably French along with English, and perhaps a smattering of Latin, and good manners. This latter was most important, and quite a variety of treatises and tracts were on hand during the fifteenth century to help the master turn out a well-mannered and courteous page. One has already been mentioned in the last quotation, the " book of urbanitie." This may have reference to a poem of about one hundred lines called *Urbanitas,*[11] composed around 1460, and dealing entirely with good manners. Such admonitions as these are sharp and quite to the point:

> . . . . . .
> When thou comeste be-fore a lorde
> In halle, yn boure or at the borde
> Hoode or Kappe thou of tho.
> . . . . . .
> Fyrste loke that thy handes be clene,
> And that thy knyf be sharpe & kene;
> And cutte thy bread & alle thy mete
> Ryghth euen as thou doste hit ete.
> . . . . . .
> Loke yn thy mowth be no mete
> When thou begynneste to drynke or speke; . . .

When in the company of ladies the page is urged to

> In chambur among ladyes bryghth
> Kepe thy tonge & spende thy syghth;
> Lawghe thou not with no grette cry,
> Ne Rage thou not with Rybawdry.

A religious ending of the poem was quite in keeping with the practicalities because, even though emphasis in chivalric education was placed on " this world," yet Christ was the model on which the knights were to base their ideals. *Urbanitas*

---

[10] *Liber Niger in Household Ordinances,* p. 45, quoted by Frederick Furnivall, editor of *The Babees Book* (London: N. Trübner and Co., for the Early English Text Society, 1868), p. ii. Hereafter referred to as *Babees Book.*

[11] *Babees Book,* pp. 13-15.

concludes with a plea to Christ to give its reader enough intelligence and wit to take its precepts to heart:

> Now, criste of his grette grace
> Geue us alle bothe wytte & space
> Welle this to knowe & Rede,
> And heuen to haue for our mede!
> Amen, Amen, so moot hit be,
> So saye we alle for charyte!

The unknown author of another such poem, the *Babees Book* (c. 1475) [12] makes it quite clear to his audience that he is instructing not old men who are quite expert in the art of " curtesy," but children, " Babees yynge." For, as he asks with charming naivete,

> For what nedys to yeve helle peynes smerte,
> Ioye vnto hevene, or water vnto the see,
> Heete to the Fyre that kan nat but hoote be?
> It nedys nouhte: therfore, O Babees yynge,
> My Book only is made for youre lernynge.

Evidently the author must have been a grammar master or teacher of some sort, because a pedagogical note creeps in when he writes:

> Else, swete children, yf there be eny worde
> That yee kenne nouht, spyrre whils yee yt ken;
> Whanne yee yt knowe, yee mowe holde yt in horde,
> Thus thurhe spyrryng yee mowe lerne at wyse men.

His directions are clear-cut and logical: first, the page is told how to approach the table at mealtime:

> Whenne yee entre into your lordis place,
> Say first " god spede "; And alle that ben byfore
> Yow in this stede, salue withe humble Face; . . .

He is then told to stand until the lord tells him he may sit; next, after having offered the lord water to wash his hands with and after grace has been said, he may, with the lord's permission, sit. Now must the page be careful, indeed, of his actions:

> And whenne your potage to yow shalle be brouhte,
> Take your sponys, and soupe by no way,
> And in youre dysshe leve nat your spone, I pray,
> Nor on the borde lenynge be yee nat sene,
> But from embrowyng the clothe yee kepe clene.

---

[12] *Babees Book*, pp. 1-9.

> Oute ouere youre dysshe your heed hee nat hynge,
> And withe fulle mouthe drynke in no wyse;
> Youre nose, your teethe, your naylles, from pykynge,
> Kepe At your mete, for so techis the wyse.

Generosity with food is advocated:

> And yf straungers withe yow be sette at mete,
> And vnto yow goode mete be brouhte or sente,
> Withe part of hit goodely yee theym Rehete,
> For yt ys nouhte ywys convenyent
> Withe yow at mete, whanne other ben present,
> Alle forto holde that vnto yow ys brouhte. . . .

Finally, when the meal is over, the young page is to clean his knives and put them away, wash his hands, then go to his lord's table, and, after grace has been said, help the lord to wash. (One is told to get the water, another to hold the towel, and still another to pour the water over the lord's hands.) The author stops short with these services:

> Other service thanne this I mythe comende
> To yow to done, but, for the tyme is shorte,
> I putte theym nouhte in this lytyl Reporte,
>
> .   .   .   .

A much more complete manual of instructions was written in the fifteenth century by one who was well-qualified for such a task. John Russell was, as he says in the introductory and concluding lines of his work, *The Boke of Nurture*,[13] usher and marshal to Humphrey the Duke of Gloucester, a " prynce of highe degre," and delighted in his teaching, quitting only when forced to by " croked age." Russell started his book as so many of the medieval tellers of tales did, with the fanciful little device of having the narrator meet a young man wandering in the forest, anxious to be taught the duties of any or all the offices in a lord's household.[14] The narrator then takes it upon himself to instruct the youth in these matters, in this all-inclusive manual. These are some of the subjects treated: the panter or butler, his duties, including

---

[13] *Babees Book*, pp. 117-199.
[14] Compare the similar treatment in Ramón Lull's *Le Libre del Orde de Cauayleria* (translated and printed by William Caxton under the title of *The Book of the Ordre of Chyvalry*; edited by Alfred T. P. Byles; London: Oxford University Press, for the Early English Text Society, 1926).

the broaching of wine, of fruits and cheese, and of the care of wines in wood; names of sweet wines; how to make Ypocras; the botery, how to lay the table-cloth; how to wrap up bread stately; how to make the surnape; how to manage at table; simple conditions or rules for good behavior for every servant; the " connynge of kervynge "; fumosities; the carving of flesh; baked meats, and how to carve; fried meats; pottages; different sauces; the courses of a " flesh " dinner; the courses of a fish dinner; sauces for fish; the office of a chamberlain; the wardrobes (how to put the lord to bed, and prepare his bedroom); how to prepare a lord's bath; and the office of usher and marshall.[15] Surely this must have been a profitable handbook for the " Maister of Henxmen " of King Edward's court!

Still another popular work was that ascribed to John Lydgate around 1460, and considered by Cornish [16] as the common manual of good manners which all young people studied, *Stans Puer ad Mensam*.[17] In addition to the usual admonitions of how to behave at the table, there are a few remarks on the character of children, with bits of psychology thrown in:

> Be soft in mesure, not hasti, but treteable;
> Ouer soft is nought in no maner thing;
> To children longith not to be vengeable,
> Soone meued and soone fightinge;
> And as it is remembrid bi writynge,
> Wrathhe of children is ouercome soone,
> With the partis of an appil ben made at oon.
> In children werre is now mirthe & now debate
> In her quarel is no violence,
> Now pleie, now wepinge, & seelde in oon state . . .

Then Lydgate reminds us that " to spare the rod spoils the child," a very common maxim during the Middle Ages:

> To her pleyntis geue no credence;
> A rodde reformeth al her necligence;
> in her corage no rancour dooth abide,
> who that sparith the rodde all vertues settith a-side.

---

[15] Cf. also *A Fifteenth Century Courtesy Book and Two Fifteenth Century Franciscan Rules*, edited by R. W. Chambers and Walter W. Seton (London: Paul, Trench, Trübner and Co., for the Early English Text Society, 1914), pp. 1-22.

[16] *Op. cit.*, p. 64.   [17] *Babees Book*, pp. 27-33.

Probably the first ABC book ever to appear in English was the one which appeared in the third decade of the fifteenth century, entitled *The ABC of Aristotle*,[18] although there is nothing of Aristotle in it save its title and its closing line, reminiscent of the "golden mean." Because it represents the forerunner of a series of ABC books that appeared in the sixteenth century and are still appearing in the twentieth century, I quote it in full:

> Who-so wilneth to be wijs, & worschip desirith,
> Lerne he oo lettir & looke on anothir
> Of the a. b. c. of aristotil: argue not agen that:
> It is councel for right manye clerkis & knyghtis a thousand,
> And eek it myghte ameende a man ful ofte
> For to leerne lore of oo lettir & his lijf saue;
> For to myche of ony thing was neuere holsum
> Reede ofte on this rolle, & rewle thou ther aftir;
> Who-so be greued in his goost, gouerne him bettir;
> Blame he not the barn that this a. b. c. made,
> But wite he his wickid will & his werk aftir;
> It schal neuere greue a good man though the gilti be meendid.
> Now herkeneth & heerith how y bigynne.

> A. to amerose, to aunterose, ne argue not to myche.
> B. to bolde, ne to bisi, ne boorde not to large.
> C. to curteis, to cruel, ne care not to sore.
> D. to dul, ne to dreedful, ne drinke not to ofte.
> E. to elenge, ne to excellent, ne to eernesful neither.
> F. to fers, ne to famuler, but freendli of cheere.
> G. to glad, ne to gloriose, & gelosie thou hate.
> H. to hasti, ne to hardi, ne to heuy in thine herte.
> I. to iettynge, ne to iangelinge, ne iape not to ofte.
> K. to kinde, ne to kepynge, & be waar of knaue tacchis.
> L. to looth for to leene, ne to liberal of goodis.
> M. to medelus, ne to myrie, but as mesure wole it meeue.
> N. to noiose, ne to nyce, ne use no new iettis.
> O. to orped, ne to ouerthwart, & oothis thou hate.
> P. to presing, ne to preuy with princis ne with dukis;
> Q. to queynte, ne to quarelose, but queeme weel youre souereyns.
> R. to riotus, to reueling, ne rage not to rudeli.
> S. to straunge, ne to stirynge, ne straungeli to stare.
> T. to toilose, ne to talewijs, for temperaunce is beest.
> V. to venemose, ne to veniable, & voide al violonye.
> W. to wielde, ne to wrathful, neither waaste, ne waade not to depe,
> For a mesurable meene is euere the beste of alle.

The letters X, Y, and Z must have presented too great a barrier to the composer to overcome. Anyway, they are not present, in this alphabetical version, at least.

---

[18] *Ibid.*, pp. 11-12.

These moral and mannerly poetic works just mentioned are but a few of the ones available to English tutors of the fifteenth century, master of henchmen, teachers at the court schools, and at the religious houses where the training of gentlemen's sons was carried on. Bishops and abbots were served in the same way by the noble youths sent to them by their parents and guardians, as well as by the young clerks whom they brought up to become chaplains, scholars, and churchmen.[19] William Roper says that Sir Thomas More was

> . . . receaved into the house of the right reuerend, wise and learned prelate Cardinale Mourton . . . The Cardinal . . . wold often say of him vnto the nobles that divers tymes dined with him, ' This child here wayting at the table, whosoeuer shall liue to see it, will proue a mervalous man,' [20]

Evidently Richard Pace was sent at an early age to Thomas Langton, Bishop of Winchester, to board and to school, for Pace says in his *De Fructu*:

> For he (Langton) considered the humanities to be of such great value that he provided for boys and youths to be taught in a private school of his own. And he was delighted to hear the scholars repeat to him at night the lessons given them by the teacher during the day. In this competition, he who had admirably distinguished himself went away with a present of something suitable to his character, after having been praised in the most refined manner. And if any seemed to him to be dull, but nevertheless not lacking in good will, he did not just put the blame on nature, but exhorted him to struggle diligently with his nature, holding before him the examples of others who had previously done this. But if he observed someone ignorant of letters not because of his ability but because of his own negligence, he reproved him with the wisest of words and showed by arguments that nothing would ever turn out happily for him whom it did not shame to be disdainful of such virtues. . . .[21]

Thomas Warton remarks that:

> It appears to have been customary for the governors of the most considerable convents, especially those that were honoured with the mitre, to receive into their own private lodgings the sons of the principal families of the neighbourhood for education. About the year 1450, Thos. Bromele, abbot of the mitred monastery of Hyde near Winchester, entertained in his own abbatial house within that monas-

---

[19] Cornish, *op. cit.*, p. 60.
[20] *The Lyfe of Sir Thomas More, Knight* (edited by Elsie Vaughan Hitchcock; London: Oxford University Press, for the Early English Text Society, 1935), p. 5.
[21] Richard Pace, *De Fructu* (Basil: N. N., 1517), pp. 27-28. Author's translation.

tery eight young gentlemen, or *gentiles pueri*, who were placed there
for the purpose of literary instruction, and constantly dined at the
abbot's table. I will not scruple to give the original words, which are
more particular and expressive, of the obscure record which preserves
this curious anecdote of monastic life. 'Pro octo gentilibus pueris
apud dominum abbatem studii causa perhendinantibus, et ad mensam
domini victitantibus, cum garcionibus suis ipsos comitantibus, hoc
anno, XVII l. IX S. Capiendo pro. . . .' . . . And this seems to
have been an established practice of the abbot of Glastonbury:
'whose apartment in the Abbey was a kind of well-disciplined court,
where the sons of noblemen and young gentlemen were wont to be
sent for virtuous education, who returned thence home excellently
accomplished.' [22]

Metrical romances were full of allusions as to what a child
of noble lineage should be and was taught. For example, in
King Horn [23] are these lines:

> Stiward, tak nu here
> Mi fundlyng for to lere
> Of thine mestere,
> Of wude and of riuere,
> And tech him to harpe
> With his nayles scharpe,
> Biuore me to kerue,
> And of the cupe serue.
> Thu tech him of alle the liste
> That thu euere of wiste,
> And his feiren thou wise
> Into others seruise:
> Horn thu underuonge,
> And tech him of harpe and songe.

Again, the education of a nobleman's son is described in the
Romance of Guy of Warwick: [24]

> Guye a foster fader hadde
> That him lerned and also redde
> Of wode, of Ryuer, of all game:
> Heraude of Arderne was his name
> He was curteys, and well taughte,
> Guye he lerned and forgate him naughte;
> Mikell he kouthe of haukes and houndes
> Of Ostours, of Faukons of grete moundes
> .   .   .   .

[22] Thomas Warton, *History of English Poetry* (edited by W.
Carew Hazlitt; London: Reeves and Turner, 1871), IV, 9.
[23] *King Horn*, in *Middle English Metrical Romances* (edited by
Walter Hoyt French and Charles Brockway Hale; New York:
Prentice-Hall, Inc., 1930), p. 32.
[24] *The Romance of Guy of Warwick* (edited by Dr. Julius Zupitza;
London: Trübner and Co., for the Early English Text Society, 1883,
1887, 1891), I, 12, 13, 185.

> Whan the Erle to the mete sette was,
> Guye stode before him in that plaas,
>
> .   .   .   .
>
> Than at Chequer with the meyne
> Before that maide pleyden they
> The first game they haue sette,
> And the Styward it loste withoute lette.

And in *Tryamore* [25] we are told that

> The child was taught great nurterye;
> a Master had him vnder his care,
>   & taught him *curtesie*

The pages were required to wait not only on the lords of the castle, but on the ladies, too, and it was from the latter that the young boys learned to play chess, an accomplishment much to be admired, and the rudiments of gallantry. However, the most important part of a page's education was the outdoor exercises and the military skill that was developed in such practical ways as wrestling, boxing, running, riding, tilting at the ring, quintain, bull and bear baiting, hunting, and hawking. By the time the page was fourteen or fifteen, and eligible to begin his work as a squire, he had gained at least an elementary knowledge of reading, writing, languages, music, etiquette, gallantry, and chess-playing, as well as athletic skill in outdoor activities.

The years between fourteen and twenty-one were but a continuation of the previous seven-year period. Now the squire made use of his instruction in manners in a practical way. To him belonged the duty of attending and waiting on his lord, of offering him personal military as well as personal domestic service.

> The squier has his hernays dyght;
> He did right als his mayster red;
> His stede, his armurs he him led. [26]

If the lord were important and wealthy, he was apt to have a number of squires: one for his chamber, one for carving, one for dress and for other services, etc. [27] When the lord ventured forth into battle, the squire went with him, taking care

[25] *Tryamore*, quoted by Furnivall, *Babees Book*, p. v.
[26] *Ywain and Gawain*, *Middle English Metrical Romances*, p. 503.
[27] Mills, *op. cit.*, I, 40.

of his armor, his steed, presenting him with a fresh lance when necessary, and keeping close to him at all times so that he might render him any assistance that might be called for. This was the culmination of all the squire's studying—he was fulfilling that principle of education that has existed for centuries: learn to do by doing. This is portrayed in the romance of *Ipomadon*, where Ipomadon, having fallen in love with a neighboring princess, goes to her court to enter her service, and one of the first tests she gives him is to see if he knows how to serve.

> The lady callyd hur botelere:
> ' This cupe of gold thou shalt take here,
>   And gyffe hit to younde man;
> To buttrey dore lede hym with the,
> Therwith of wyne to serue me:
>   We shall see yf he can.'
> The butteler hym the cuppe betoke
> And he was fayne and not foresoke;
>   To the chylde sayde he thanne,
> ' It ys my ladyes byddynge
> That off wyne thou shall here bring.'
> In covrte thus he began.[28]

Needless to say, Ipomadon passed the test successfully—he had been well trained as a page and squire!

That knighthood and chivalry were on the wane by the latter part of the fifteenth century is clearly indicated by the translation and publication of Ramon Lull's *Book of the Ordre of Chyualry* by William Caxton in 1485, in order to stimulate an interest in the practices which Caxton felt were being neglected by the nobles. The fifteenth century was a transitional one, and chivalry was one of the many old customs and practices that were being discarded. The wars, both foreign and domestic, helped to bring about such a state. Even the people, in 1349, petitioned Parliament for liberty to commute by a pecuniary fine the obligation to receive knighthood.[29] Since war was the profession of the upper classes of the Middle Ages, and the art of modern warfare was slowly evolving so that the chivalric knight was gradually being displaced, it was only natural that a change had to come.

[28] *Ipomadon, Middle English Metrical Romances*, p. 653.
[29] Mills, *op. cit.*, I, 100.

10

However, there is always an " educational lag "; methods of instruction are usually behind social changes and the " old guard " never gives up without a fight. Consequently, chivalric education was still being given, even though but negligently, and it was this state of indifference that Caxton was trying to overcome in his little book. In despair he asks:

> . . . O ye knyghtes of Englond where is the custome and vsage of noble chyualry that was vsed in tho dayes / what do ye now / but go to the baynes & playe att dyse And some not well aduysed vse not honest and good rule ageyn all ordre of knyghthode / leue this / leue it and rede the noble volumes of saynt graal of lancelot / of galaad / of Trystram / of perse forest / of percyual / of gawayn / & many mo / Ther shalle ye see manhode / curtosye & gentylnesse / And loke in latter dayes of the noble actes syth the cõquest / as in kyng Rychard dayes cuer du lyon / Edward the fyrste / and the thyrd / and his noble sones / Syre Robert knolles / syr Iohan Hawkwode / Sir Iohan chaũdos / & Syre gaultier Manny rede froissart / And also behold that vyctoryous and noble kynge Harry the fyfthe / and the captayns vnder him his noble bretheren / Therle of Salysbury Montagu / and many other whoos names shyne gloryously by their vertuous noblesse & actes that they did in thonour of thordre of chyualry / Allas what doo ye / but slepe & take ease / and ar all dysordred fro chyualry / I wold demaunde a question yf I shold not displease / how many knyghtes ben ther now in Englond [30] / that haue thuse and thexcercyse of a knyghte / that is to wete / that he knoweth his hors / & his hors hym / that is to saye / he beynge redy at a poynt to haue al thyng that longeth to a knyght / an hors that is accordyng and broken after his hand / his armures and harnoys mete and syttyng / & so forth / et cetera / I suppose and a due serche shold be made / ther shold be many founden that lacke / the more pyte is / j wold it pleasyd oure souerayne lord that twyes or thryes in a yere / or at lest ones he wold do crye Iustes of pees / to thende that euery knyght shold haue hors and harneys / and also that vse and craft of a knyght / and also to tornoye one ageynst one / or ii ageynst ii / And the best to haue a prys / a dyamond or Iewel / suche as shold please the prynce / This shold cause gentylmen to resorte to thauncyent custõmes of chyualry to grete fame and renõmee / And also to be alwey redy to serue / theyr prynce whan he shalle calle them / or haue nede / Thenne late euery man that is come of noble blood and entendeth to come to the noble ordre of chyualry / rede this lytyl book / and doo therafter / in kepyng the lore and commaundements therein comprysed / And thenne I doubte not he shall atteyne to thordre of chyualry / et cetera / . . . [31]

---

[30] Cf. also *A Relation of the Island of England*, p. 39, whose author remarks : " Of these lords, who are called *milites* (knights), there are very few left, and those diminish daily. But the present King Henry [Henry VII] has appointed certain military services, to be performed by some of his own dependants [sic] and familiars, who he knows can be trusted on any urgent occasion; and can be kept on a much smaller number of fees, costing him, it is said, on an average of 60 nobles *per annum*, which are equal to 120 florins of the Rhine."

[31] *The Book of the Ordre of Chyualry*, pp. 122-125.

However, Caxton's hand could not stay the march of time, and not many years were to pass before the knight was to become a mere courtier.

The duties of a knight were many: to defend the faith, to defend his lord and maintain justice, to hunt and exercise himself in arms, to maintain the land, to be brave, to defend the weak and helpless, to protect the people, to punish thieves and criminals, to eschew false swearing and impurity, to challenge traitors to mortal combat, and to take care of his horse.[32] In consideration of these prerequisites, a squire should be examined by a knight of great integrity to make sure that the squire loves and fears God, is not too young when knighted, is nobly born, that his "custommes and maners" are up to par, that he is valorous, that he is rich enough to sustain the expenses of his rank, that he is physically fit, has done no treacherous deed, is not vainglorious or a flatterer, nor has any gross vices.[33] These characteristics are indicative of the perfect knight and squire of the thirteenth century; by the fifteenth century the requirements were not so ideal, but, on the other hand, much more practical. To be a knight in the fifteenth century, actually there were only three requirements: that the candidate was nobly-born, was of sufficient wealth to maintain his position, and had been educated in the knightly manner. Many men never advanced beyond the stage of squire simply because of the great expense that devolved on those who entered knighthood. These requirements, however, could sometimes be set aside, as was the case in knighting a man after he had done some heroic deed on a battlefield.

The ceremony of ordaining a knight, the climax of knightly education, must have been an impressive one.[34] The night before was spent in fasting and prayer. After the knight had confessed his sins, bathed himself so that both his soul and body were pure, he was placed in bed, the bed signifying eternal rest. After he was asleep, attendants clothed him in a white shirt, symbolical of the purity of his new character, and

---

[32] *Ibid.*, pp. 24-46, 48-54.   [33] *Ibid.*, pp. 47-48, 55-65.
[34] This paragraph is based on *Book of the Ordre of Chyualry*, pp. 66-76; Mills, *op. cit.*, I, 48-55; and Eby and Arrowood, *op. cit.*, p. 801.

a red garment was thrown over him, to mark his resolution to spill his blood in the cause of his faith. The inauguration took place in church, where the knight's sword was blest, the oath was taken, and where the exterior marks of chivalry were given. Kneeling before his king or lord, the knight took his vows and was struck lightly on the neck by his sword. Lords and ladies alike gave him the various pieces of his harness, the gold chain, sword-belt, and spurs. Immediately after the ceremony, the knight vaulted on his horse and went through the town, showing himself to the populace and receiving their acclamations with pride and joy, and distributing largess in return. The rest of the day was spent in feasting and rejoicing, and no wonder—this was one of the greatest events, if not the greatest, in a nobleman's life.

Even during the fifteenth century the ceremony of the preparation and ordination of a knight had changed very little. There is extant in the British Museum an article on the making of knights that is concerned with the coronation of Henry VI on November 6, 1429, an article headed " Manner of making of a knight after the custom of England in time of peace, and at the coronation; that is Knights of the Bath." Following is a synopsis of the article:[35]

1. The knight designate is received at the royal court, and is provided with two squires of honour, or governors.
2. " And if the Esquire do come before dinner, he shall carry up one dish of the first courst to the King's table."
3. The squire is conducted to his chamber.
4. In the evening, a bath is prepared and a number of knights and squires proceed with minstrelsy to the chamber.
5. The squire enters the bath, only the chosen knights and the governors being present. The chief knight sprinkles water on his shoulders and instructs him in the Order.
6. The squire is dried and clothed, and the barber takes the bath as his fee.
7. The squire is conducted to the chapel.
8. The knights take leave of him.
9. Only the squire, the governors, the priest, the chandler, and the watch remain for the vigil, which lasts throughout the night and terminates with confession, mattins, [sic] and mass.
10-12. The ceremonies of the mass, with the offering of the taper and the penny to the glory of God and the knight who is about to officiate are described. The squire then goes to bed until later in the

---

[35] *The Book of the Ordre of Chyualry, Appendix*, pp. 129-131. Editor's condensation.

day, and his bed is decorated while he sleeps. The ceremonious dressing of the squire is described in detail.

13. The squire rides to court, preceded by a youth carrying his sword and spurs.

14. The marshal takes the horse for his fee.

15. The king commands the two noblest knights to fasten the squire's spurs, and he himself girds on the sword.

16. The king kisses the knight, saying, "Be thou a good knight." The new knight then pledges himself at the high altar to maintain the rights of the Church.

17. He offers his sword on the altar. "All which being accomplished, he is to take a draught of wine."

18. As he leaves the chapel, the master-cook says, "I, the King's master-cook, am come to receive your spurs as my fee; and if you do anything contrary to the order of Knighthood, (which God forbid!) I shall hack your spurs from your heels."

19. He then sits with the knights at dinner, "but he must neither eat nor drink at the table, nor spit, nor look about him, more than a bride."

20. In his chamber the knight is disrobed and his robes are given to the King of Arms.

21. He is dressed in a blue robe, with a "lace of white silk" on his shoulder. He must wear this until he achieves some honour or renown in arms; then a prince, "or most noble lady," will cut it off.

22. The knight thanks the King for the honour bestowed on him.

23. The governors ask for their fees and take their leave.

All the essential early practices are included in this fifteenth century ceremony, with a few variations, but the rituals are more formal. It is easy to see why one of the main qualifications for a knight was wealth!

Chivalric Education for Girls

The education of girls and young women was by no means neglected, as is readily seen in the fact that it was under the ladies of the castle that some of the young pages first learned their letters and gallantry. Girls were sent away from their homes to be placed in castles and manors just as the boys were. The Paston Letters are full of allusions to this type of education. Margaret Paston writes to John Paston in 1470 that:

. . . for asmych as he [Margaret's cousin, Calthorp] can not be payd of his tenaunts as he hat befor this tyme, he purposith to lesse his howshold, and to leve the streytlyer. Wharfor he desireth me to pur-vey for your suster Anne; he seth she waxeth hygh, and it wer tyme to purvey her a marriage.[36]

[36] *Paston Letters* (edited by James Gairdner; London: Chatto and Windus, 1904), V, 93.

Evidently it did not suit the Pastons to take Anne back, for, in the same letter, Margaret continues,

> I pray you commune with my Cosyn Clere at London, and wete how he is dysposyd to her ward, and send me word, for I shall be fayn to send for her, and with me she shall but lese her tyme, and with ought she wull be the better occupied she shall oftyn tymes meve me and put me in gret inquieteness. Remembr what labour I had with your suster, therfor do your parte to help her forth, that may be to your wurchiep and myn. . . .

Anne must have been quite a problem child to her brother's wife! Probably the real reason behind Calthorp's desire to be rid of John Paston's sister was her disobedience to him, a trait which seemed to run in the family, for earlier John's cousin, Elizabeth Clere had written to him that John's sister was misbehaving:

> . . . and sche hath sen Esterne the most part be betyn onys in the weke, and some tyme twyes on o day, and hir hed broken in to or thre places. . . .[37]

This practice of sending girls away from home must some-times have resulted in a strain on family ties.

John Hevenyngham, knight, also had trouble placing his cousin Anneys Loveday and asked his cousin Margaret:

> . . . yff that hit please you to have hyr with you to in to the tyme that a mastris may be purveyeid for hir, I pray you ther off, I shall contente you ffor hir boarde, that ye shall be wel pleased. . . .[38]

Margaret Paston would not place her daughter out until her husband agreed to it. She wrote to her son John Paston the Younger:

> I grete you wele, letyng you wete that as for your sustrys beyng with my Lady, if your fader wull aggrey thereto I hold me right wele pleasyd; for I wuld be right glad that she shuld do her servyse be for any other, if she cowde do that shuld pleas my ladyes good grace. Wherfor I wuld that ye shuld speke to your fader therof and lete hym wete that I am pleasid that she shuld be ther yf he wuld, fur I wuld be right glad and she myght be preferrid by marriage or be servyce, so that it myght be to her wurchep and profight in dischargyng of her frendis. . . .[39]

Just what these maidens learned in the castle is in some doubt, but we know that they must have learned at first-hand

---

[37] *Ibid.*, II, 110.   [38] *Ibid.*, II, 237.   [39] *Ibid.*, IV, 213.

how to run and manage a household, for often the lady had to take charge of the estate while her husband was off to battle. More than likely the maiden dressed her lady and learned to converse with her in French and to sing and play a musical instrument. Needlework, too, was probably one of her accomplishments. She learned enough Latin at least to repeat her prayers; perhaps in some instances her training included the seven arts. In the *Romance of Guy of Warwick*, Felice la Belle, the daughter of the Lord of Buckingham, was quite well-educated:

> She was thereto curteys and free ywys,
> And in the .vii artes well lerned, withoute mys.
> All the .vii artis she kouthe well,
> Noon better that euere man herde tell.
> Hir maisters were thider come
> Oute of Tholouse all and some;
> White and hoore all they were,
> Bisy they were that mayden to lere;
> And they hir lerned of Astronomye,
> Of Ars-meotrik, and of geometrye.
> Of Sophestrie she was also witty,
> Of Rethoric, and of other clergye;
> Lerned she was in musyke;
> Of clergie was hir noon like.[40]

Chess was learned, too, for we have countless allusions to the ladies of the castle playing with the pages and squires.[41]

The letters written by the various feminine members of the Paston family testify as to their ability to read and write English. Even though such abiilty were not widespread, at least some ladies possessed those accomplishments. Sir John Paston, courting a certain " Mastresse Annes " wrote her that he was pleased she could " reed Inglyshe "—then she could read his love letters to her.[42] A little later on he speaks of her abiilty to sing well with a harp.[43]

One gentleman of the fourteenth century, Knight Geoffrey de la Tour Landry, was an ardent advocate of education for women, at least in reading, and, composing a book of instructions for the edification of his daughters, which was later to

[40] *Romance of Guy of Warwick*, I, 7.
[41] See above.
[42] *Paston Letters*, IV, 301.   [43] *Ibid.*, V, 274.

become a popular manual for girls, he expressed his sentiments in this fashion:

How be it there be such men that have opinion that they would not that their wives nor their daughters should know no thing of the scripture: as touching unto the holy scripture, it is no force though women meddle not nor know but little thereof but for to read; every woman it is the better than can read and have knowing of the law of God, and for to have been learned to have virtue and science to withstand the perils of the soul, and for to use and exercise the works of their savement, for that is thing approved and necessary to all women.[44]

This *Book of the Knight of La Tour Landry* was a manual of deportment that was used extensively for girls of noble birth in France, England, and parts of Germany, from the year of its appearance (1371) to well into the Renaissance.[45] The treatise was written expressly for the knight's daughters, for in the Prologue the author remarks:

I purposed to make a little book in the which I could write the good conditions and deeds of ladies and gentlewoman . . . to the intent that my daughters should take example of fair continuance and good manners . . . whereupon they might learn and see both good and evil of the time past, and for to keep them in good cleanness, and from all evil in the time coming . . .

His work is full of meaty stories, morals, and words of wisdom, with examples drawn from the Bible, stories of saints, and chronicles of England, France, and Greece, as well as famous classical stories. Such traits as piety, courtesy, charity, obedience, temperance, modesty, and chastity are urged to be cultivated, and the anecdotes illustrating these virtues are extremely pointed, in some instances. The knight was firm in his medieval belief that women should rigorously subject themselves to their husbands. For instance, " A woman ought not to strive with her husband, nor give him no displeasure nor answer her husband afore strangers ";[46] and " Every woman ought to restrain wrath, and to please and suffer her husband, and he be wroth, with fair language, and *not to go away from him.*" [47] Amusing bits of advice such as these fill the book: " Be humble and devout at Church; don't

[44] *The Book of the Knight of La Tour Landry* (edited by G. S. Taylor; London: The Verona Society, 1930), p. 97.
[45] *Ibid.*, Introduction.
[46] *Ibid.*, pp. 21-22.   [47] *Ibid.*, p. 77.

jangle "; [48] " No woman should eat no licerous morsel in the absence of her husband "; [49] " In saying your prayers at mass or in other place, be not like the crane or the tortoise (i. e., twisting or turning)." [50] Ladies must sometimes have allowed themselves to be won over to the delights of the liquid potion and over-eating, for the knight warns his daughters to

. . . beware of that foul sin and vice of drunkenness, and of other delicious of overmuch eating; for once upon the day to eat and drink is angelic; and two times it is the life of man and woman; and for to eat oftimes after the fleshy appetite, it is the wholly life of a beast.[51]

It is easy to see why a little book such as this with its matter-of-fact, practical rules as to feminine chastity, piety, obedience, and other such virtues, was so popular, and why it was held up as an ideal textbook for well-bred young ladies.

Insistence on temperance again appears in a manuscript of about 1430 entitled " How the Good Wijf taughte Hir Doughter," [52] one of the most practical tracts of all, where there appears this advice:

In town, don't roam about, or get drunk on your cloth money. Where good ale is flowing, drink moderately. If you get drunk too often, you'll be in disgrace.

Drunkenness certainly seems to have been one of the not-so-nice characteristics of a lady. The maiden is reminded that one of her first major concerns is to run a household:

Don't be too sharp or too easy with your household; put them to work at what needs most to be done. . . . If your husband is away, make your people work and treat them according to what they have accomplished. . . . Pay your people on the day set for salaries, and be generous to them.

That the " good wife " thinks her advice is important is seen in this statement:

> Betere were a child vnbore
> Than vntaught of wijs lore,
> Mi leue child.

That well-born girls were sometimes sent to nunneries to receive an education is a well-known fact, but how much

---

[48] *Ibid.*, p. 34.　　　　　　[50] *Ibid.*, p. 13.
[49] *Ibid.*, p. 19.　　　　　　[51] *Ibid.*, p. 95.
[52] *The Babees Book*, pp. 36-47. Marginal notes.

they actually learned there is doubtful. Miss Eileen Power has made a very careful and very thorough study of the question of education in the convent, and has summarized her results as to the educational attainments of English nuns in the later Middle Ages: [53]

1. Reading and singing the services of the church.
2. Sometimes, but not always, writing.
3. Latin very rarely after the thirteenth century.
4. French very rarely after the fourteenth century.
5. Some needlework and embroidery.
6. Perhaps an elementary knowledge of physic, which was the possession of most ladies of their class.

The translation of the offices used by the Sisters of the Briggitine Monastery at Sion, at Isleworth, during the fifteenth and sixteenth centuries bears out Miss Power's conclusions.[54] The author, presumably Dr. Thomas Gascoigne, of Merton College, Oxford, Vice-Chancellor and Chancellor, during the years 1434-1445, explained in his introduction that his work, *The Myroure of oure Ladye*, was printed

. . . at the desyre and instance of the worshypfull and deuoute lady Abbesse of the worshypfull Monastery of Syon, and the reuerende fadre in God Generall confessoure of the same . . .

in order to render the services intelligible to the sisters who were unable to read Latin. In fact, some could not understand even the English, and the translator, in order to remedy this, explained the passages as he went along. Here is the passage *verbatim* in which he explains his reasons for his translation:

But forasmoche as many of you, though ye can synge and rede, yet ye can not se what the meanynge therof ys: therefore to the onely worshyp and praysyng of oure lord Jesu Chryste and of hys moste mercyfull mother oure lady and to the gostly comforte and profyte of youre soules I haue drawen youre legende and all youre seruyce in to Englyshe, that ye shulde se by thevnderstondyng thereof, how worthy and holy praysynge of oure gloryous Lady is contente therein, & the more deuoutely and knowyngly synge yt & rede yt and say yt to her worshyp. And in many places where the nakyd letter is thoughe yt be set in englyshe, ys not easy for some symple soulles to vnderstonde; I expounde yt and declare yt more openly, other before the letter, or after or else fourthewyth togyther.[55]

---

[53] Eileen Power, *Medieval English Nunneries* (Cambridge: University Press, 1922), p. 260.
[54] *The Myroure of oure Ladye* (edited by John Henry Blunt; London: N. Trübner and Co., for the Early English Text Society, 1873).
[55] *Ibid.*, p. 2.

In keeping with this, the *Rule of St. Benet* was put into English for the same purpose as the example above, except that in one version men as well as women were included as lacking latinity. One version [56] has these lines:

> Monkes & als all leryd men
> In latyn may it lyghtly ken,
> And wytt tharby how thay sall wyrk
> To sarue god and haly kyrk.
> Bott tyll women to mak it couth,
> That leris no latyn in thar youth,
> In inglis is it ordand here,
> So that thay may it lyghtly lere.

The Caxton Abstract says in its introduction:

Here felowyth a compendious abstracte translate unto englysshe out of the holy rule of saynt Benet for men and wymmen, of the habyte thereof, the whiche understonde lytyll laten or none to the entent that they may often rede execute the hole rewll and the better kepe it than it is accordyng to the abyte and their streyte professyon so that the welle of their sowlys and better enxample of that holy relygyon maye be the sonner had and knowen.

While it is unsafe to generalize on the strength of two or three examples, yet it seems pretty evident that nuns were not too well fortified with a knowledge and understanding of Latin; it is, therefore, reasonable to conclude that little or no Latin was taught to their charges.

The statement that it was the general custom among the English nuns to receive children for education is subject to several limitations:

1. By no means did all nunneries take children, and those which did seldom had large schools.

2. The children who received a convent education were drawn from the upper and wealthy middle classes.

3. The practice of receiving children was a purely financial expedient on the part of the nuns, at first forbidden, afterwards restricted,

---

[56] "The Northern Metrical Version of the Rule of St. Benet" in *Three Middle-English Versions of the Rule of St. Benet* (edited by Ernst A. Koch; London: Paul, Trench, Trübner and Co., Ltd. for the Early English Text Society, 1902), p. 48. Cf. also "The Thirde Order of Seynt Franceys and The Rewle of Sustris Menouresses Enclosid" in *A Fifteenth-Century Courtesy Book and Two Fifteenth-Century Franciscan Rules*, pp. 25-119. The implication is plain also in Sebastian Brant's *The Ship of Fools* (translated by Alexander Barclay; Edinburgh: William Paterson, 1874), in the lines

> Eche is not lettred that nowe is made a lorde
> Nor eche a clerke that hath a benefyce.

and always frowned upon by the bishops, who regarded it as subversive of discipline.

⁴ The education which the children received from the nuns, so far as book-learning as distinct from nurture, was extremely exiguous.⁵⁷

Leach, who also has done some very thorough research on this matter of education in the convents of England, says,

> . . . no evidence whatsoever has been produced of what was taught in nunneries. That . . . something must have been taught, if only to keep the children employed, is highly probable. That the teaching included learning the Lord's Prayer, &., by heart may be conceded. Probably Fuller is right in guessing that it included reading; but it is only a guess. One would guess that it included sewing and spinning. As for its including Latin, no evidence is forthcoming, and it is difficult to see how those who did not know Latin could teach it.⁵⁸

Although Leach does not mention the teaching of writing, that art must have been taught to some extent, for the voluminous correspondence of the fifteenth century includes many letters written by the feminine sex, and sporadic references to it in literature. Power to some extent agrees with this.⁵⁹

Since only two professions were open to women of high birth in the fifteenth century, that of nun and that of mistress of a manor, the type of education that the feminine sex received suited them very well. Manners, morals, music, and practical management in household affairs, a little writing and a little reading sufficed for the latter, while reading, some writing, a few prayers and rituals, singing, and needlework formed the basis of education for the nuns.

Gild Education

Education in England in the fifteenth century was of a definite, practical nature. Song schools trained youngsters to be able to take part in the singing of the Mass; grammar schools gave the rudiments of formal subjects for those preparing to enter holy orders; and the universities carried further the education of those of clerical position. Gild educa-

---

⁵⁷ Power, *op. cit.*, pp. 261-262.
⁵⁸ Leach, " Medieval Education of Women," *Journal of Education*, XXXIII (new series), 838-841.
⁵⁹ *Op. cit.*, p. 277.

tion, that system of instruction that pertains to craftwork, particularly emphasized the utilitarian aspect of education as a whole, and made very definite contributions to the structure of education in the way of insistence upon perfection in vocational training, in the foundation of some few grammar schools, and in making possible some elementary instruction for the children of gild members through the endowment of chantries or the support of gild priests.

The word " gild " has come down to us from the Saxon " gyldan," and meant originally a " rateable payment." Miss Lucy Smith [60] says that it was only natural that the brotherhoods, by their inherent power of making what internal rules they pleased, should gather a regular rate, or " gilde," from each of the number for their common expenses. A secondary meaning of " brotherhood " thereupon became attached to these societies because of the regular payments which distinguished them.[61] The gild as we know it meant an association of persons who met for mutual aid and protection, for social purposes, for worship, and for the regulation of trade and commerce. There were three classes of gilds : the religious-social, the merchant, and the craft. The religious-social gild was probably the oldest type of gild,[62] and usually had such religious and charitable objects as : the endowment of a chantry and a priest to say masses for the souls of dead members ; help for the poor and sick ; burials ; care of roads and the building of bridges ; care of pilgrims ; veneration of certain religious mysteries ; and the performance of religious plays. Its members belonged to all sorts of trade ; there was no distinction made. After the Norman Conquest and the ascendancy of William the Conqueror to the throne of England, trade revived and expanded, and there grew up the

[60] *English Gilds* (edited by Toulmin Smith; London : N. Trübner and Co., for the Early English Text Society, 1870), p. xix.
[61] Joseph Malet Lambert, *Two Thousand Years of Gild Life* (Hull : Brown & Sons, 1891), p. 38.
[62] Lujo Brentano, in the Introduction to Toulmin Smith's edition of *English Gilds*, p. lxxiii, claims that the religious fraternities of Christianity, when they came to the North, amalgamated with the heathen sacrificial societies which they found there, and that from this union arose the religious gilds of the Middle Ages.

Gild Merchant, the central idea of which was the monopoly of the regular trade privileges.[63] Gross [64] says that it may safely be stated that at least one-third—and probably a much greater proportion—of the boroughs were endowed with this type of gild in the thirteenth century. He also remarks:

> . . . the influence of the Gild Merchant manifested itself, not in the origin, but in the development, of the municipal constitution; . . . it was one of the most important privileges constituting the 'liber burgus' of the twelfth and thirteenth centuries; and, . . . in conjunction with other liberties, it aided in evolving the later legal idea of technical municipal incorporation, but was never actually equivalent to the latter.[65]

Free commercial intercourse was shackled by the Gild Merchant: merchants not franchised by the Gild had to pay a toll on all wares they were allowed to buy or sell. The Gild

> . . . aimed to reduce free competition to a minimum, regarded what we now consider legitimate speculation as a crime, deflected from the town every powerful current of trade, mercilessly obliterated the spirit of mercantile enterprise, and crushed out every stimulus to extensive production.[66]

The medieval craft gild may be defined as " an association of skilled workers, who normally dwelt within the walls of the same town and pursued the same occupation." [67] The gild organization had spread rapidly to all the branches of industries and trades, and by the beginning of the fifteenth century the country was securely bound and fettered in its vise, with the craft gild in the ascendancy. When the craftsmen of a trade grew to be sufficient in number, they immediately wanted to band together to protect and monopolize their trade, and no better way was at hand than to emulate the organization already in existence and so popular. It was the same old medieval love of systematization, seen in the organization of knowledge by the Scholastics, that made the gild system so attractive to the workers. According to Ashley

[63] Lambert, op. cit., p. 97.
[64] Charles Gross, The Gild Merchant (Oxford: Clarendon Press, 1890), I, 22.
[65] Ibid., I, 105.
[66] Ibid., I, 50-51.
[67] Ephraim Lipson, The Economic History of England (London: Charles & Adam Black, 1937), I, 308.

there were other motives that stimulated this general movement toward gild formation:

The gild corresponded so closely to the social tendencies of the time,—the disposition to seek for local or class franchises rather than general liberties, the love of pageantry and public display, the desire to insure the soul's future by means of alms and masses,—that it became the universal form of association.[68]

The privilege of monopoly and the right to enforce their regulations made the craftsmen solicit the aid of the town, and seek the approval of the mayor and the aldermen in organizing their craft gild. For many craftsmen, this was but an additional step; among many of the same craft there already existed a religious fraternity,[69] and in many cases they merely almalgamated.

As the craft gilds grew in number, the gild merchant was weakened, and its circle of activity dimiinshed; its disintegration occurred in the fourteenth and fifteenth centuries, the period in which the craft gilds attained supremacy.[70] By the fifteenth century, every occupation came to have an organization of its own, similar to other gilds, with regular meetings, elected officers, prescribed payments for common purposes, the right of search, certain powers of jurisdiction, common religious interests or practices, and a defined position in the civic constitution.[71]

The break-up of the manorial system was, of course, of great importance in this new economic movement. Commutation of services, money from which enabled the lords to hire free laborers, and the alienation of the demesne, were two factors which did much to promote this break-up.[72] The Black Death brought about a scarcity of laborers and wages consequently rose. The government tried to control the rise of the laboring class but its efforts to check this growth were unsuccessful. Such vain attempts are clearly shown by a glance at the Statutes. First, in 1345, it was enacted that the " villein's son could not be set to letters, or educated at

[68] William James Ashley, *An Introduction to English Economic History and Theory* (N. Y.: G. P. Putnam's Sons, 1906), II, 74-75.
[69] *Ibid.*, II, 74.   [71] Ashley, *op. cit.*, II, 74.
[70] Gross, *op. cit.*, I, 115 and 117.   [72] Lipson, *op. cit.*, I, 88.

school, or apprenticed to a free handicraft, except the lord gave his consent." [73] Then, in 1388, in an effort to keep a supply of laborers on the manors, it was decreed:

> . . . That he or she, which use to labour at the plough and cart, or other labour or service of husbandry, till they be of the age of twelve years, that from thenceforth they shall abide at the same labour, without being put to any mystery or handicraft.[74]

Complaints of the lords that fathers and mothers who had no land, rent, nor other living, were apprenticing their children to crafts, " within the cities and boroughs of the said realm," and thus depriving them of laborers, caused Henry IV to pass a law refusing to allow any children to become apprentices unless the parents possessed property to the value of twenty shillings per year.[75] That this last enactment was easily circumvented is shown in a bill of contempt and trespass brought in 1428 by a certain Symon Welles against Richard Claidich for having taken as apprentice Thomas Fermery, whose parents did not possess the twenty shillings required. The defense which Richard Claidich, writer of the court-hand, pleaded was that the statute said nothing about " a son or daughter putting himself or herself as they may please." Claidich won the suit.[76] The next year the mayor, aldermen, and Commons of the city of London appealed to the king to permit any free man [77] to put his son or daughter as apprentice to any free man,[78] regardless of property ownership, and in due course of time this was granted.[79] Following repeal of this statute, the laboring class was legislatively recognized and continued on its course in the gild system. It is plain to see that by the fifteenth century industry was becoming more attractive than agriculture.[80]

---

[73] *Calendar Patent Rolls*, Edward III (1343-1345), VI.
[74] *Statutes-at-Large*, II, 301-302.
[75] *Ibid.*, II, 472-473.
[76] *Calendar of Letter-Books of the City of London* (edited by Reginald R. Sharpe; London: John Edward Francis, 1899-), *Letter Book K*, p. 87.
[77] One who had the right to trade or exercise a craft.
[78] *Calendar of Letter-Books, Letter Book K*, pp. 104-105.
[79] *Statutes-at-Large*, III, 130.
[80] As Lipson says (*op. cit.*, I, 321), ". . . it offered a wider scope to men of initiative and enterprise, and opened up a field of opportunity

It was the craft gilds' rigid system of apprenticeship that gave them their power, controlled the amount and quality of work produced, and supplied a system of vocational education that has yet to meet its equal.

Apprenticeship was in reality a " contractual relationship involving mutual obligations on the part of master and apprentice alike." [81] The parents, desiring their child be taught a craft, selected a competent and skilled master and placed him under that master's care, *in loco parentis*, as it were. An article of indenture was drawn up and signed, usually in the gild hall in the presence of the wardens of the gild, in which both parties agreed to coöperate for mutual advantage. Ashley [82] gives an indenture of apprenticeship to a carpenter in 1409, in which it is agreed that the master

. . . shall provide John, his apprentice, with food, clothing, and other necessaries, according as it is fitting that such an apprentice should be provided for, for the first four years, and also all the instruments pertaining to the carpenter's art, with which he may have to work in the service of his master; and in the fifth year the aforesaid John shall find himself in everything, except that his master shall find him in all the instruments, Anglicé the *tools*, with which he shall have to work, and he shall receive from his master 20 s. And in the sixth year he shall receive from his master 40 s. for everything.

An indenture of an apprentice to a fisherman made in 1459 is still more explicit:

This indenture made between John Gibbs of Penzance in the county of Cornwall of the one part, and John Goffe, Spaniard, of the other part, witnesses that the aforesaid John Goffe has put himself to the aforesaid John Gibbs to learn the craft of fishing, and to stay with him as apprentice and to serve from the feast of Phillip and James next to come after the date of these presents until the end of eight years then next ensuing and fully complete; throughout which term the aforesaid John Goffe shall well and faithfully serve the aforesaid John Gibbs and Agnes his wife as his masters and lords, shall keep their secrets, shall everywhere willingly do their lawful and honourable commands, shall do his masters no injury nor see injury done to them by others, but prevent the same as far as he can, shall not waste his master's goods nor lend them to any man without his special command. And the aforesaid John Gibbs and Agnes his wife shall teach, train, and inform or cause the aforesaid John Goffe, their apprentice, to be informed in the craft of fishing in the best way they know, chastising

---

where wealth and prestige lay within the grasp of all who could prove themselves worthy by their skill and resources."

[81] Lipson, *op. cit.*, I, 309.
[82] *Op. cit.*, II, 87.

11

him duly and finding for the same John, their apprentice, food, clothing linen and woollen, and shoes, sufficiently, as befits such an apprentice to be found, during the term aforesaid. And at the end of the term aforesaid the aforesaid John Goffe shall have of the aforesaid John Gibbs and Agnes his wife 20 s. sterling without any fraud. In witness whereof the parties aforesaid have interchangeable set their seals to the parts of this indenture. These witnesses: Richard Bascawen, Robert Martyn, and Robert Cosyn, and many others. Given at Penzance, 1 April in the 37th year of the reign of King Henry the Sixth after the Conquest of England.[83]

This indenture is typical of the care which was taken in binding over an apprentice to a master; every point is well taken: the term carefully specified, what is to be included in the apprentice's obligations to his master, and vice-versa, the agreement of the master to pay a certain fee at the end of the apprenticeship to the apprentice (probably to be used in setting up the new master in his life-work), and witnesses to sign the indenture.

A fee was usually required both of the master and the apprentices when the master took on an apprentice, but there was no fixed sum. The Craft of Glovers, in Hull, in 1499, required that the master must pay to the gild " xijd. for every prentice "; [84] the Fullers of Lincoln demanded that " if anyone wishes to learn the craft, no one shall teach it to him until he has given two pence to wax "; [85] while the Tailors of Lincoln decided that

. . . if any master of the gild takes anyone to live with him as an apprentice, in order to learn the work of the tailor's craft, the apprentice shall pay two shilling to the gild, or his master for him, or else the master shall lose his gildship.[86]

The Gild of the Tailors in Exeter, in its ordinances of 1466, likewise required a fee:

Also hit is ordeyned, by the Master and Wardons and all the hole crafte, that every persone of the sayd Crafte that takethe aprentys, shall brynge hym before the Master and Wardons, and there to have his Indenture in-rolled, and the Master to paye xij d. for the in-rollment; and this to be done w^tin twel-moth and a day, or else to lose his

[83] Ancient Deeds, A10022, quoted by A. E. Bland, P. A. Brown, and R. H. Tawney, *English Economic History, Select Documents* (London: G. Bell and Sons, Ltd., 1933), pp. 147-148.

[84] Lambert, *op. cit.*, p. 216.

[85] Smith, *op. cit.*, p. 179.   [86] *Ibid.*, p. 182.

fredom of the crafte for ever more. . . . And every prentes . . . that is inrolled and trewly seruethe his cownand, shall pay a spone of silver, . . . and shall elde a brekefast to the forsayd Master and Wardons.[87]

Evidently feasting the company with a breakfast was customary when an apprentice completed his term and entered the gild as a freeman: the Gild of Ringers of Bristol made the same provision.[88] There seems to have been a tendency in the fifteenth and sixteenth centuries for the gilds to raise the fee of the apprentices in order to check the number of new members.[89]

The length of the term of apprenticeship varied, but in the main seven years was considered a sufficient time in which to master the principles of good workmanship and to secure a thorough training.[90] However, we find some terms lasting for eight years,[91] while in others the time was extended to ten and twelve years.[92] These longer terms, however, were exceptional.

How many apprentices a master should have working under him was a burning, controversial question, and one which was finally settled during the fifteenth century by permitting the masters to enroll no more than two or three apprentices. The common complaint of the craftsmen was that work was scarce. In 1435, the Craft of Girdelers appealed to the Mayor and Aldermen, complaining that an old ordinance of the craft, to the effect that no one of the gild should have more than two apprentices together, had never

---

[87] *Ibid.*, p. 299.
[88] This was analogous to the bachelor's feast at the university.
[89] O. Jocelyn Dunlop, *English Apprenticeship and Child Labor* (N. Y.: Macmillan Co., 1912), pp. 46-47.
[90] Gild of Weavers, Gild of Glovers, Lambert, *op. cit.*, pp. 204-206, 215-217; Lipson, *op. cit.*, I, 314-315; Gild of Barbers, *Coventry Leet Book* (edited by Mary D. Harris; London: Paul, Trench, Trübner, and Co., for the Early English Text Society, 1907), I, 224-226; Gilds of Barbers, Fullers, Hoopers in Bristol, *The Little Red Book of Bristol* (edited by Francis B. Bickley; Bristol: W. Crofton Hemmons, 1900), II, 138, 142, 163; *Liber Albus* (translated by Henry Thomas Riley; London: Richard Griffin and Co., 1861), pp. 237, 330, 598; and Dunlop, *op. cit.*, p. 35.
[91] *Vide* above for the indenture of a fisherman; Ashley, *op. cit.*, II, 86 and 87.
[92] Newcastle Adventures, Goldsmiths, and Ironmongers, cited by Dunlop, *op. cit.*, p. 47.

been enrolled in the Gildhall, and that, since no penalty had been attached to its non-observance, some craftsmen had taken many apprentices,

. . . in so much that nowe adayes ther is so gret abondaunce of apprentices of the seid craft that many freemen of the same craft which have but small quantitee of goodes of their owen and were wont to live by the work that thei made to other men of the same craft may now have no werk with in the seid craft but some of hem be come Waterberers and laborers and some of hem gone home ageyn to her owen contreys and gone to cart and plough and leven this Citee for ever to grete repreef and sclaundre aswele to all this worthy citee as to the craft aforeseid.[93]

They therefore requested that this ruling be enrolled in the Gildhall, with a fine of one hundred shillings if it were not kept. This was granted. Probably the main object of such restriction [94] was the prevention of too much competition against the skilled worker in the person of child labor. Ashley says:

In London it seems to have been usual to regulate the number of apprentices in accordance with the master's rank in the company. ' It shall be lawful,' says the ordinances of the Founders, ' to every Brother of the Craft, being out of the Clothing, that is able with his own stuff and goods to teche and find an Apprentice, to have one and no more at once, except he shew his Complaynt to the Chamb'ln, (of the city), and if he finds him perfect and able, to have two apprentices and no more. . . . Those of the Clothing to have two Apprentices and no more at once. And to him that has been Warden iii and no more. The upper Warden to have iiii and no more at once.' Similarly ' it was enacted by the Master and Wardens of the Skinners, with the assent of the Sixteen of the Fellowship of Corpus Christi, that one who has been Master shall have in seven years four apprentices, Wardens three, and others two.' [95]

For the ordinary craftsman, though, the custom seems to have been a limitation of two.

During the whole time of the apprenticeship the gild exercised a close supervision over the master and his apprentices,

[93] *Calendar of Letter Books, Letter Book K.*, p. 200; *Letter Book L*, pp. 201-202; *Liber Albus*, p. 330.

[94] The Weavers of Hull, the Founders and Brewers of London, Lethersellers and Mercers, and Tailors, were all limited to one, two, or three apprentices. Most gilds permitted the workmen to accept a third apprentice a year or two before his two apprentices left him in order that he would not be left with an ignorant, unskilled learner when the two apprentices' terms expired.

[95] *Op. cit.*, II, 91-92, quoting Williams, *Founders*, II (1489), and *Trans. Lond. and Mid. Arch. Soc.*, V. 106 (1486).

through a system of inspection that was one of the greatest contributions of the gilds. The primary purposes of inspection were the condemnation and prevention of poor workmanship and regulation of wages.[96] However, just as much emphasis was laid on moral education as was put on vocational training, and the inspectors both of the craft and the religious gilds investigated this, too. The workmen had to be upright and just and a good example to his students, or he was heavily fined. The Trinity Gild of Lynn provided that:

. . . if any brother was found guilty and convicted of any notorious scandalous falsehood to the loss or disgrace of the guild, he should be deprived [of his guild] and never be reconciled, but looked upon as a convict and perjured person.[97]

Reverence for one's superiors was insisted on:

. . . none of our brethren shall come into the guild before the aldermen and his brethren capped, or hooded, or barefooted, or in any other rude or rustick manner, and if he does he shall pay 4 d. for alms.[98]

In the Gild of the Assumption, Cambridge, definite types of misconduct were listed:

If any of the brethren be wont to wander in the streets at night without good cause or wont to play chess, dice, or be caught in suspect company or conducting himself improperly, whereof the fraternity may be disturbed or defamed, and if after two warnings from the rectors he will not amend, he shall be expelled forever and lose all benefit of the gild, and be pronounced by the Bishop of Ely or his official a perjurer and canonically punished.[99]

---

[96] In 1406, the Fullers of Bristol enacted " that four good men of the said craft may be elected every year among them and sworn before the Mayor to present legally all manner of defaults which hereafter shall be found in the said craft, having power to survey twice a week the said defaults and also to correct the servants and labourers of the same craft within the franchise of Bristol to the end that the said servants and labourers do not take more salary than was customary in former times and was ordained of record. . . . And in case that any of the said masters pay more to the said labourers than is before ordained that then they shall incur the penalty on every occasion of 2 s., that is to say 12 d to the Commonalty and 12 d to the craft aforesaid." *Little Red Book of Bristol*, II, 76-78. This rigid inspection was typical of all the craft gilds and did much to keep the level of workmanship high.

[97] Gross, *op. cit.*, II, 116.

[98] *Ibid.*, II, 167.

[99] *Cambridge Gild Records* (edited by Mary Bateson; Cambridge: for the Antiquarian Society, Octavo Series, XXXIX, 1903), 73-74.

The master in turn was responsible for the moral as well as vocational behavior of those whom he employed [100] and was allowed to chastise them if it were necessary.[101] The punishment for infractions of rules of either behavior was pecuniary —evidently the gilds were determined to produce good citizens as well as good workmen.

When an apprentice had completed his work term he was ready for the final step of admittance into the gild as a master workman and into the borough or city as a citizen.[102] Even after serving his term of at least seven years, the apprentice would not always be admitted to the gild; in some cases he had to be judged by other masters or the wardens of the gild as " able and well-instructed," [103] or " able in connyng and of good and true condicion to occupie the said Crafte." [104] Sometimes two or three years passed before the apprentice was able to gain admittance to the gild, and during this time, in the capacity of a " journeyman," he accumulated enough capital to set up his own workshop.[105] Then at last he was a master, able to carry on his trade and take in apprentices himself. The following fifteenth-century oath epitomizes the master's entrance into the gild:

> . . . This hear you, Mayor and ye Brethren of the Gilde, that I truly the customs of my Gilde shall lawfully hold, and my Gild in all things serve. I shall lote and scot with my brethren of the Gild, whether I dwell in the town frauncheses, or in the Bishop Fee, or in any other place. Also I shall warne Mr. Mayor and the good folks of the town if I know any man that merchandizeth within the fraunches of this town, that been able to enter into the Chapman Gilde. And also I shall be obedient and ready at Mr. Mayor's commandement and sommons; and the good customs and fraunchisses of this town to my power I shall maintain, as God me help and all Saynts.[106]

---

[100] Ordinances (1477) of Weavers of Bury St. Edmund, *Historical Manuscript Commission, 14th Report,* Appendix, VIII, 135.

[101] *Vide* above, p. 151, the indenture of a fisherman; Ordinances of Worcester (1467) in Toulmin Smith's *English Gilds,* p. 390; Records of Leicester, iii, 50, in Lipson, *op. cit.,* I, 311.

[102] The two were usually synonymous in the fifteenth century.

[103] Cordwainers (1408) and Dyers (1407), *Little Red Book of Bristol,* II, 84 and 104.

[104] Weavers, *Little Red Book of Bristol,* II, 126; *Calendar of Letter Books, Letter Book* L, pp. 201-202.

[105] Lipson, *op. cit.,* I, 327.

[106] Leicester Gilds, Gross, *op. cit.,* II, 138-139.

The gilds not only provided for this thorough system of vocational and moral training, but also indirectly afforded a kind of " social" education through participation in the pageants and plays held by some of the gilds, in religious feasts, in the mutual aid and charity given to its members, and in its business transactions.[107] Lipson [108] sums up this contribution:

It [apprenticeship] was intended to fashion not only good craftsmen but good citizens, inspired with loyalty to their city, and willing to give active service on its behalf when summoned to the field or the council chamber. In medieval times the status of citizenship involved real responsibilities; and apprenticeship served as a period of initiation in the public duties which awaited the future citizen.

However, it is the ideal of technical training and good craftsmanship for which the medieval gilds are particularly noted.

The gilds made another contribution to education in England through the founding of new schools or the maintenance of those already in existence. It is extremely difficult to tease out any such information concerning those schools, partly because of the inaccessibility of records, and partly because the records available either do not mention them or are very vague about the dates of their foundation. In 1389, the twelfth year of Richard II's rule, it was ordered that the " Masters, Wardens, and Overlookers of all the Mysteries and Crafts " send to the King's Council in Chancery copies of their letters patent, and that the " Masters and Wardens of All the Gilds and Brotherhoods " return all details as to the foundation, statutes, and properties of their gilds. Toulmin Smith [109] has printed about seventy-five of these ordinances, Cornelius Walford [110] has abstracted about ninety-four of these returns, and H. F. Westlake [111] has done the same for about four hundred gilds, but references to schools are very, very slim. The most prolific sources of information are

[107] The records are full of such functions, given in minute detail.
[108] *Op. cit.*, p. 313.
[109] *Op. cit.*
[110] *Gilds: Their Origins, Constitutions, Objects, and Later History* (printed for private circulation, 1870).
[111] *The Parish Gilds of Medieval England* (N. Y.: Macmillan Co., 1919).

the commissions and extracts from the certificates and warrants under the Chantries Act of 37 Henry VIII and 1 Edward VI, published in Arthur F. Leach's *English Schools at the Reformation*. These certificates indicate that a large majority of the gilds in England were maintaining schools at the time of the investigation (1546-1548). It must be remembered, however, that not all the returns are published; the chantry certificates seldom give the date of the founding of the schools or the gilds, so that many of them may have come later than the fifteenth century; and the craft gilds were not included in the Dissolution Acts. A survey of these certificates indicate that the following gilds maintained either a school or a schoolmaster:

1. Trinity Gild, Chipping Norton
2. Trinity Gild, Coventry
3. Trinity Gild, Deddington
4. Gild of Our Lady and St. Katherine, Eccleshall
5. Trinity Gild, Finchingfield
6. Trinity Gild, Hornchurch
7. St. Peter's Gild, Lavenham
8. The Goldsmiths' and Mercers' Gilds, London
9. The Palmers' Gild, Ludlow
10. A gild at Northallerton
11. Our Lady Gild, Burford
12. Our Lady Gild, Pickering
13. Holy Cross Gild, Stratford-on-Avon
14. A gild at Ashwell
15. Trinity Gild, Barnard Castle, Durham
16. A gild at Brayles
17. St. John the Baptist Gild, Chilton by Clare
18. Trinity Gild, Wisbeche
19. Trinity Gild, Worcester
20. Our Lady Gild, Middleton
21. Our Lady Gild, Topcliffe
22. St. Laurence Gild, Ashburton
23. Morrow Mass Gild (sometimes called Corpus Christi Gild), Chelmsford
24. Trinity Gild, Louthe
25. Trinity Gild, Nottingham
26. Corpus Christi Gild, Stamford

Leach has made a chronological list of all the schools mentioned in the Chantry Acts, regardless of their origin, and has traced as far as possible the first mention of their foundation. Of the ninety-eight schools listed, of which there is evidence as to their existence prior to the sixteenth century, sixteen were maintained or controlled by gilds. Seven of these are indicated as fifteenth-century foundations: Deddington (1445-6), Chilton by Clare (1446), Deritend (1448), Chipping Norton (1451), Ashwell (1477), Prittlewell (1477), and Stockport,[112] the school founded by Sir Edmund Shaw in 1478 and entrusted to his own company of goldsmiths. Not included in this list, but certainly a school under the care of a gild is the school at Farthinghoe, founded in 1443 by one John Abbot, mercer, who made his own " mistere " of mercers trustees of it.[113] While the school at Appleby was actually a chantry school, nevertheless there is indirect evidence of gild or lay control in an indenture made on the twenty-fifth of March, 1478, when the mayor, bailiffs, and commonalty of Appleby granted to Sir Thomas Whynfell, chaplain, some chantries under the condition that he would keep " or cause to be kept by a fit person, yearly, at all fit and proper times a . . . grammar school." This was not a free school, however, as the indenture goes on to say that the schoolmaster was to take from the scholars the " school fee and customary payments according to the ancient custom of the school aforesaid." [114]

There are other scattered references to the interest in education evinced by the gilds in the fifteenth century. In the Preston Gild Merchant Roll of 1415,[115] Richard Marshall, a " scolemaister," is mentioned as having paid an admission fee of three shillings. He may have been employed to teach the children of the members of the gild, or the children of the town. In 1429, in Coventry the Gild of Weavers declared that John Pynchard, the " skolemayster of Grammer " could live where he was for forty shillings a year, provided that as long as he stayed there he taught school.[116] Ten years later, the mayor and several members of his council conferred with the prior and agreed to permit the prior to occupy a school so long as he did not interfere with the citizens' privilege of

[112] Nicholas Carlisle, *op. cit.*, I, 125-126, and Leach, *Schools of Medieval England*, p. 245.
[113] *Educational Charters*, pp. 415-417.
[114] Leach, *Schools of Medieval England*, pp. 268-269.
[115] William Alexander Abram, *Memorials of the Preston Guilds* (Preston: George, J. G. and T. Toulmin, 1882), p. 14.
[116] *Coventry Leet Book*, I, 118.

sending their children to the school of their choice, the implication being that there were several schools in Coventry.[117]
The gild of Stratford had maintained a school some years
previous to the fifteenth century, but in 1416-17 the school,
formerly housed in the gild's hall, the House of St. Mary,
followed the schoolmaster to Rood House in Church Street,
where he dwelled. A few years later the gild built a school
house in Church Street some yards south of the chapel, at a
cost of approximately ten pounds.[118] The school was endowed
in 1482 by Master Thomas Jolyffe, gild priest.[119] There were
several schoolmasters in the gild during the years 1453-1478,
among them Robert Wyncote, Thomas Caunton, and Richard
Fox.[120] Another gild that may be cited as promoting education, indirectly, at least, is the Trinity Gild of Lynn, which
directed some of its profits toward " poor clerks keeping
schools." [121]

A more or less desultory kind of teaching must have been
taking place during this time—that given by the gild priests.
Nearly every gild had one or more priests attached to it,
either for the purpose of celebrating mass, or to help keep the
gild's records. The minutes of the various gilds are full of
allusions to such persons. It stands to reason that these
priests spent a good deal of their time giving the rudiments of
education to the youngsters, just as the chantry and stipendiary priests (and many of the gild priests were supported
in the same way) were accustomed to do in their free time.
That there was a demand for some sort of schooling for the
sons of the burghers other than the purely formal secondary
education offered in the traditional Latin grammar schools
is seen in Rotheram foundation [122] for those " youths endowed
with the light and sharpness of ability, who do not all wish

---

[117] *Ibid.*, p. 190.
[118] *Minutes and Accounts of the Corporation of Stratford-upon-Avon
and Other Records* (transcribed by Richard Savage; Oxford: Frederick Hall, for the Dugdale Society, 1921-1924), I, xv. The appointment
of the schoolmaster had to have the full consent of all the aldermen.
Westlake, *op. cit.*, p. 114.
[119] *Educational Charters*, pp. 380-387.
[120] *Ibid.*, pp. 378-381.
[121] Gross, *op. cit.*, II, 160.   [122] See p. 117.

to attain the dignity and elevation of the priesthood." Surely, then, these gild priests must have given a more practical type of schooling and instruction, perhaps with the emphasis on the utilitarian subjects of arithmetic, and writing and reading in the native English language as well as Latin. Gild transactions had to be kept, and the accounts figured, and while nearly all the gilds had clerks for such purposes, the individual masters must have leaned somewhat heavily on the brighter youngsters who showed an aptitude for figures and neat penmanship.[123] Then, too, those who showed such aptitude may have gone on to the universities where specialized courses in business training were being given for those who wished to avail themselves of such opportunities. All in all, the gilds, directly or indirectly, made a distinct contribution toward weakening the firm hold and control which the Church exercised over education. A new class had arisen and was demanding its place in the sun politically, economically, and educationally. The Renaissance in England had begun.

AUTHOR'S NOTE: Legal education will be considered in a later study.

---

[123] Occasionally we run across an indenture which stipulates that the master should provide an apprentice with schooling. For example, a haberdasher in 1462 took an apprentice for twelve years, but the master undertook to provide him with two years of schooling, the first year and a half to learn grammar, and the next half year to learn to write. *Early Chancery Proceedings*, 19, No. 491, quoted by L. F. Salzmann in *English Industries of the Middle Ages* (London: Constable and Co., Ltd., 1913), pp. 229-230.

BIBLIOGRAPHY *

‧ I. Primary Sources

The Babees Book, The Bokes of Nurture of Hugh Rhodes and John Russell, Wynkyn de Worde's Boke of Kervynge, The Booke of Demeanor, The Boke of Curtasye, Seager's Schoole of Vertu, etc. (edited by Frederick J. Furnivall; London: N. Trübner and Co., for the Early English Text Society, 1868).

> This volume, ably edited by Frederick J. Furnivall, consists of numerous treatises and manuals of deportment for children of noble birth. It is an extremely valuable source of materials used for educational purposes in the fifteenth century.

The Book of the Knight of La Tour-Landry (edited by G. S. Taylor; London: The Verona Society, 1930).

> A manual of deportment for girls of noble birth, which appeared in the late fourteenth century, and which was used etxensively in France, England, and parts of Germany until well into the Renaissance.

Brant, Sebastian, *The Ship of Fools* (translated by Alexander Barclay; Edinburgh: William Paterson, 1874). 2 vols.

> A fifteenth century poem which contains allusions to the state of ignorance of the clergy.

Bristol, England

> *The Little Red Book of Bristol* (edited by Francis B. Bickley; Bristol: W. Crofton Hemmons, 1900). 2 vols.

> > Contains the early records of the city of Bristol. Volume II has those that refer to the gilds in the fifteenth century. There are many valuable references to apprenticeship regulations.

Calendar of the Close Rolls
> See under Great Britain. Public Record Office.

Calendar of Letter Books of the City of London
> See under London. Corporation.

Calendar of the Patent Rolls
> See under Great Britain. Public Record Office.

Cambridge Gild Records (edited by Mary Bateson; Cambridge: University Press, for the Cambridge Antiquarian Society, Octavo Series, 1903).

> Records of the gilds of Cambridge, ably edited by Miss Bateson. Invaluable for the early history of gilds.

The Cely Papers (edited by Henry Elliot Maiden; London: Longmans, Green and Co., for the Royal Historical Society, Camden Series, 1900).

> These papers consist of selections from the correspondence and memoranda of the Cely family, who were merchants of the Staple. Of inferential rather than direct use for this study. The papers date 1475-1488.

The Conventry Leet Book (edited by Mary D. Harris; London: Paul,

---

* This bibliography is not meant to be exhaustive. Only those references are included which are quoted or used directly in this study.

Trench, Trübner and Co., for the Early English Text Society, 1907-1913). 4 vols.
> Records of the city of Coventry. Has great value to students interested in the legal, social, and topographical aspects of the city.

The Dean's Register of Oriel (1446-1661) (edited by G. C. Richards and H. E. Salter; Oxford: The Clarendon Press, for the Oxford Historical Society, 1926).
> A record of the decrees passed at College meetings. Because of the scarcity of records, less than three printed pages are devoted to the fifteenth century.

Documents Relating to the University and Colleges of Cambridge (London: Longman, Brown, Green and Longmans, 1852). 3 vols.
> Volume I contains documents relating to Cambridge in the fifteenth century, and is invaluable for information of all kinds concerning the university.

Educational Charters and Documents (edited by Arthur F. Leach; Cambridge: University Press, 1911).
> A collection of selected educational charters and documents of England from earliest times. Invaluable to students of education.

Epistolae Academicae Oxoniensis (edited by the Rev. Henry Anstey; Oxford: Clarendon Press, for the Oxford Historical Society, 1898). 2 vols.
> A collection of letters and miscellaneous documents illustrative of academic life and studies at Oxford in the fifteenth century. English summaries (sometimes very inadequate) preface the letters.

Epistolae Obscurorum Virorum: (The Latin text with an English Rendering, Notes, and an Historical Introduction by Francis Griffin Stokes; London: Chatto and Windus, 1925).
> A series of anonymous satirical letters, written early in the sixteenth century, and sometimes ascribed to Erasmus. Some are diatribes against the heavy pedantic style of the medievalists of that time.

Extracts from Matthew Stokys Esquire Bedel His Book Appendix A of George Peacock, *Observations on the Statutes of the University of Cambridge* (London: John W. Parker, 1841).
> Particularly good for a description of medieval ceremony of the inception of a Master of Grammar at Cambridge University.

A Fifteenth-Century Courtesy Book and Two Fifteenth-Century Franciscan Rules (edited by R. W. Chambers and Walter W. Seton; London: Paul, Trench, Trübner and Co., for Early English Text Society, 1914).
> The first part of this volume contains suggestions for manners and morals; the second part contains the English versions of the religious rules, English because of the alleged lack of knowledge of Latin on the part of the nuns.

Formularies Which Bear on the History of Oxford (edited by H. E. Salter, W. A. Pantin, H. G. Richardson; Oxford: Clarendon Press, for the Oxford Historical Society, 1942). 2 vols.
> Literary and legal documents which give an insight into the style of medieval English writers and teachers. Excellent introductions to the contents by the editor.

Fortescue, Sir John, *De Laudibus Legum Anglie* (edited by S. B.

Chrimes; Cambridge: University Press, 1942. Cambridge Studies in Legal History.).

A fifteenth-century book on English law and the legal profession by an illustrious lawyer of that time. Several chapters are devoted to the education of lawyers.

Grace Books, containing the Proctor's Accounts and Other Records of the University of Cambridge (Cambridge: University Press, for the Cambridge Antiquarian Society, 1897, 1903, 1905). 2 vols.

Grace Book A, covering the years 1454-1488, edited by Stanley M. Leathes, and Grace Book B, covering the years 1488-1511, edited by Mary Bateson, give a wealth of academic and financial information concerning Cambridge. Both volumes have excellent introductions.

Great Britain. Historical Manuscripts Commission

Second Report of the Royal Commission on Historical Manuscripts (London: Eyre and Spottiswoode, 1871).

Fourth Report of the Royal Commission on Historical Manuscripts (London: Eyre and Spottiswoode, 1874).

Great Britain. Public Record Office

Calendar of the Close Rolls, Henry IV, 1399-1413 (London: His Majesty's Stationery Office, 1927-1938). 5 vols.

Calendar of the Close Rolls, Henry V, 1413-1422 (London: His Majesty's Stationery Office, 1929-1932). 2 vols.

Calendar of the Close Rolls, Henry VI, 1422-1447 (London: His Majesty's Stationery Office, 1933-1937). 4 vols.

Calendar of the Patent Rolls, Henry IV, 1399-1413 (London: His Majesty's Stationery Office, 1903-1909). 4 vols.

Calendar of the Patent Rolls, Henry V, 1413-1422 (London: His Majesty's Stationery Office, 1910-1911). 2 vols.

Calendar of the Patent Rolls, Henry VI, 1422-1461 (London: His Majesty's Stationery Office, 1901-1911). 6 vols.

Calendar of the Patent Rolls, Edward IV, 1461-1467 (London: His Majesty's Stationery Office, 1897).

Calendar of the Patent Rolls, Edward IV, Henry VI, 1467-1477 (London: His Majesty's Stationery Office, 1900).

Calendar of the Patent Rolls, Edward IV, Edward V, Richard III, 1476-1485 (London: His Majesty's Stationery Office, 1901).

Calendar of the Patent Rolls, Henry VII, 1485-1509 (London: His Majesty's Stationery Office, 1914-1916). 2 vols.

The Calendar of Close Rolls consists of records of writs, mandates, subsidies, truces, treaties, proclamations, etc., while the Calendar of Patent Rolls includes entries of grants of lands, offices, privileges charters, pardons, etc. The latter is particularly fruitful with regard to the charters, licences and grants to the universities.

Letters and Papers Illustrative of the Reigns of Richard III and Henry VII (edited by James Gairdner; London: Longman, Green, Longman and Roberts, for *Rerum Britannicorum Medii Aevi Scriptores,* 1861-1863). 2 vols.

Documents and papers pertaining to political, diplomatic, and military events.

Materials for a History of the Reign of Henry VII (edited by

William Campbell; London: Longman and Co., for the *Rerum Britannicorum Medii Aevi Scriptores*, 1873-1877). 2 vols.

Miscellaneous documents containing information about personages and events of this era.

Munimenta Academica (edited by Henry Anstey; London: Longmans, Green, Reader, and Dyer, for the *Rerum Britannicorum Medii Aevi Scriptores,* 1868). 2 vols.

Until the appearance of Mr. Strickland Gibson's *Statuta Antiqua Oxoniensis* in 1931, these volumes were probably the most prolific printed sources of information about the statutes, privileges, and regulations of early Oxford. This is still a monumental work.

Great Britain. *The Statutes at Large of England and Great Britain.* (Cambridge: University Press, 1762—).

Vol. II, 15 Edward III to 13 Henry IV, 1341-1411 (Cambridge: University Press, 1762).

Vol. III, 1 Henry V to 23 Edward IV, 1413-1482 (Cambridge: University Press, 1762).

Vol. IV, 1 Richard III to 31 Henry VIII, 1483-1539 (Cambridge: University Press, 1763).

Letters and Papers Illustrative of the Reigns of Richard III and Henry VII
See under Great Britain. Public Record Office

London. Corporation
Calendar of Letter Books of the City of London (edited by Reginald R. Sharpe; London: John Edward Francis, 1899—)
Letter Book I, circa A. D. 1400-1422
Letter Book K, temp. Henry VI
Letter Book L, temp. Henry VII
Materials on the civic affairs and usages of London.

Liber Albus: The White Book of the City of London (translated from the original Latin and Anglo-Norman by Henry Thomas Riley; London: Richard Griffin and Co., 1861).

This volume contains much valuable material on social conditions, usages, and institutions of the city of London in the thirteenth and fourteenth centuries. There are some scattered references to apprenticeship.

Lull, Ramón, *Le Libre del Ordre de Cauayleria* (translated and printed by William Caxton; edited by Alfred T. P. Byles; London: Oxford University Press, for the Early English Text Society, 1926).

This translation by Caxton was primarily to revive interest in the institution of knighthood. Excellent details of chivalry.

Materials for a History of the Reign of Henry VII
See under Great Britain. Public Record Office

Medieval Archives of the University of Oxford (edited by Herbert E. Salter; Oxford: Clarendon Press, for the Oxford Historical Society, 1920-1921). 2 vols.

Volume I contains the privilege and similar deeds preserved in the university archives, title deeds of university property, etc., while Volume II has, among other things, the rolls of Proctors' Accounts for the years 1464 to 1497.

Middle English Metrical Romances (edited by Walter Hoyt French and Charles Brockway Hale; New York: Prentice-Hall, Inc., 1930).

A collection of metrical romances which abound in descriptions of the life and education of noble men and women.

Minutes and Accounts of the Corporation of Stratford-upon-Avon and Other Records (transcribed by Richard Savage; Oxford: Frederick Hall, for the Dugdale Society, 1921-1929). 2 vols.

These volumes are too late for the fifteenth century (1553-1620), but the introduction to Volume I contains a reference to the school and schoolmaster maintained by the gild.

Munimenta Academica
See under Great Britain. Public Record Office

Myroure of oure Ladye (edited by John Henry Blunt; London: N. Trübner and Co., for the Early English Text Society, 1873).

A translation of the offices used by the Sisters of the Briggitine Monastery at Sion, Isleworth, commonly attributed to Dr. Thomas Gascoigne, one-time Chancellor of Oxford University during the years 1434-1445.

Pace, Richard, *De Fructu* (Basil: n. n., 1517).

A Latin essay by an English intellectual of the late fifteenth and early sixteenth century. It describes in part the type of education provided in the private school of Thomas Langton, Bishop of Winchester.

The Paston Letters (edited by James Gairdner; London: Chatto and Windus, 1904). 6 vols.

A collection of letters written to and by the members of the Paston family and their servants in the fifteenth century. The letters are replete with allusions to social, cultural, domestic, and foreign affairs. Many of the letters contain references to the educational customs of the times.

Plumpton Correspondence (edited by Thomas Stapleton; London: John Bowyer Nichols and Son, for the Camden Society, 1839).

A series of letters, mostly domestic, written in the reigns of Edward IV, Richard III, Henry VII, and Henry VIII. The correspondence is of the same general type as the Paston letters, although not as copious nor as valuable.

The Privileges of the University of Cambridge (edited by George Dyer; London: Longman and Co., 1824). 2 vols.

A collection of the various privileges of Cambridge University dating from 1229 A. D. More detailed accounts can be found in the Patent Rolls, Close Rolls, and Charter Rolls.

Register of the University of Oxford (edited by Charles William Boase; Oxford: Clarendon Press, for the Oxford Historical Society, 1885). 2 vols.

Volume I lists chronologically for the years 1449 to 1463 and 1505 to 1571 the students of Oxford. Many of the names have, in addition to the years of their inception, the degrees taken. Much incidental information about graces, books read, positions held, etc. is included by the editor.

Registrum Annalium Collegii Mertonensis (edited by Herbert E. Salter; Oxford: The Clarendon Press, for the Oxford Historical Society, 1923).

Only about half of this volume can be used for the fifteenth century, but the material is prolific, including such information as the contents of Merton's treasury, lists of fellows, rules for the use of books, dispensations and graces, announcements of gifts, scrutinies, and a host of other daily incidents in collegiate life.

Registrum Cancellarii Oxoniensis (edited by Herbert E. Salter; Oxford: Clarendon Press, for the Oxford Historical Society, 1932). 2 vols.

These two volumes are devoted to the Acts of the Chancellors of Oxford during the years 1434 to 1458. Mr. Salter has in his introduction a very full account of the duties of the chancellor, and has printed the chronological lists of chancellors, commissaries, *cancellarii nati,* proctors, and bedels. In addition, in the appendices, he has very carefully listed the halls of Oxford and their probable location, and has compiled a list of books mentioned in the register.

Registrum Collegii Exoniensis (edited by Charles William Boase; Oxford: Clarendon Press, for the Oxford Historical Society, 1894).

The editor has written a history of the college, which prefaces the register and some of the early documents of Exeter. Excellent material.

The Regulations and Establishment of the Household of Henry Algernon Percy, the Fifth Earl of Northumberland, at His Castles of Wresill and Lekinfield (London: William Pickering, 1827).

A record book of the household of Henry Algernon Percy, Fifth Earl of Northumberland. Contains references to the presence of young sons of noblemen in the household.

A Relation of the Island of England (translated from the Italian by Charlotte A. Sneyd; London: John Bowyer Nichols and Son, for the Camden Society, 1847).

An account of English customs by an Italian who visited England during the reign of Henry VII. The passage referring to the English custom of sending children away from home at the tender age of seven to be educated elsewhere is enlightening.

The Romance of Guy of Warwick (edited by Dr. Julius Zupitza; London: N. Trübner and Co., for the Early English Text Society, 1883, 1887, 1891). 3 volumes.

A metrical romance of the middle ages, which is full of allusions to the training of nobles and noblemen's sons.

Statuta Antiqua Universitatis Oxoniensis (edited by Strickland Gibson; Oxford: Clarendon Press, 1931).

The early statutes of Oxford University, very carefully and ably edited by Mr. Gibson. Their chronological sequence has been more exactly determined by this editor.

Smith, Toulmin, editor, *English Gilds* (London: N. Trübner and Co., for the Early English Text Society, 1870).

The original ordinances of approximately one hundred early English Gilds. An invaluable printed collection for any one working in that field.

Stow, John: *A Survay of London* (edited by Henry Morley; London: George Rutledge and Sons, Ltd., 1890).

An interesting and rather valuable account of London in the sixteenth century by a writer of that time. Several pages are devoted to the grammar and law schools of London.

Three Middle-English Versions of the Rule of St. Benet (edited by

12

Dr. Ernest A. Koch; London: Paul, Trench, Trübner, and Co., Ltd., for the Early English Text Society, 1902.
English versions of the Latin Rule of St. Benet. The preface indicates the reason for translation: ignorance of Latin on the part of the sisters.

II. Secondary Sources *

A. The Universities

Boase, Charles W., " Exeter College," *The Colleges of Oxford, Their History and Traditions* (edited by Andrew Clark; London: Methuen and Co., 1891).

Broderick. George C., " Merton College," *The Colleges of Oxford, Their History and Traditions* (edited by Andrew Clark; London: Methuen and Co., 1891).

*Clark, Andrew, editor: *The Colleges of Oxford, Their History and Traditions* (London: Methuen and Co., 1891).

—— " Lincoln College," *The Colleges of Oxford, Their History and Traditions* (edited by Andrew Clark; London: Methuen and Co., 1891).

Clark, John Willis, *Cambridge* (London: Seeley, Jackson and Halliday, 1881).

Collected Papers of Henry Bradshaw (Cambridge: University Press, 1889).

Conybeare, F. C., " University College," *The Colleges of Oxford, Their History and Traditions* (edited by Andrew Clark; London: Methuen and Co., 1891).

*Cooper, Charles Henry, *Annals of Cambridge* (London: Warwick and Co., 1842-1853). 5 vols.

*—— *Memorials of Cambridge* (Cambridge: William Metcalfe, 1860). 3 vols.

Driver, G. R., " Magdalen College Library," *Oxford Bibliographical Society, Proceedings and Papers,* II (1927-1930), 145-200.

Fuller, Thomas, *The History of the University of Cambridge* (London: Thomas Tegg, 1840).

Hartshorne, Charles Henry, *The Book Rarities in the University of Cambridge* (London: Longman, Rees, Orme, Brown and Green, 1829).

James, Montague Rhodes, *A Descriptive Catalogue of the Manuscripts in the Library of Corpus Christi College, Cambridge* (Cambridge: University Press, 1912). 2 volumes.

—— *A Descriptive Catalogue of the Manuscripts in the Library of Pembroke College, Cambridge* (Cambridge: University Press, 1905).

Legge, M. Dominica, " William of Kingsmill—A Fifteenth Century Teacher of French in Oxford," *Studies in French Language and Medieval Literature,* presented to Mildred K. Pope, 1939, 241-246.

Lyte, H. C. Maxwell, *A History of Eton College* (London: Macmillan and Co., 1875).

Magrath, J. R., " Queen's College," *The Colleges of Oxford, Their*

---

* The volumes marked with an asterisk are considered by the author to be either the most valuable, the most scholarly, or the most useful for this particular study.

History and Traditions (edited by Andrew Clark; London: Methuen and Co., 1891).

*Mallet, Charles Edward, *A History of the University of Oxford* (New York: Longmans, Green and Co., 1924, 1928). 3 vols.

*Mullinger, James Bass, *The University of Cambridge* (Cambridge: University Press, 1873).

Oman, C. W. C., "All Souls College," *The Colleges of Oxford, Their History and Traditions* (edited by Andrew Clark; London: Methuen and Co., 1891).

Parker, James, *The Early History of Oxford* (Oxford: Clarendon Press, for the Oxford Historical Society, 1885).

Peacock, George, *Observations on the Statutes of the University of Cambridge* (London: John W. Parker, 1841).

Petriburg, M., "Some Library Correspondence of Humphrey, Duke of Gloucester," *English Historical Review*, X (1895), 99-104.

Ragatz, Lowell Joseph, *Glimpses of Oxford during the Thirteenth, Fourteenth, and Fifteenth Centuries* (Washington: Paul Pearlman, n. d.).

Rashdall, Hastings, "New College," *The Colleges of Oxford, Their History and Traditions* (edited by Andrew Clark; London: Methuen and Co., 1891).

*———— *The Universities of Europe in the Middle Ages* (original edition; Oxford: Clarendon Press, 1895). 2 vols.

*———— *The Universities of Europe in the Middle Ages* (new edition by F. M. Powicke and A. B. Emden; Oxford: Clarendon Press, 1936). 3 vols.

Richardson, Henry Gerald, "Business Training in Medieval Oxford," *American Historical Review*, XLVI (Jan., 1941), 259-280.

———— "An Oxford Teacher of the Fifteenth Century," *John Rylands Library*, Bulletin XXIII (1939), 436-457.

Salter, Herbert E., *Medieval Oxford* (Oxford: Clarendon Press, for the Oxford Historical Society, 1936).

Sandars, Samuel, "An Annotated List of Books Printed on Vellum To Be Found in the University and College Libraries at Cambridge," *Cambridge Antiquarian Society*, No. XV (1878), 1-80.

Schachner, Nathan, *The Medieval Universities* (London: George Allen and Unwin, Ltd., 1938).

Seebohm, Frederick, *The Oxford Reformers* (second edition; London: Longmans, Green and Co., 1869).

Shadwell, C. L., "Oriel College," *The Colleges of Oxford, Their History and Traditions* (edited by Andrew Clark; London: Methuen and Co., 1891).

Stanier, Robert Spencer, *Magdalen School* (Oxford: Clarendon Press, for the Oxford Historical Society, 1940).

*Weiss, Robert, *Humanism in England During the Fifteenth Century* (Oxford: Basil Blackwell, 1941).

Wilson, H. A., "Magdalen College," *The Colleges of Oxford, Their History and Traditions* (edited by Andrew Clark; London: Methuen and Co., 1891).

B. Social, Political, and Intellectual Backgrounds

Abram, Annie, *English Life and Manners in the Later Middle Ages* (London: George Routledge and Sons, Ltd., 1913).

*Adams, George Burton, *Civilization during the Middle Ages* (revised edition; N. Y.: Charles Scribner's Sons, 1922).

Adamson, Robert, " Roger Bacon," *Dictionary of National Biography* (new edition), I, 846-850.

Arrowood, Charles F., " Sir John Fortescue on the Education of Rulers," *Speculum*, X (1935), 404-410.

Aurner, Nellie Slayton, *Caxton: Mirrour of Fifteenth-Century Letters* (Boston: Houghton Mifflin Co., 1926).

Birch, T. Bruce, editor, *De Sacramento Altaris of William of Ockham* (Burlington, Iowa: Lutheran Literary Board, 1930).

Cornish, F. Warre, *Chivalry* (London: Swan Sonnenschein and Co., Ltd., Social England Series, 1908).

Coulton, George Gordon, *Life in the Middle Ages* (Cambridge: University Press, 1928-1930). 4 vols.

*—— *Medieval Studies* (first series, second revised edition; London: Simpkin, Marshall, Hamilton, Kent and Co., Ltd., 1915).

*—— *Studies in Medieval Thought* (London: Thomas Nelson and Sons, Ltd., 1940).

Dale, Edmund, *National Life and Character in the Mirror of Early English Literature* (Cambridge: University Press, 1907).

Davey, Henry, *History of English Music* (London: J. Curwen and Sons, 1895).

Davis, Henry William C., *Medieval England* (a new edition of Barnard's *Companion to English History;* Oxford: Clarendon Press, 1924).

Denton, William, *England in the Fifteenth Century* (London: George Bell and Sons, 1888).

Draper, John William, *Intellectual Development of Europe* (London: George Bell and Sons, 1896). 2 vols.

*Gilson, Etienne, *La Philosophie au Moyen Age* (Paris: Payot, 1925).

*—— *The Spirit of Medieval Philosophy* (translated by A. H. C. Downes; N. Y.: Charles Scribner's Sons, 1936).

Kingsford, C. L., *Prejudice and Promise in XVth Century England* (Oxford: The Clarendon Press, 1925).

Lang, Paul Henry, *Music in Western Civilization* (New York: W. W. Dutton and Co., Inc., 1941).

Louard, Henry Richards, " Robert Grosseteste," *Dictionary of National Biography* (new edition), VIII, 718-721.

Maurice, Frederick Denison, *Modern Philosophy* (London: Griffith, Bohn, and Co., 1862).

McFarlane, K. B., " England: The Lancastrian Kings, 1399-1461," *Cambridge Medieval History*, VIII (1936), 362-417.

Mills, Charles, *The History of Chivalry* (London: Longman, Hurst, Rees, Orme, Brown, and Green, 1825). 2 vols.

Moody, Ernest A., *The Logic of William Ockham* (N. Y.: Sheed and Ward, Inc., 1935).

Munro, Dana Carleton, and Sellery, George Clarke, editors, *Medieval Civilization* (New York: The Century Co., 1920).

Painter, Sydney, *Chivalric Ideas and Practices in Medieval France* (Baltimore: The Johns Hopkins Press, 1940).

*Poole, Reginald Lane, *Illustrations of the History of Medieval Thought and Learning* (second edition, revised; N. Y.: Macmillan Co., 1920).

*—— " William of Ockham," *Dictionary of National Biography* (new edition), XIV, 802-807.

Rickaby, Joseph, S. J., *Scholasticism* (London: Constable and Co., Ltd., 1911).

Riggs, James McMullen, " Duns Scotus," *Dictionary of National Biography* (new edition), VI, 216-220.

Roper, William, *The Life of Sir Thomas Moore, Knight* (edited by Elsie Vaughn Hitchcock; London: Oxford University Press, for the Early English Text Society, 1935).

Sandys, John Edwin, *A History of Classical Scholarship* (Cambridge: University Press, 1903-1908). 3 vols.

Schwegler, Albert, *A History of Philosophy in Epitome* (translated from the first edition by Julius H. Seelye; N. Y.: D. Appleton and Co., 1905).

*Taylor, Henry Osborn, *The Medieval Mind* (second edition; London: Macmillan and Co., Ltd., 1914), 2 vols.

Thompson, James Westfall, *The Literacy of the Laity in the Middle Ages* (University of California Publications in Education, Vol. 9, Berkeley, California: University of California Press, 1939).

Townsend, William J., *The Great Schoolmen of the Middle Ages* (N. Y.: G. E. Steckert and Co., 1920).

Trevelyan, George Macaulay, *England in the Age of Wycliffe* (N. Y.: Longmans, Green and Co., 1935).

*———— *History of England* (London: Longmans, Green, and Co., Ltd., 1927).

Ueberweg, Friederich, *History of Philosophy* (translated from the fourth German edition by George S. Morris; N. Y.: Scribner, Armstrong, and Co., 1876). 2 vols.

*Vickers, Kenneth H., *England in the Later Middle Ages* (London: Methuen and Co., 1931).

Walsh, James Joseph, *The Thirteenth, Greatest of Centuries* (N. Y.: Fordham University Press, 1937).

Warton, Thomas, *The History of English Poetry* (edited by W. Carew Hazlitt; London: Reeves and Turner, 1871). 4 volumes.

Williams, C. H., " England: The Yorkist Kings—1461-1485." *Cambridge Medieval History*, VIII (1936), 418-449.

Woodward, William H., *Studies in Education* (Cambridge: University Press, 1906).

*Wulf, Maurice de, *History of Medieval Philosophy* (third edition, translated by P. Coffey; London: Longmans, Green and Co., 1909).

———— *Philosophy and Civilization in the Middle Ages* (Princeton: Princeton University Press, 1922).

C. Schools

Anderson, Lewis F., *History of Common School Education* (N. Y.: Henry Holt & Co., 1909).

Carlisle, Nicholas, *A Concise Description of the Endowed Grammar Schools in England and Wales* (London: Baldwin, Cradock, and Joy, 1818). 2 vols.

Cubberley, Ellwood P., *The 'History of Education* (New York: Houghton Mifflin Co., 1920).

Davidson, Thomas, *A History of Education* (N. Y.: Charles Scribner's Sons, 1900).

Drane, Augusta Theodosia, *Christian Schools and Scholars* (New York: G. E. Stechert and Co., 1910).

*Eby, Frederick and Arrowood, Charles Flinn, *The History and Philosophy of Education Ancient and Medieval* (New York: Prentice-Hall, Inc., 1940).

Hazlitt, W. Carew, *Schools, Schoolbooks, and Schoolmasters* (London: J. W. Jarvis and Son, 1888).

Leach, Arthur F., *Early Yorkshire Schools* (London: J. B. Nichols and Sons, 1899). 2 vols.

*———— *English Schools at the Reformation* (Westminster: Archibald Constable and Co., 1896).

———— "Medieval Education of Women," *Journal of Education* (new series), XXXII (1910), 838-841.

*———— *Schools of Medieval England* (New York: Macmillan Co., 1915).

McCormick, Patrick J., *History of Education* (revised by Frank P. Cassidy; Washington, D. C.: Catholic Education Press, 1946).

Messenger, James Franklin, *An Interpretative History of Education* (N. Y.: Thomas Y. Crowell Co., 1931).

*Montmorency, J. E. G. de, *State Intervention in English Education* (Cambridge: University Press, 1902).

Mulhern, James, *A History of Education* (N. Y.: The Ronald Press Co., 1946).

*Parry, A. W., *Education in England in the Middle Ages* (London: University Tutorial Press, Ltd., 1920).

Potter, G. R., "Education in the Fourteenth and Fifteenth Centuries," *Cambridge Medieval History,* VIII (1936), 688-717.

*Power, Eileen, *Medieval English Nunneries* (Cambridge: University Press, 1922).

Staunton, Howard, *The Great Schools of England* (new edition; London: Daldy, Isbister and Co., 1877).

Walker, T. A., "English and Scottish Education. Universities and Public Schools to the Time of Colet," *Cambridge History of English Literature,* II (1932), 341-371.

Watson, Foster, *The Old Grammar Schools* (Cambridge: University Press, 1916).

D. Economic Backgrounds

Abram, William Alexander, *Memorials of the Preston Guilds* (Preston: George, J. G. & T. Toulmin, 1882).

*Ashley, William James, *An Introduction to English Economic History and Theory* (New York: G. P. Putnam's Sons, 1906). 2 vols.

Bland, A. E., Brown, P. A., Tawney, R. H., *English Economic History, Select Documents* (London: G. Bell and Sons, Ltd., 1933).

*Dunlop, O. Jocelyn, *English Apprenticeship and Child Labor* (N. Y.: The Macmillan Co., 1912).

*Gross, Charles, *The Gild Merchant* (Oxford: Clarendon Press, 1890). 2 vols.

Lambert, Joseph Malet, *Two Thousand Years of Gild Life* (Hull: A. Brown and Sons, 1891).

*Lipson, Ephraim, *The Economic History of England* (seventh edition, revised; London: Adam and Charles Black, 1937).

Rogers, James E. Thorold, *Six Centuries of Work and Wages* (N. Y.: G. P. Putnam's Sons, 1884).

Salzman, L. F., *English Industries of the Middle Ages* (London: Constable and Co., Ltd., 1913).

Walford, Cornelius, *Gilds: Their Origins, Constitutions, Objects, and Later History* (printed for private circulation, 1879).

Westlake, H. F., *The Parish Gilds of Medieval England* (N. Y.: Macmillan Co., 1919).

INDEX